WHAT'S CLASS GOT TO DO WITH IT?

WHAT'S CLASS GOT TO DO WITH IT?

AMERICAN SOCIETY IN THE TWENTY-FIRST CENTURY

EDITED BY MICHAEL ZWEIG

ILR PRESS AN IMPRINT OF
CORNELL UNIVERSITY PRESS
ITHACA AND LONDON

First published 2004 by Cornell University Press
First printing, Cornell Paperbacks, 2004

Printed in the United States of America

Library of Congress Cataloging-in-Publication Data

What's class got to do with it? : American society in the twenty-first century / edited by Michael Zweig.
    p. cm.
    Includes bibliographical references and index.
    ISBN 0-8014-4259-1 (cloth : alk. paper) — ISBN 0-8014-8899-0 (pbk. : alk. paper)
    1. Social classes—United States.   2. Working class—United States.   3. United States—Social conditions—21st century. I. Zweig, Michael, 1942–
    HN90.S6.W43 2004
    305.5'0973—dc22

                                  2003023064

Cornell University Press strives to use environmentally responsible suppliers and materials to the fullest extent possible in the publishing of its books. Such materials include vegetable-based, low-VOC inks and acid-free papers that are recycled, totally chlorine-free, or partly composed of nonwood fibers. For further information, visit our website at www.cornellpress.cornell.edu.

Cloth printing   10 9 8 7 6 5 4 3 2 1
Paperback printing   10 9 8 7 6 5 4 3 2 1

CONTENTS

ACKNOWLEDGMENTS

Many people have made this book possible. The contributors have my thanks for their work and their care in meeting deadlines. Anonymous reviewers made valuable suggestions for many chapters. My own chapter benefited greatly from comments by Kathy Chamberlain, Esther Cohen, Jay D. Mazur, John Roslak, and Robert Sauté, who also provided research assistance. Ruth Misheloff edited an early version of the manuscript with care and intelligence. Fran Benson saw the value of this collection from the beginning and shepherded the manuscript through all stages of review at Cornell University Press. It has been a pleasure working with the staff of the Press, who have been thorough, prompt, and helpful at every step.

John Russo and Sherry Linkon have pioneered the creation of working class studies, and I thank them for the generosity of spirit they have shown since I first met them in 1999. Since then, the State University of New York at Stony Brook has come to support the Center for Study of Working Class Life and the development of working class studies in the social sciences. My thanks go to President Shirley Strum Kenny and many others at Stony Brook who have encouraged this line of inquiry, and who helped to make possible the How Class Works conference in 2002, which provided the initial testing ground for most of the chapters in this book.

WHAT'S CLASS GOT TO DO WITH IT?

INTRODUCTION
THE CHALLENGE OF WORKING CLASS STUDIES

Michael Zweig

I.

The long silence about class in the United States is finally coming to an end. In the early years of the twenty-first century, as capitalism has emerged triumphant from the Cold War and capitalists are asserting their power ever more brazenly in the United States and around the world, the central importance of class in American life is increasingly obvious for all to see. Euphemisms about the middle class and consumer society are no longer persuasive when chief executives pay themselves tens of millions of dollars while their employees are thrown out of work with ruined pensions. When huge tax cuts go to the richest 1 percent of the population while workers suffer the burdens of lost public services, people wonder if we're really all in this together. Working people notice that the tiny amounts they get in tax relief are more than eaten up by the consequences of the resulting fiscal crisis.[1] They wonder what is going on when attention to the corporate scandals of Enron, WorldCom, Arthur Andersen, and so many other firms has been buried deep in the rubble of a war costing tens of billions of dollars.

Whether in regard to the economy or issues of war and peace, class is central to our everyday lives. Yet class has not been as visible as race or gender, not nearly as much a part of our conversations and sense of ourselves as these and other "identities." We are of course all individuals, but our individuality and personal life chances are shaped—limited or enhanced—by the economic and social class in which we have grown up and in which we exist as adults.

Even though "class" is an abstract category of social analysis, class is real. Since social abstractions can seem far removed from real life, it may help to consider two other abstractions that have important consequences for flesh-and-blood individuals: race and gender. Suppose you knew there were men and women because you could see the difference, but you didn't know about the socially constructed concept of "gender." You would be missing something vitally important about the people you see. You would have only a surface appreciation of their lives. If, based only on direct observation of skin color, you knew there were white people and black people, but you didn't know about "race" in modern society, you would be ignorant of one of the most important determinants of the experience of those white and black people. Gender and race are abstractions, yet they are powerful, concrete influences in everyone's lives. They carry significant meaning despite wide differences in experience within the populations of men, women, whites, blacks.

Similarly, suppose that based on your observation of work sites and labor markets you knew there were workers and employers, but you didn't recognize the existence of class. You would be blind to a most important characteristic of the individual workers and employers you were observing, something that has tremendous influence in their lives. Despite the wide variety of experiences and identities among individual workers, capitalists, and middle class people, it still makes sense to acknowledge the existence and importance of class in modern society. In fact, without a class analysis we would have only the most superficial knowledge of our own lives and the experiences of others we observe in economic and political activity.

This book is meant as a resource for the newly emerging field of working class studies, which is dedicated to an exploration of class as it plays out in all of our lives. Later in this introduction I define classes, using power as the basic guide rather than income or lifestyle. This introduction also explores the historical context for working class studies in the United States. The chapters that follow explore four themes.

First we look at the "mosaic of class, race, and gender." Classes aren't uniform, nor are races or genders. The working class is made up of men and women of all races and nationalities. If you look at the population of white people, or African Americans, or other racial and ethnic groups, you will find workers among them, but all kinds of middle class people and capitalists as well. The same is true of course for men and women. This complicated mosaic of identities, corresponding to complex arrangements of power, means that class analysis isn't a simple matter of fitting people into neat categories. In the first part of the book we see how our understanding of class can be informed by knowing the operation of race and gender in our lives. We see that no meaning of class is fully independent of race and gender, because a person's experience of class position depends on the person's race, ethnicity, and gender. At the same time, we see how an appreciation of class can illuminate some of the complexities of racial and gender experience.

We then turn to the operation of class in the global economy. Here we see how globalization, the spread of capitalist institutions to most countries around the world since the end of the Cold War in the early 1990s, has affected working people and national economies. We find that very little separates the domestic U.S. economy from the global economy. As workers have lost ground in the United States, the same has been happening around the world. At home and abroad, income, wealth, and power have become much more unequally distributed.[2]

This fact is not lost on U.S. strategic thinkers and military planners. The United States Space Command, presenting a justification for placing and operating U.S. military weapons in space, warns: "Although unlikely to be challenged by a global peer competitor, the United States will continue to be challenged regionally. The globalization of the world economy will continue, with a widening between the 'haves' and 'have-nots.'"[3]

Usually, what we mean by "haves" and "have-nots" is "rich" and "poor." In U.S. popular culture and political conversation, we tend to talk about class in terms of income, assuming that the United States has a broad "middle class" that includes most people, with some rich people at the top and some poor people at the bottom. By world income standards, most workers and even the poor in the United States do pretty well, so when U.S. strategic planners refer to the world's "have-nots," most Americans think of someone else, far away. But, as the chapters in the second part of this book establish, if we understand class in a different way, not in terms of income but in terms of power, new relationships and the possibility of new political alignments emerge. They suggest a basis for linking most Americans with the world's have-nots, separating us from the haves in important ways, and opening the door to new approaches to doing politics and building social movements.

The two chapters on class and public policy in the third part of this book use class analysis to investigate the lived experience of American workers in the last decades of the twentieth and early part of the twenty-first century. Here we see the close connections between working people and the poor. We see how the decline of union power has contributed to the decline in living standards that workers experience, and how public policy in the United States has been shaped by class power to the detriment of working people.

In the final three chapters, on class and young adults, the authors explore the operation of class in the lives of young workers and working class students attending colleges and universities. Here we see that class has important cultural aspects with psychological implications. These in turn expose useful but often painful questions for the education process itself, allowing faculty as well as students to think in new ways about the experience of higher education when viewed through the lens of class.

II.

Before turning to the aspects of class explored in the four parts of this book, we need to define clearly the terms of discussion. When people in the United States talk about class, it is often in ways that hide its most important parts. We tend to think about class in terms of income, or the lifestyles that income can buy. The essays in this book contribute to the growing field of working class studies by understanding class instead as mainly a question of economic and political power.

Power doesn't exist alone within an individual or a group. Power exists as a relationship between and among different people or groups. This means that we cannot talk about one class of people alone, without looking at relationships between that class and others. Working class studies, then, necessarily involves the study of other classes, most importantly the capitalist class. But in working class studies, we look at all classes in society from the point of view of working people—their lives, experiences, needs, and interests.

The working class is made up of people who, when they go to work or when they act as citizens, have comparatively little power or authority. They are the people who do their jobs under more or less close supervision, who have little control over the pace or the content of their work, who aren't the boss of anyone. They are blue-collar people like construction and factory workers, and white-collar workers like bank tellers and writers of routine computer code. They work to produce and distribute goods, or in service industries or government agencies. They are skilled and unskilled, engaged in over five hundred different occupations tracked by the U.S. Department of Labor: agricultural laborers, baggage handlers, cashiers, flight attendants, home health care aides, machinists, secretaries, short order cooks, sound technicians, truck drivers. In the United States, working class people are by far the majority of the population. Over eighty-eight million people were in working class occupations in 2002, comprising 62 percent of the labor force.[4]

On the other side of the basic power relation in a capitalist society is the capitalist class, those most senior executives who direct and control the corporations that employ the private-sector working class. These are the "captains of industry" and finance, CEOs, chief financial officers, chief operating officers, members of boards of directors, those whose decisions dominate the workplace and the economy, and whose economic power often translates into dominant power in the realms of politics, culture, the media, and even religion. Capitalists comprise about 2 percent of the U.S. labor force.

There are big differences among capitalists in the degree of power they wield, particularly in the geographic extent of that power. The CEO of a business employing one hundred people in a city of fifty thousand might well be an important figure on the local scene, but not necessarily in state or regional affairs. On the national scale, power is principally in the hands of those who control the largest corporations, those employing over five hundred people. Of the over twenty-one million business enterprises in the United States, only sixteen thousand employ that many. They are controlled by around two hundred thousand people, fewer than two-tenths of 1 percent of the labor force.

Even among the powerful, power is concentrated at the top. It's one thing to control a single large corporation, another to sit on multiple corporate boards and be in a position to coordinate strategies across corporations. In fact, if we count only those people who sit on multiple boards, so-called interlocking directors, they could all fit into Yankee Stadium. They and the top political leaders in all branches of the federal government constitute a U.S. "ruling class" at the pinnacle of national power.

Capitalists are rich, of course. But when vice-president Dick Cheney invited a select few to help him formulate the country's energy policy shortly after the new Bush administration came into office in 2001, he didn't invite "rich people." He invited people who were leaders in the energy industry, capitalists. The fact that they were also rich was incidental. Capitalists are rich people who control far more than their personal wealth. They control the wealth of the nation, concentrated as it is in the largest few thousand corporations. There is no lobby in Washington representing "rich people." Lobbyists represent various industries or associations of industries that sometimes coordinate their efforts on behalf of industry in general. They represent the interests that capitalists bring to legislative and regulatory matters.

Something similar operates for the working class. Over thirteen million people are in unions in the United States. Most of these unions—like the United Auto Workers (UAW); the American Federation of State, County, and Municipal Employees (AFSCME); the Carpenters; and the International Brotherhood of Teamsters (IBT)—maintain offices in Washington and in major and even smaller cities where their members work. In addition to engaging in collective bargaining at the workplace, these unions lobby for their members and occasionally coordinate their efforts to lobby for broader working class interests. Sixty-eight unions have joined under the umbrella of the American Federation of Labor, Congress of Industrial Organizations (AFL-CIO) to pool resources and try to advance the interests of working people in general. These organizations represent workers, not "the poor" or "middle-income people," even though some workers are poor and some have an income equal to that of some in the middle class.[5]

In between the capitalist and the working classes is the middle class. The "middle class" gets a lot of attention in the media and political commentary in the United States, but this term is almost always used to describe people in the middle of the income distribution. People sometimes talk about "middle class workers," referring to people who work for a wage but live comfortable if modest lives. Especially in goods-producing industries, unionized workers have been able to win wages that allow home ownership, paid vacations, nice cars, home entertainment centers, and other consumer amenities.

When class is understood in terms of income or lifestyle, these workers are sometimes called "middle class." Even leaders of the workers' unions use the term to emphasize the gains unions have been able to win for working people. "Middle class workers" are supposed to be "most people," those with stable jobs and solid values based in the work ethic, as opposed to poor people—those on welfare or the "underclass"—on one side, and "the rich" on the other. When people think about classes in terms of "rich, middle, and poor," almost everyone ends up in the middle.

Understanding class in terms of power throws a different light on the subject. In this view, middle class people are in the middle of the power grid that has workers and capitalists at its poles. The middle class includes professional people like doctors, lawyers, accountants, and university professors. Most people in the "professional middle class" are not self-employed. They work for private companies or public agencies, receive salaries, and answer to supervisors. In these ways they are like workers.

But if we compare professional middle class people with well-paid workers, we see important differences. A unionized auto assembly worker doing a lot of overtime makes enough money to live the lifestyle of a "middle class worker," even more money than some professors or lawyers. But a well-paid unionized machinist or electrician or autoworker is still part of the working class. Professors and lawyers have a degree of autonomy and control at work that autoworkers don't have. The difference is a question of class.

It is also misleading to equate the working class as a whole with its best-paid unionized members. Only 9 percent of private sector workers belong to unions, and millions of them are low-paid service employees. The relatively well-paid manufacturing industries are not typical of American business, and they are shrinking as a proportion of the total economy.

The middle class also includes supervisors in the business world, ranging from line foremen to senior managers below the top decision-making executives. As with the professional middle class, some people in the supervisory middle class are close to working people in income and lifestyle. We see this mostly at the lower levels of supervision, as with line foremen or other first-level supervisors. They often are promoted from the ranks of workers, continue to live in working class areas, and socialize with working class friends. But a foreman is not a worker when it comes to the power grid. The foreman is on the floor to represent the owner, to execute orders in the management chain of command. The foreman is in the middle—between the workers and the owners. When a worker becomes a supervisor, he or she enters the middle class. But just as the well-paid "middle class worker" is atypical, so "working class bosses" make up a small fraction of supervisory and managerial personnel in the U.S. economy.

We see something similar with small business owners, the third component of the middle class. Some come out of the working class and continue to have personal and cultural ties to their roots. But these connections do not change the fact that workers aspire to have their own business to escape the regimentation of working class jobs, seeking instead the freedom to "be my own boss." That freedom, regardless of how much it might be limited by competitive pressures in the marketplace and how many hours the owner must work to make a go of it, puts the small business owner in a different class from workers.

At the other end of the business scale, senior managers and high-level corporate attorneys and accountants share quite a bit with the capitalists they serve. They have considerable authority, make a lot of money, and revolve in the same social circles. But they are not the final decision makers. They are at a qualitatively different level in the power grid from those they serve, who pay them well for their service but retain ultimate authority. They, too, are in the middle class.

In all three sections of the middle class—professionals, supervisors, and small business owners—there are fuzzy borders with the working class and with the capitalists. Yet the differences in power, independence, and life circumstances among these classes support the idea of a separate middle class. The middle class is about 36 percent of the labor force in the United States—sizable, but far from the majority, far from the "typical" American.

Like the working class and the capitalists, the middle class is represented in the political process by professional associations and small business groups. There is no "middle-income" lobby, but there are, for example, the Trial Lawyers Association, the American Medical Association, the American Association of University Professors, the National Association of Realtors.

Clearly, classes are not monolithic collections of socially identical people. We have seen that each class contains quite a bit of variation. Rather than sharp dividing lines, the borders between them are porous and ambiguous—important areas to study and better understand. Also, beyond the differences in occupations and relative power within classes, which lead to differences in incomes, wealth, and lifestyles, each class contains men and women of every race, nationality, and creed. Yet, despite these rich internal variations and ambiguous borders, a qualitative difference remains between the life experience of the working class compared with that of the professional and managerial middle class, to say nothing of differences both of these have with the capitalists.

III.

A look at the last sixty years of U.S. history indicates that silence has descended over the topic of class, and how that silencing has been related all the while to sharp class conflict in economic and political matters. In the twenty-five years following the end of World War II, workers in the United States won substantial increases in living standards through the power of unions in collective bargaining. Since the late 1970s, however, these historic gains in workers' living standards have come under increasing attack in industry after industry. "Concession bargaining," in which unions are forced to give back previously won wages and benefits, have come to characterize collective bargaining in basic industry. Corporate threats to move production overseas have become more widespread and more effective in manufacturing, business services, and other sectors of the economy that can take advantage of the new "free-trade" environment of NAFTA and the WTO.[6] The result has been a systematic, long-term decline in union strength and workers' living standards coupled with a steady increase in profits going to corporations and wealth going to the capitalists who run them.[7]

Class differences play out in power relations on the job, where most people work under the direction of a relatively small number of senior executives. In larger firms these executives extend their power to the shop floor through intermediate layers of management. Where there is no union to protect them, workers are employed "at the pleasure of" the boss. Unions arise first and foremost to give workers an opportunity to match the power of the boss through the countervailing power of concerted collective action. In the United States at the start of the twenty-first century, a large majority of working people want to be in unions, though fewer than 15 percent actually are. Well-documented implacable hostility to unions by employers, often involving practices that violate U.S. law and international human rights standards, makes it difficult for workers to realize their desires by organizing into unions for collective bargaining.[8]

The contest is about more than money paid out and received in wages and benefits. Workers also turn to unions to secure a measure of respect at work, to be treated "like human beings" instead of in arbitrary and demeaning ways. These issues are often more important than money, both to the workers and to their employers, who typically offer pay raises at the last moment to try to defeat union organizing campaigns and preserve their power. Seniority provisions, grievance procedures, and work rules all operate to protect the worker from the boss, and all depend for their success on the organized strength of workers taken together. Even the money end of the agreement isn't just about money; it is about the ability of workers to secure a "fair" share of the product they create and a "living" wage that provides a decent life for the worker and his or her family. These concerns and conflicts arise in every industry, for every occupational group of workers. They are problems of class, even though individuals who may have little else in common experience them in different settings. The right to organize into unions and conflicts over contract terms are clearly class questions.

Given this country's rich history of confrontations—sometimes violent—between workers and capitalists, it is ironic that the prevailing culture so rarely admits the existence of class, the reality of class conflict. From the beginning of the nineteenth century until now, capitalists have used every means of judicial restraint, police and military power, and private armies of goons and thugs to suppress unions, while workers have resisted by using militant methods of mass organizing.[9]

Those who present class as a question of income instead of power entirely miss this history. They fail to see the continuing array of attacks the working class suffers, and dismiss the possibility that the working class could again mobilize power on a massive scale in the United States. When explicit talk of class warfare emerged on the national scene in early 2003 in the context of President George W. Bush's tax proposals, it seemed to some that Bush himself was launching such warfare. But one commentator dismissed the possibility of class-based mass opposition to this tax relief for the rich, citing evidence that many Americans mistakenly believe themselves to be rich, or aspire to be even though they aren't. He concluded that attacking the rich in American politics is a strategy bound to fail.[10]

If class conflict is represented as an attack by the poor on the rich, it may not find resonance with most Americans. But if class conflict is represented as what it *is*, a contest of power to decide which interests will be served in the workplace and by public policy, a contest in which the interests of working people are different from those of capitalists, most Americans, and certainly most workers, get it. It turns out that class struggle is as American as cherry pie.

Class divisions operate in public policy as well as in corporate structures. Class can be found in the differential impact of such everyday elements as tax burdens, the pattern of government service cuts in a fiscal crisis, and the privatization of public services and imposition of markets and private enterprise for the provision of such basic services as health care and education. Class operates in regulatory policy and in government action (and inaction) related to collective bargaining and the ability of workers to organize unions. Class divisions even extend to foreign affairs, affecting the rules of international trade and investment, the structure of alliances, definitions of friend and foe, and the decision to make war.

For many decades the capitalists have been on the offensive in this contest, but, happily for the majority of people, in some periods of the twentieth century the tide went the other way. During the Progressive Era and through World War I, reformers expanded the regulatory powers of the state to limit the excessive market power of trusts, impose quality standards on food processing, and otherwise constrain the alarming power of the new large corporations. There was widespread public vilification of the plutocratic capitalist with cigar and top hat. The Triangle Shirtwaist fire in 1911 and the Lawrence (Massachusetts) textile strike in 1912, among other incidents of harsh working class suffering at the hands of employers, contributed to a public atmosphere in which restrictions on union activity loosened a bit and more workers were able to organize.

But following the 1917 Russian Revolution, the business community—fearful revolution might be contagious—fought back with an anti-Bolshevik campaign marked by the arrest of ten thousand active workers in the January 1, 1920, Palmer Raids and the summary deportation of over four hundred of them. The 1920s were a period of weak unions and strong companies, a time when the president of the United States would say, "The business of America is business."[11]

The Depression of the 1930s brought with it widespread discontent with the suffering that came from the obvious failure of capitalism as a system and the failure of capitalists as a class to secure progress for the country. Powerful strike waves shook the country as workers demanded recognition for their unions. New Deal legislation brought the national government's power to bear on the side of the working class, securing their legal right to a union of their own choosing, making it illegal for employers to interfere with organizing and requiring them to bargain with the unions workers chose to represent them. In the latter half of the 1930s, over four million workers joined unions. Path-breaking Depression-era legislation also established the Social Security system, unemployment compensation, and public welfare for the destitute (called "relief" at first); created the first minimum wage; and made time and a half for overtime the law for millions of workers.[12]

President Franklin D. Roosevelt's role in securing these reforms earned him the bitter hatred of many capitalists, who saw him as a traitor to his own class. Other capitalists saw his policies as a necessary and wise response to the extreme conditions of the time. But once the Depression was history and World War II had ended with the United States a preeminent world power, a reaction set in. As millions of workers engaged in a renewed cycle of strikes immediately after the war (during the war, unions had signed no-strike pledges and, except in rare instances of the grossest provocation, kept production going at full pace to support the war effort), capitalists came to agree that working class power had gotten out of hand and took steps to assert their own power more forcefully.

The working class has been on the defensive ever since. The capitalists' offensive against labor has had several interconnected elements.[13] In the area of legislation, Congress passed the Taft-Hartley Act in 1947. The law greatly restricts the tactics of solidarity workers can use to organize unions. Among its provisions, it became illegal to organize a secondary boycott, in which people are urged to stop buying from a company that buys, sells, or uses products made by another company that is resisting a union organizing drive or refusing to negotiate. In the 1970s, for example, when farm workers in California tried to force growers to bargain with the United Farm Workers Union, it was legal to organize a primary boycott of grapes grown on certain farms, but illegal to organize a secondary boycott of supermarkets that sold the disputed grapes.

Taft-Hartley also allows states to pass legislation that makes illegal a collective bargaining agreement requiring all workers covered by a contract to belong to, or pay dues to, a union, even though all the workers get the full benefits of the contract. More than twenty states have adopted these so-called right-to-work laws, which greatly weaken union bargaining power and political strength. The fact that many of these right-to-work states are in the South has helped to secure the region as a safe haven for corporations fleeing unions in the Northeast and Midwest. To this day southern workers are the lowest paid and least unionized in the United States.

In 1947 Congress passed Taft-Hartley and overrode President Truman's veto of it as the Cold War was starting and anticommunism was beginning to grip the country. The act made it illegal for a communist to be a union officer and required union members to take an oath swearing they were not communists as a condition of taking union office. The resulting purge of left-wing unionists went far beyond the relatively few Communist Party members who were then officers. In the context of the general anticommunist hysteria encouraged by years of congressional hearings conducted by the House Un-American Activities Committee (HUAC) and several Senate committees, including the one Senator Joseph McCarthy chaired, many liberal critics of capitalism were also silenced. Anyone with an explicit working class sympathy or sharp class-based hostility to capitalist power was completely marginalized, and sometimes even jailed. The purge of the Left went far beyond the union movement, extending also to writers, movie directors and actors, academics, schoolteachers, and journalists.[14]

By the time the American Federation of Labor and the Congress of Industrial Organizations merged in 1955 to form the AFL-CIO, a federation of almost all unions in the country, the purge of class-oriented labor leaders was almost complete. This merger, which created a unified labor movement with over a third of all workers in the country protected by collective bargaining, marked the high point of union strength in U.S. history. But ironically, without class-based leadership and organizing among workers, and with increasingly hostile corporate practices in labor relations, workers were not able to build on that strength. It has been downhill for unions ever since.

A parallel positive effort to redirect the labor movement accompanied the deliberate campaign to tame unions through purges of the Left. In the period following World War II, business, government, and cooperative unions worked to establish and strengthen a number of labor studies and industrial relations programs at premier universities across the country, including Harvard, Berkeley, Cornell, and the Universities of Michigan and Wisconsin. These programs were designed to promote a sympathetic understanding of collective bargaining, in the context of mutual respect of each side for the other. Faculty and staff at the centers conducted important research, published journals, and developed the new field of "labor studies." These programs also conducted training sessions for union officers and their management counterparts to acquaint both sides with commonly accepted and legally sanctioned methods of collective bargaining and contract administration.

But class analysis was not welcome in labor studies. The field was permeated by Cold War liberalism that accepted the legitimacy of capitalism at home and U.S. power abroad. Anticommunism dominated the field to such an extent that the Industrial Relations Research Association (IRRA), the professional society for labor studies, was the only academic organization in the social sciences in which no New Left, radical caucus or trend developed during the 1960s and 1970s. When, in January 2002, the annual meetings of the IRRA included a session titled "Is Class Relevant in Industrial Relations Studies?" it was the first time in the association's fifty-five year history that class was explicitly addressed in one of its sessions.[15] Even then, it was accepted for the program only in the form of a question, rather than with the more assertive title originally proposed, "The Relevance of Class in Industrial Relations Studies."[16]

In the context of general anticommunism and the purges and isolation of almost everyone associated with class analysis during the Cold War, class disappeared from polite conversation. In its absence, workers came to be known as "consumers" or "middle class." Income and lifestyle became the markers of class. The focus of attention in economic matters turned from production to consumption, as summed up in Walter Reuther's famous question to the auto executive who proudly showed the UAW president the latest automated equipment that would substitute for workers in the factory: "Very interesting, but who will buy the cars?"

The capitalists' counterattack against labor began just after World War II, but it wasn't until 1973 that power relations had reversed to the point at which working class living standards began to decline absolutely.[17] It took until 1979 for union strength to become so eroded that concession bargaining came to dominate collective bargaining, first in the auto industry, then throughout the economy in the 1980s. President Ronald Reagan set new standards for antiunion, antiworking class action when he fired over eleven thousand air traffic controllers in 1981 when they struck, not for more money, but for additional periods of rest during their work hours to relieve the tensions of the job. Reagan's action destroyed the Professional Air Traffic Controllers' Organization (PATCO), a union that had supported him in his election campaign the previous year.

The George W. Bush administration has continued the broad assault on unions in the Reagan tradition. In the debates establishing the new Department of Homeland Security, President Bush demanded that workers in the new department be stripped of their union protections and right to collective bargaining. He wanted the utmost flexibility in personnel matters and suggested that unions undermine national security. The result was loss of union protection for 180,000 workers and professional employees who had been represented by the American Federation of Government Employees (AFGE) before their agencies were transferred to the new department.

This theme was picked up in a remarkably Orwellian display of "up is down and down is up" thinking by the National Right to Work Legal Defense and Education Fund in a letter they circulated in early 2003. They sought funds to oppose "the union bosses' drive to use the national emergencies we face today to grab more power." The letter said the drive "presents a clear and present danger to the security of the United States," and claimed that this behavior is "not surprising, given the history of how Big Labor notoriously exploited the Second World War" to "expand its power at the expense of the war effort." Many union leaders objected to the letter in the strongest terms; one such leader was Harold A. Schaitberger, president of the International Association of Firefighters, who has been trying to extend collective bargaining protection to fire fighters in so-called right-to-work states. Schaitberger said, "How dare you question the patriotism of the nation's firefighters and their elected union officials, all of whom have crawled down a burning hallway, faced uncontrolled flames, and risked their lives countless times for the citizens of our great nation. . . . I have never felt more outrage, astonishment, and utter disgust than I feel today."[18]

The lies and distortions involved in these attacks on labor take us back to the days of the "un-American activities" hearings and McCarthyite investigations into alleged domestic subversion that marked the 1940s and 1950s. Now, as then, such attacks are motivated by an explicit fear of the power working people can wield. They are happening at a time when the president of the United States has the authority to declare unilaterally, without any prospect of judicial review, anyone to be an enemy combatant and have that person arrested and held indefinitely without bail, without access to anyone other than his or her captors, not even a lawyer. But, unlike during the Vietnam War period, in early 2003, at a time of a limitless and vaguely defined war on terror and the projection of U.S. military power around the world, significant sections of organized labor openly opposed the war with Iraq and questioned the interests such a war and subsequent occupation would advance.[19] By the end of 2003, U.S. Labor Against the War had brought dozens of large locals and international unions together in a National Labor Assembly for Peace that declared:

> We propose to create a voice within the labor movement that is an energetic advocate for policies that strengthen international institutions so

that conflicts between nations can be resolved through diplomacy rather than war. We seek a U.S. foreign policy that promotes global economic and social justice, not the use of military force. We want our government to meet human needs, not cater to corporate greed.[20]

Are we experiencing class warfare in the United States? President Bush and Republican commentators feared it might be so, characterizing criticisms of their policies and challenges to corporate behavior as evidence of class warfare being waged by irresponsible opponents.[21] They use the old rhetorical trick that labels an opposing argument in a way that suggests it should be disregarded without their having to answer it. They ridicule and dismiss their critics for even hinting that such a thing as "class warfare" could be going on, or that "class warfare" has any legitimate place in American political conversation.

They protest too much. Of course class warfare is going on. Capitalists have been waging it relentlessly for over fifty years, and for generations before that, and it continues to this day in virulent and destructive forms. Class has played a central part in U.S. history from the beginning, finding explicit expression in the policy calculations capitalists have made, and slave owners, merchants, and landowners before them.[22] Capitalists have long believed that workers *as a class* need to be strictly disciplined and controlled.

Until the middle of the twentieth century class was also an explicit part of working people's understanding of their place in society, and they attempted a variety of organizational forms to assert their own class interests.[23] As our future now unfolds and becomes new history, class will surely continue to play a crucial role. Capitalists understand this, whether the rest of us recognize it or not.

It is not a simple matter to make history, to act in a way that helps to shape events and influence outcomes on a social scale. At any given moment it may not be at all obvious what to do. It takes careful thought and meticulous organization to make and then implement the best decisions. Capitalists have their think tanks devoted to strategic matters, places like the Heritage Foundation, the Cato Institute, the Brookings Institution. Capitalists have PACs, trade associations, and other organizations trying to make history that benefits them. On college and university campuses there are many centers of learning devoted to understanding and promoting the interests of capitalists. Their scholars defend the dominant role of markets and the capitalist system, domestically and globally, and take as their agenda defining and solving the problems of this system from the point of view of capitalist interests.

By comparison, the working class has only the most meager resources.

Still, as the early twenty-first century unfolds, many leaders and activists in the labor movement and other social movements are showing renewed interest in the subject of class. Scholars, intellectuals, and journalists are taking note. Labor studies programs are paying new attention. There are more open challenges to the legitimacy of capitalist domination and more interest in organizing working people and their middle class allies to engage in class politics.

Working class studies—an attempt to understand how class works to shape our lives and the larger society—is arising in this social and intellectual ferment. In an analogous way, black studies and other ethnic studies programs developed in the context of the powerful civil rights movements of the 1960s and 1970s, and women's studies developed in the midst of the feminist social movement of those years. Working class studies is taking shape in the context of ever-more-obvious class divisions and growing movements of resistance to capitalist power stimulated by the human suffering and environmental disruption it entails.

Capitalists and their defenders sometimes decry working class studies, portraying it as a lamentable venture into bankrupt, outdated, and ideologically motivated "class struggle politics," as women's studies and black studies were once (and still are) resisted by those whose power they challenge. But class power leaves tracks. If we learn to discern them, we can better understand the particularities and complexity of power and be in a better position to influence history as it is made. The outcome is not predetermined. In every present moment, the future is in the balance, shaped in some important measure by the understanding and organizational capacity of the classes contending for power.

The fact that classes are not monolithic has important consequences in this process. Not every worker will be sympathetic to working class politics or want to join a union. Not every capitalist supports the extreme forms of capitalist power and market ideology that the George W. Bush administration and its backers have championed. Some workers will prefer to express sympathy for the capitalists and aspire to be one of them, while some capitalists will willingly make personal and corporate sacrifices to satisfy the needs of their own and other workers. Still, there is a basic conflict in class interests that divides worker from capitalist on a social scale, whatever the opinions and values of individual workers or capitalists, based in the way a capitalist economy organizes production, generates profit, and distributes goods and services to the people.[24] The middle class, caught in the midst of this basic power grid, is in a particularly complicated place.

There is an old saying in the labor movement to the effect that "the boss is your best organizer." Most people would prefer to avoid confrontations at work. Most people prefer not to participate in mass demonstrations, engage in building unions, or organize social movements, wishing instead to lead calmer lives devoted to family and personal interests. But people are driven to take these actions from time to time by intolerable conditions, disrespectful treatment, and evidence of gross injustice, to themselves and to their neighbors. To the degree that capitalists are responsible, it is they themselves who stimulate the class struggle, even as they denounce and seek to avoid it.

Talk of class and class conflict naturally brings to mind the nineteenth-century social critic Karl Marx and his theory of social revolution. But Marx did not invent or discover classes; they were known long before him. Nor did he discover that the capitalists' profits originate in the labor of the workers they employ and correspond to the product those workers create, taken from them by their employers. Adam Smith, the eighteenth-century founder of modern economics and a staunch defender of capitalism as it was coming into being, described this process in detail in his pioneering study of capitalism, *The Wealth of Nations*, published ninety years before Marx's *Capital*. Marx's contribution to class analysis is contained in the double claim that class conflict drives history, and that the working class in particular will become the revolutionary force that brings capitalism to an end.[25] Throughout the twentieth century, with a combination of social reform and military power, the capitalist class managed to defeat or marginalize nearly every attempt to end its rule and bring the working class to power. Still, whether or not Marx was wrong about revolution in the long run, classes exist and class conflicts continue. In society as on the shop floor, capitalists will bear significant responsibility for the history that results.

Class is an enormous topic with many facets. No single book can cover all, or even many, of its important elements. It will take a fully developed framework of working class studies engaging scholars and activists throughout the world to make a serious dent in the problem. The articles in this collection raise important issues that deserve further investigation. We hope they will stimulate discussion and even controversy in classrooms, union halls, professional academic settings, wherever people come together and discuss what's going on in the world. In these discussions, new voices are heard through which deeper understandings of class and society will emerge.

PART I

THE MOSAIC OF CLASS, RACE, AND GENDER

In the great triumvirate of class, race, and gender, class has receded from view since the 1960s as the civil rights and women's movements have shaken the country and focused popular and academic attention on other urgent matters. Now, with the ever-bolder assertion of capitalist power in the United States and across the globe in the post–Cold War era, class is coming back into focus. Working class studies investigates how class operates, not in isolation from race and gender, but in ways that seek to understand the complex interactions among these different aspects of power and experience.

In the United States, we have capitalist women, capitalist blacks, Hispanics, Asians, and other nationalities. Despite this variety, capitalists are disproportionately white men. White men are also, to a lesser degree, disproportionately found in the middle class, which is more mixed by race and gender. In 1996, women were 46 percent of the employed labor force and held 44 percent of middle class jobs and 47 percent of working class jobs. Blacks and Hispanics also had significant membership in the middle class as well as the working class but were disproportionately more likely to be in the working class and less likely in the middle class. Within each class, because of continuing racism and male chauvinism, women and minorities have tended to hold the lower paying, less powerful positions.[1]

Lack of clarity about class can lead to problems when addressing the concerns women and minorities raise in their social movements and can undermine the interests of the working class as well. When we take class to be a matter of income, for example, and see the world divided into rich, middle class, and poor people, we open the door to some of the most common and most pernicious misunderstandings about American society: that most poor people are black or Hispanic, and that poverty is a women's issue. In fact, in 1999 two-thirds of all poor people were white, and more than three-quarters of all black people were not poor.[2]

It is true that poverty affects minorities and women disproportionately. But if we treat poverty as a race issue or a gender problem only, we miss its class component, the unstable work environment and low wages with few benefits that make most people poor. The tendency is then to blame poverty either on the failings of the poor themselves, a view fed by the racism and male chauvinism that supposes "the poor" to be inferior, or to blame white people and men as the perpetrators. In both scenarios, capitalism disappears, and no attention is paid to the role of markets in creating and perpetuating poverty. Racializing poverty also separates the antipoverty movement from the over two million white men who are poor in this country. Poverty is a class problem. Addressing poverty requires a realignment of class power.

But it would be a mistake to reduce the problem of poverty to one of class alone, since the continuing force of racism and male chauvinism means that women and minorities suffer particularly hard from poverty. That extra suffering, within class experience, must be addressed by challenging racism and male chauvinism directly, as they operate within the working class as well as within the larger society where capitalists make the rules.

It is a complicated task to trace the intricate patterns of power and often conflicting interests, sometimes within an individual, that constitute the mosaic of class, race, and gender. In her chapter here, **DOROTHY SUE COBBLE** examines women's activism in the union movement from the 1930s to the 1960s, the period between the suffragist movement and the second wave of feminism that began in the mid-1960s. In this period the dominant wing of feminism centered its attention on issues of class. Yet it sought to build not only the labor movement but also a *different* labor movement, one that took up the particular needs of women workers and welcomed women into leadership positions. Cobble examines some of the conflicts this activism created that divided women by class, relating those conflicts also to gender divisions in the working class. Recovering this history allows us to see that feminism did not die out in the decades between its generally recognized two waves, nor was the labor movement uniformly or simply a class uprising.

Class and race have been inextricably linked since the first settlements in the New World.[3] **BILL FLETCHER** looks at this history to explain the low level of class-consciousness among workers in the United States. As capitalism generates competition among workers in the labor market, race divides workers in a special way to make classwide unity rare. Fletcher also observes that the dominant role of the United States in the world contributes to "imperial consciousness" among workers, especially the native born, further dividing the working class by immigrant status and effectively disrupting international working class solidarity. To address this weakness, Fletcher proposes that workers in the United States create "social justice unionism" with a broad agenda that encourages class awareness and solidarity.

JEFF LUSTIG also looks at the long history of race in the United States. He points out that class consciousness does not arise spontaneously from conditions of oppression and exploitation. Because our interpretations of experience are filtered through politics and ideology, including views on race, the experience of class in the United States has always been merged with the experience of race. He recounts how racism weakened the reforms of the New Deal by exempting farm labor and domestic workers from Social Security coverage and wage and hour protections. Most black workers were in these occupations and therefore exempt, their white employers free from these obligations to them. This race difference in treatment of the working class was the requirement southern Democratic Party senators and representatives demanded before they would vote for the programs. Lustig pays special attention to the idea of "whiteness," which he characterizes as a cross-class alliance of white workers and white capitalists (and southern planters in slavery times). He uses racial history, especially among whites, in a critique of traditional theories of class that focus exclusively on economic conditions.

The connection between race and class has played an important role in the history of repression and terror in the United States. The Ku Klux Klan is rightly known as a racist organization that terrorizes black people. But the Klan also lynched union organizers throughout the South and fomented hatred against Catholics, almost all of whom were working class, and Jews, who tended to be liberal and antiracist. During the "un-American activities" hearings in the HUAC and McCarthy era, investigators looking for communist sympathizers routinely focused on whites who opposed racism.

Cobble, Fletcher, and Lustig help us to see why class never appears in pure form. Even though class has its roots in economic relationships, the people in classes are enmeshed in complicated networks of race and gender as well. While each of these "identities" has a certain integrity, none exists in isolation, and none can be understood without taking the others into account.

WHEN FEMINISM HAD CLASS

Dorothy Sue Cobble

Twenty-three-year-old Myra Wolfgang strode to the middle of one of Detroit's forty Woolworth's five-and-dime stores in 1937 and signaled for the planned sit-down strike of salesclerks and counter waitresses to begin. The main Woolworth's store was already on strike, and the Hotel Employees and Restaurant Employees Union (HERE) was threatening to escalate the shutdown to all the stores in Detroit. Wolfgang was an art school dropout from a Jewish Lithuanian immigrant family. A natural orator with a wicked wit, she had already given her share of soapbox speeches for radical causes as a teenager before settling down to union organizing in her early twenties. Nicknamed the "battling belle of Detroit" by the local media, she eventually became an international vice president of HERE. But in the 1940s and 1950s, Wolfgang ran the union's Detroit Joint Council, which bargained contracts for the thousands of union cooks, bartenders, food servers, dishwashers, and maids in Detroit's downtown hotels and restaurants. She relished a good fight with employers, particularly over issues close to her heart. A lifelong member of the National Association for the Advancement of Colored People (NAACP), she insisted, for example, on sending out racially integrated crews from the union's hiring hall in the late 1940s and 1950s, rejecting such standard employer requests as "black waiters only, white gloves required."

In the 1960s, Wolfgang, now in her fifties, led a sleep-in at the Michigan statehouse to persuade legislators to raise the minimum wage. She also brought Hugh Hefner to the bargaining table to talk about the work-

Portions of this chapter are drawn from Dorothy Sue Cobble, *The Other Women's Movement: Workplace Justice and Social Rights in Modern America* (Princeton: Princeton University Press, 2004); and from Dorothy Sue Cobble, "Lost Visions of Equality: The Labor Origins of the Next Women's Movement," *Labor's Heritage* 12 (winter/spring 2003): 6–24.

ing conditions of Playboy bunnies at his Detroit club. HERE eventually won a national contract covering all the Playboy clubs by 1969, but Detroit was the first to go union. In the initial bargaining sessions in 1964, Wolfgang and her negotiating team debated with management over the exact length in inches of the bunny suit, that is, how much of the food server's body would be covered. They proposed creating rules not just for bunnies but for *customers*—rules such as "look but do not touch." And they challenged the Playboy practice of firing bunnies as they aged and suffered what management called "loss of bunny image," a somewhat nebulous concept according to the union but not in the eyes of the Playboy Club. Bunny image faded, Playboy literature warned, at the precise moment bunnies developed such employee defects as "crinkling eyelids, sagging breasts, crepey necks, and drooping derrieres."

These fascinating and somewhat atypical labor-management conversations came only after an extensive seven-month organizing campaign. Wolfgang launched her assault by sending her younger daughter, seventeen-year-old Martha, in as a union "salt," shortly after the Detroit club opened in 1963. She was promptly hired, despite being underage. Martha then fed Mom a steady diet of useful information, particularly about the club's wage policies, or rather its *no-wage* policies. Bunnies, it turned out, were expected to support themselves solely on customer tips. Wolfgang and her volunteers picketed the club, wearing bunny suits and carrying signs that read: "Don't be a bunny, work for money." They also secured favorable media coverage, lots of it. To the delight of scribbling reporters, Wolfgang "scoffed at the bunny costume as 'more bare than hare' and insisted that the entire Playboy philosophy was a 'gross perpetuation of the idea that women should be obscene and not heard.'"

I first stumbled across Wolfgang—or, better put, she reached out and grabbed me—when I came across her papers some years ago in the Walter P. Reuther labor archives in Detroit. It was not just her entertaining antics that kept me awake. I was intrigued by her *political philosophy*, particularly her gender politics. She considered herself a feminist, and she was outspoken about her commitment to end sex discrimination. Yet at the same time, Wolfgang lobbied against the Equal Rights Amendment (ERA) until 1972, and she led the national committee against repeal of woman-only state protective laws. She also accused Betty Friedan, author of the feminist best-seller *The Feminine Mystique* (1963) and the first president of the National Organization for Women (NOW), of demeaning household labor, romanticizing wage work, and caring not a whit about the needs of the majority of women. Indeed, in a 1970 Detroit debate between Wolfgang and Friedan hosted by Women's Studies at Wayne State University, things rapidly devolved into mutual name-calling. Friedan called Wolfgang an "Aunt Tom" for being subservient to the "labor bosses" and Wolfgang returned the favor, calling Friedan the "Chamber of Commerce's Aunt Tom."[1]

My curiosity roused, I set out to discover more about the Myra Wolfgangs of the post-Depression decades. I came to understand that there were multiple and competing visions of how to achieve women's equality in the so-called doldrum years[2]—the supposedly quiescent trough of feminist reform between the 1920s and the 1960s. Moreover, the Wolfgangs of the world, far from being oddities, were the *dominant* wing of feminism in that era. In other words, a feminism that put class and social justice at its core did not end with the Progressive-era generation of women reformers. Indeed, stimulated by the rise of a new labor movement in the 1930s and the heady experiences of World War II, it emerged refashioned and modernized by the end of the war. And significantly, unlike the social justice feminism of an earlier era, it was led by *labor* women, women who identified with and worked in the labor movement, arguably the largest and most powerful social movement of the period.

But why hasn't this history been told before? Why aren't the reform efforts of labor women part of the standard narrative of postwar labor and women's history? In part, the absence results from long-standing gender biases that are still operative among many historians of labor. Labor history as a field takes as its primary focus male workers and their activities in the public wage-earning arena. Gender as a category of historical analysis remains external to the narrative and theoretical frame.[3] Yet labor women also are missing from the history of American *feminism*. Indeed, the scholarship on American feminism has a class problem. The history of feminism is largely the story of the efforts of white middle class and elite women to solve their *own* problems. The efforts of working class and minority women to achieve gender justice, as *they* define it, are relegated to the historical margins, if they appear at all.[4]

The labor women reformers featured in this chapter also had a class problem, but theirs was of a different sort. The class problem for them was, in many ways, what I assume it is for many readers of this volume, that is, how to create a *new* politics of class—one that recognizes the multiplicity of class experience and that refuses to take any single class identity or location as representative of the whole. In pursuing their aims, they chose to work closely with the labor movement, and they embraced many of its fundamental tenets. But at the same time, they sought to create a *different* labor movement, one that would include women fully in its governance and in its agenda. In so doing, they were pioneering an alternative feminism, a feminism that took class seriously and that sought a gender equality that would meet the needs of the majority of women, not just the few. The history of this forgotten generation of women labor reformers can help us envision a new class politics and a new, more inclusive feminism, one that would once again have class.

THE OTHER LABOR MOVEMENT

We have much to learn from our foremothers, even those who lived, worked, and organized in that supposedly benighted prefeminist era before the 1960s. Their generation came of age in the midst of depression and war. Many were "Rosies" who took on wartime jobs and at the war's end supposedly returned to the home and embraced a conservative gender ideology centered on domesticity. Yet the majority of women war workers were working class and had jobs *before* the war. The majority also kept on working *afterward*. Many of these women turned their energies in the postwar decades to building unions and to making those unions more responsive to the needs of women.

The story of union growth in the *1930s* is an oft-told tale. But for labor *women*, the 1940s proved just as crucial. The labor movement feminized substantially during the 1940s, adding millions of women to its ranks. The number of women in the labor movement skyrocketed in wartime and then plummeted immediately after the war, but what often gets lost is that the number rebounded in the late 1940s and then remained *far above* the 1930s levels in both *absolute* and *percentage* terms. By 1953, three million women were union members, a far cry from the eight hundred thousand who belonged in 1940, and the percentage of unionists who were women had doubled since 1940, reaching 18 percent. In addition, some two million women belonged to labor auxiliaries. Auxiliaries took in the wives, daughters, mothers, sisters, and, on occasion, "friends" of union men. By the 1940s, many of these women were also wage earners, albeit in unorganized sectors. Although not accorded the full rights and benefits of union membership in the international unions, central labor councils, and labor federations that issued their charters of affiliation, women auxiliary members defined themselves as an integral part of the labor movement, and they participated actively in its political and economic life.[5]

These women union and auxiliary members comprise an "other labor movement" as well as an "other women's movement." This "other women's movement," as Karen Nussbaum, the former head of the AFL-CIO Working Women's Department, enjoys pointing out, is still the largest women's movement in the country, registering over six million women, a fact not lost on the *Wall Street Journal*. In reporting the January

2002 release of U.S. government statistics on union membership, which revealed a 1 percent loss in male membership, down to nine and a half million, and a close to 1.5 percent gain in the number of women, up to almost seven million, the newspaper opened its story with the query "Women's Movement?"[6]

In addition to the rise in the number of women who belonged to unions, the 1940s witnessed the move of women into local, regional, and national *leadership* positions in the labor movement. This development should not be confused with gender parity in union leadership, by any stretch of the imagination. Nevertheless, the power and influence of women in unions increased, and a critical mass emerged of women union leaders who were committed to women's equality as well as to class and race justice. Myra Wolfgang was not alone. Many others made their mark as well: Esther Peterson, Dorothy Lowther Robinson, Gladys Dickason, and Anne Draper of the Amalgamated Clothing Workers of America (ACWA); Maida Springer-Kemp of the International Ladies' Garment Workers' Union (ILGWU); Mary Callahan and Gloria Johnson of the International Union of Electrical Workers (IUE); and a remarkable group of women at the United Auto Workers (UAW), including Caroline Dawson Davis, Lillian Hatcher, Millie Jeffrey, Olga Madar, and Dorothy Haener. Some of the most vocal and visionary labor feminists—women like Ruth Young, the first woman on the international executive board of the United Electrical Workers (UE), and Elizabeth Sasuly and Luisa Moreno of the Food, Tobacco, Agricultural, and Allied Workers of America (FTA)—disappeared from the public stage by the early 1950s, due in large part to cold war politics. But they were the exceptions, not the rule.[7]

It is impossible to give each of these women her due in a short essay. But let me offer two brief biographical sketches—one of Addie Wyatt of the United Packinghouse Workers of America (UPWA), and a second of Caroline Dawson Davis of the UAW. Hired in 1941 at Armour's meatpacking plant in Chicago, Mississippi-born Addie Wyatt, like many African American women in this period, had her first encounter with trade unionism during the war. It wasn't long before she filed her first grievance. The foreman had given her job to a newly hired white woman and reassigned her to a worse position on the "stew line." "I was very angry, and as I always did when there was something I didn't think was right, I spoke out." When the issue couldn't be resolved with the foreman, Wyatt and her union representative, a black woman steward, marched over to the plant superintendent's office. "What effect," Wyatt remembered thinking, could "two black women have talking to the two white, superior officers in the plant?" To her amazement, she and the steward won. Just as surprising was the union response when she got pregnant.

The steward explained the union's maternity clause: Wyatt could take up to a year off and her job would be held for her. "I didn't really believe them. But I thought I'd try it, and I did get my job back." By the early 1950s, her local (UPWA 437), the majority of whose members were white men, elected her as vice president. Later, she took over the presidency of the local and ran successfully for the UPWA's national executive board on a platform emphasizing women's rights and the advancement of racial minorities. In 1954, she was appointed to the UPWA staff as the first black woman national representative, a position she held for the next thirty years.[8]

Caroline Dawson Davis, who headed the UAW Women's Department from 1948 until her retirement in 1973, grew up in a poor Kentucky mining family steeped in religion and unionism. In 1934, she got a job as a drill press operator in the same Indiana auto parts plant that had hired her father. Caroline Davis had a strong anti-authoritarian streak, and, like Addie Wyatt, had a bad habit of stepping in to stand up for anyone being mistreated. Both these traits propelled her toward union activity. "The worst thing about a job to me was authority," Davis once explained. "I loved people," she continued, and "I believed in people. I never saw the difference between someone who had a title and a lot of money, and Joe Doe and Jane Doe who swept floors and dug ditches." Thirty-year-old Davis helped organize her plant in 1941, was elected vice president of UAW Local 764 in 1943, and, shortly thereafter, "moved upstairs when the union president was drafted." By 1948, Davis had taken over the reins of the UAW Women's Department. A year earlier, *Life* magazine had run a feature story on "the strikingly attractive lady labor leader," accompanied by a four-page photo spread of Davis. In one photo, Davis lounges at home reading Freud, a thinker whose ideas, she explained to the interviewer, proved indispensable to running her local union. "If I hadn't been a union leader," Davis added, "I would have been a psychiatrist."[9]

The majority of labor feminists[10] came up from the shop floor and were from working class and poor backgrounds, women like Wyatt and Davis. Yet some came from decidedly elite families—not what I expected to find when I first began my research. A generation earlier, many politically engaged college women would have moved into settlement house work, or joined the National Consumers' League, or pursued a career in social welfare. But in the context of the 1930s, they gravitated toward the labor movement. By the 1940s many held union staff jobs as lobbyists and political action coordinators, as community service representatives, and as research and education directors. A few, like Esther Peterson, eventually moved into key government posts.

Perhaps the most influential labor feminist of her generation, Peterson grew up in Provo, Utah, where her father was the local school superintendent. She received her BA from Brigham Young University in 1927 and then pursued graduate work at Columbia Teachers College before being swept up in the dramatic labor struggles of the 1930s. She taught theater, physical education, and economics to working girls at the local YWCA, and she was on the faculty of the Bryn Mawr Summer School for Women Workers until the school closed its doors in 1938, after the faculty and their worker students persisted in such questionable activities as helping the college maids organize. Shortly before her fourth child was born in 1946, Peterson moved from the Education Department of the ACWA to become its first Washington-based legislative representative. Then, in 1958, she became the AFL-CIO's first woman congressional lobbyist. As Peterson tells the story, she was assigned to John F. Kennedy, the junior senator from Massachusetts, because no one thought he would amount to much. Two years later, the newly elected president tapped her to direct the U.S. Women's Bureau. Eventually, she became the highest-ranking woman official in the Kennedy administration. She is often credited with playing a key role in the establishment of the president's Commission on the Status of Women (the first federal body devoted to assessing women's status and needs), the passage of the Equal Pay Act, and other significant federal breakthroughs of the early 1960s.[11]

SOCIAL RIGHTS AND WAGE JUSTICE

By the end of World War II, this group of women labor leaders had mapped out a broad-ranging and concrete social reform agenda that would guide them into the late 1960s. It also put them in opposition to the National Woman's Party (NWP), to the policies and principles being touted by conservative employers and politicians, and, at times, to the priorities advanced by their union brothers. They came together nationally at a series of U.S. Women's Bureau conferences held for trade union women leaders between 1944 and 1946, and they continued to socialize and work together for the next twenty-five years, first through the Women's Bureau Labor Advisory Committee, a group that served as a national think tank for top women in the labor movement from 1945 to 1953, and then through the National Committee for Equal Pay, which existed from 1953 to 1965, and other ad hoc coalitions.[12]

Like their opponents in the NWP, labor feminists recognized that discrimination against women *did exist*—an assumption not widely shared in the 1940s. Their goal was not to end *all* distinctions on the basis of sex, which they feared would be the result of the passage of the ERA. They sought only to end those distinctions that *harmed* women, that is, the "unfair" or "invidious" distinctions that amounted to discrimination. Some distinctions, they felt, actually benefited the majority of women, such as the woman-only state laws setting wage floors and hour ceilings. They wanted these protections extended to men; but until that happened, the laws should be retained. This conviction was a major source of labor feminists' opposition to the ERA.

Yet the battle over the ERA was not the only source of their alienation from the feminists in the NWP. Sex discrimination was a problem, they agreed, but it was not the *only* problem. Class, race, and other kinds of inequalities needed to be addressed as well. But how? Here again, labor feminists parted ways with the more individualist, equal rights feminist tradition often celebrated in current histories. Individual opportunity, access to the market, and equal treatment with men were important and necessary. But they were also *insufficient*, particularly for poor women. Working class women, like working class men, needed *more* than access to the market or the opportunity to move into the few positions at the top. They needed to *transform* the market *and* the nature of working class jobs. To effect this transformation, labor women looked to the state and to working class organizations.

Space precludes any kind of comprehensive history of labor feminists' reform efforts, but let me briefly describe their principal concerns. Making "no bones about the fact that there are certain things women need that men don't," labor feminists sought accommodation for women's reproductive labor from employers and the state. Pregnancy was not "developed by women for their entertainment," remarked one prominent labor feminist. It was a "social function" and as such should be borne by the community.[13] Labor feminists pushed unions to negotiate improved pregnancy and maternity leaves with job and income guarantees, health coverage for women during childbirth, and contract language that would give workers more control over their work schedules and more time off for family emergencies. Labor feminists also sought to expand disability and unemployment coverage to pregnant women and mothers, fought for tax reforms that would benefit families with dependents, and lobbied repeatedly for federally funded universal child care programs. When labor feminists testified before Congress in the 1940s and early 1950s on behalf of bills amending the Social Security Act, they argued for the importance of universal health care insurance, including the cost of childbirth, and they made a strong case for the sections of the bill that provided four months of paid maternity leave. Caring labor was as deserving of social wages and state benefits as any other work, they reasoned, and the right to a life apart from wage work was an important aspect of what they called "first-class economic citizenship" for women. "Women must not be penalized for carrying out their normal functions of motherhood," Esther Peterson told a convention of international government officials in 1958. But, she ruefully added, "the achievement of our real goal of adequate maternity leave with cash payment and medical and hospital insurance for all women workers is still ahead of us."[14]

These efforts are clearly forerunners to the work-family reforms that have become increasingly central to the current women's movement. Yet the core of the labor feminist work-family agenda still has not been incorporated into today's discussions. For theirs was a reform movement aimed at solving the problems of nonprofessional women. That meant, for them, finding *collective*, not *individual*, solutions to two crucial concerns: low wages and long hours.

The solution to raising women's wages that came to predominate by the end of the 1960s was to move women into higher-paying men's jobs. But this was not the primary strategy pursued by labor feminists. Rather, throughout the 1940s and 1950s they sought to upgrade and change the way the jobs held by the majority of women were valued and paid. The wage-setting systems used by employers undervalued women's skill, productivity, and responsibility, the labor feminists claimed, and a fundamental rethinking of employer pay practices was in order. In other words, when the comparable worth movement burst onto the national stage in the 1980s, resulting in millions of dollars of pay equity raises for secretaries, nurses, and others in underpaid pink-collar jobs, the idea was not new. It had a long historical pedigree rooted in the activism of union women of a generation earlier.

From the 1940s to the 1960s, labor women urged their unions to bargain, picket, and strike over the gender wage gap. They also launched a national legislative campaign for what they called "a fair rate for the job" or "equal pay for comparable work." They succeeded in passing new equal pay laws in eighteen states in the postwar decades, and, in 1945, they introduced a bill mandating equal pay for comparable work into Congress, reintroducing it every year until an amended version passed in 1963. But the amended version was a far cry from what labor women had envisioned. "Equal" had been substituted for "comparable" and the impact of the law diluted considerably. Women should be paid the same as men when they do the same work, the labor feminists had argued; they should also receive a fair and just wage when they do different jobs.

Yet labor feminists' approach to raising women's wages in this period was not limited to calls for equal pay. They also pursued higher wages for women by supporting the extension of collective bargaining to new groups of women, by lobbying for higher minimum wage statutes, and by resuscitating labor's long-standing claim to a "living wage"—or what some historians refer to as a "family wage." The labor movement's wage demands historically were gendered: if a single wage high enough to cover dependents could be achieved, it was often assumed that men would earn it and their wives would contribute to the family economy as homemakers. Rather than abandon the family wage, labor feminists wanted to degender it, to claim it for women as well as men. A just wage recognized dependency and acknowledged that, in many instances, a wage needed to support more than the individual wage earner. This is a particularly important point, given the ideological shift today toward a "market wage," or a wage supposedly determined solely by productivity or supply-and-demand calculations.

"What's after the family wage?" social theorist Nancy Fraser asked not too long ago.[15] Well, unfortunately, the answer does not appear to be a provider or family wage for all but a wage based on what economist Eileen Appelbaum calls an "unencumbered worker ideal." This false ideal and the low wage it justifies extends to women and increasingly to men a new myth of individualism, one that denies the reality of our social interdependence and sets up a false world of always able-bodied, perpetually self-reliant individuals—entities who exist apart from community, civic life, or caregiving responsibilities. This was not the world labor feminists sought.

ENDING THE "LONG HOUR DAY"

The struggle over time in the postwar era was as gendered as the struggle over wages. Mary Anderson, the immigrant boot- and shoemaker who became the first director of the U.S. Women's Bureau in the 1920s, argued then that the problem of women's inequality would never be solved until the "long hour day" was eliminated. But by the 1940s, the labor movement was seeking time off not in the form of shorter *daily* hours, but in the form of a shorter workweek, a shorter work year and a shorter work life. In the postwar decades, the majority of unions bargained for and won paid vacations, paid sick leave, and paid retirement—what UAW president Walter Reuther called "lumps of leisure." Labor feminists, for their part, supported many of these union campaigns. At the same time, they continued to press for shorter *daily* hours, because the "lumps of leisure" approach did not do much for those juggling the "double day" of household and market work.

Rebuffed in the bargaining arena, labor feminists turned to legislation. They were optimistic that the Fair Labor Standards Act (FLSA), the federal law covering wages and hours that many had helped pass in 1938, could be strengthened. Yet the state hour laws that covered women only—some forty-three states had such laws in 1957—offered even better protection against the long hour day. Many state laws set ceilings on *daily* and *weekly* hours and forbid *any* work beyond those maximums. In contrast, the FLSA used the disincentive of time-and-a-half overtime pay after a forty-hour week to discourage long hours, but it did not forbid them. The FLSA approach, many thought, was an inadequate check on employer power and on the competitive market's relentless drive toward longer hours. Throughout the 1940s and 1950s, then, labor feminists sought to preserve existing state hour laws and, where possible, extend them to men. The opportunity to earn was important, they pointed out, but so was a work time policy that reined in market work and allowed for the right *not* to work as well as the right *to* work.

But the sex-based state hour laws were repealed, and no new effective mechanisms for limiting work time were identified. Rather, the FLSA became the nation's primary regulatory approach to limiting long hours. Recognized as increasingly problematic today, its weakness is certainly part of the reason why work hours in the United States are longer than in any other industrialized country.[16]

AN UNFINISHED AGENDA

At the risk of oversimplifying the rich and complex history of postwar social justice feminism, let me conclude by drawing attention to a few of the principles that I take to be both central to that movement and worth reclaiming by those contemplating a feminist class politics for the future. The labor feminists who led the other women's movement in the decades following the Depression articulated their own distinct and evolving vision of women's equality. They sought social as well as individual rights, and the reform agenda they championed—just wages, protection against long hours and overwork, and the social supports and job flexibility necessary to care for their families and communities—launched a debate over employment practices that carries on today. Yet the social and gender inequities they identified have not been resolved. Indeed, economic inequality is on the rise, and the burdens that once bore down largely on working class women—long hours, the incompatibility of parenting and employment, and the lack of societal support for caring labor—are increasingly the problems of everyone. Ending those inequities for the majority of women will depend on a new class politics emerging within the larger women's movement as well as within organized labor.

Such an effort could profitably take many of its pages from its mid-twentieth-century foremothers. The labor feminists whose stories are told here recognized multiple sources of inequality and injustice, and they tried to build a politics that addressed these problems *simultaneously*. Gender, race, and other identities were not add-ons to class experience but inseparable features of it. The question for labor feminists was not whether class or gender or race should be given priority, but how social movements can incorporate difference and how coalitions across difference can be sustained. For the labor movement, that meant understanding that workers come in all sizes and shapes, and that there is no *one* class identity or consciousness because there is no *one* worker.[17] For the women's movement, it meant understanding that women differ among themselves, that is, that there is no one experience of gender, of gender exploitation, or even of gender liberation. Labor feminists believed, as do I, that the strongest political bonds are those that grow out of acknowledging differences as well as commonalities.

HOW RACE ENTERS CLASS IN THE UNITED STATES

Bill Fletcher Jr.

One of the most important political questions in working class studies is: What factors account for the surprisingly low level of class consciousness in the U.S. working class? Clearly there is no one explanation for this. Race, gender, American pragmatism, the westward expansion, identification with the empire . . . all of these have a major impact in terms of undermining class consciousness.

Nevertheless, I would argue that the trip wire of U.S. progressive politics and movements has principally been one of race, and the failure to appreciate the impact of race on class has led to misguided political strategies, as well as flights into magical thinking. Drawing from the works of W. E. B. DuBois and Ted Allen, as well as several other theorists, I wish to offer some views on the national and international significance of this question of the relationship of race and class. I wish to also draw on my own experience in the U.S. trade union movement in advancing these thoughts.

In the early part of the twentieth century, one of the foremost organizers for the Industrial Workers of the World, an African American named Ben Fletcher—no relation as far as I can tell—stated the following: *"Organized labor, for the most part, be it radical or conservative, thinks and acts in the terms of the White Race."* This is a very damning statement and one that should force us to reflect on its premise and conclusions. Many other trade unionists of color have, at various times, reached a similar conclusion. To put it in other terms: white trade unionists frequently put their whiteness ahead of their being working class. This approach, I would suggest, does not simply play itself out in the domestic realm, but has implications for the relation of the U.S.—and specifically white—working class to the global proletariat.

As an increasing number of theorists have suggested, "whiteness," as an aspect of the discourse on race, is a sociopolitical construct. "Race," in the way that we currently understand it, emerged first in the context of the English invasion and colonization of Ireland, and later it was transmuted with the African slave trade and the invasion of the Western hemisphere.

Race, as DuBois, Allen, David Roediger,[1] and many others have noted, is about social control rather than about biology. Science is increasingly demonstrating the commonality of humanity, whereby the similarities far outweigh the differences. If this is the case, then what is this matter of social control? Social control of what—or who—over what?

Class speaks to one's relationship to the means of production, distribution, and exchange. It speaks, in other words, to issues of power. It does not summarize the entirety of one's existence, but it does speak to the very basic power relationships in a society.

The defining feature of U.S. society is that of being capitalist. To paraphrase John Kenneth Galbraith, one of the main reasons that economists like to stay away from the term "capitalism," and instead use terms like "free market," is that when one uses the term "capitalism" one understands who is in control!

Capitalism engenders competition for limited resources within the working class. This competition is not a Machiavellian conspiracy; it exists at the heart of the system. The resources may be jobs, income, or, as much of the world is presently discovering, water. In any case, the nature of the system is to promote competition. There are never enough resources—no matter what the form—to serve the existing population because of the manner in which resources are divided up. The surplus, whether the surplus value produced by the workers themselves, or the societal surplus, is not up for some sort of equitable distribution.

All of this leaves aside intent. Intent is irrelevant. It is for this reason that capitalism is correctly described as an amoral system. There is no morality contained in it.

The competition for limited resources places one section of the working class at odds with other sections. This internal contradiction in the working class is a source of delight for the capitalists. Members of the working class are crabs in the barrel, so to speak. In response to this competition, trade unions developed, originally as guilds and later as the organizations that we would recognize today.

This basic understanding is critical: the divide-and-conquer element of capitalism is not something that has to be introduced from outside of the system. It exists within the system, much like a virus.

Divide-and-conquer at a general level alone is not enough to ensure the continuation of the system. The settlers who arrived in the original colonies, that is, the laboring element among the settlers, were in competition for limited resources. Yet the newly emerging capitalist system needed more than the fundamental tension that it produces. It is in this light that one witnesses the fusion of what comes to be known as race with the capitalist system. As my friend and mentor Manning Marable is fond of saying—and I am fond of quoting—U.S. capitalism can never be understood as some sort of capitalism in the abstract, but must be understood as racial capitalism.

The fusion of race and capitalism emerged in the 1600s, as is well documented by scholars such as Ted Allen and Lerone Bennett Jr.[2] The process took place over at least one hundred years and was accomplished through legislation and brutal repression. And it took place in the context of the development of a *settler state*, that is, an artificial creation resulting from the displacement of the indigenous population and repopulation by an alien people.

Race and settlerism introduced a dramatic alteration in class relations and composition. Race and settlerism suggested a more important "other" or "them" in the dichotomy of "them" and "us." In the initial stages of the conquest, the contradiction between the settler and the indigenous person was the overwhelming dichotomy. The Africans and Europeans brought to the New World were *both* brought as bond servants or indentured servants. The Africans, of course, had little choice in the matter of their forced "immigration" to these lands, but the fact that they were not initially slaves for life is noteworthy. They could, after serving out their "time," gain their freedom and own land. This mass of bond servants, however, created problems for the colonial ruling class, a point that Ted Allen documents. The contradictions between the bond servant workforce and the colonial ruling class necessitated the introduction of a more forceful wedge.

As you will note, I speak of both race and settlerism. I must credit J. Sakai for his work on this question of settlerism.[3] I do not necessarily agree with all of his conclusions, but I believe that his formulation is particularly important in terms of understanding the reality of the United States. The early years of the colonies held multiple significant contradictions: between the bond servants and the colonial ruling class; among the bond servants (either due to basic competition or due to race); and the contradictions between the settler population and the indigenous people. The uniting of the notion of whiteness and that of being a settler created the notion of a *relevant population,* or, to put it somewhat differently, it defined who was a "human being" or a "civilized person" versus who was a "barbarian" or "inferior." A similar process unfolded in Ireland much earlier, during the English conquest.

Class contradictions in the U.S., in time, came to be defined largely in the context of race and settlerism. By this I mean that the notion of a working class is almost always modified by race or ethnicity, rather than being a generic category. This was compounded, particularly in the twentieth century, with gender. To talk about "working class interests" in the absence of a racial context has been, for the most part, an abstraction. Why? Such references fail to acknowledge the brutal split in the working class that has existed since the inception of the North American settler state and continues to influence the reality of class politics in the United States. For the sake of clarification let me note that I am *not* saying that the United States lacks a working class. I am saying that this class has multiple interests, often-contradictory interests that are affected by race, ethnicity, gender, and empire.

I would like to make one more point about settlerism. Settlerism was another successful means of redefining "them" and "us" in explicitly nonclass terms. The interests of Native American miners, for instance, could not be paired with those of Anglo miners because the Native Americans were not part of the relevant population, at least from a settler point of view. They were considered to be outsiders and remained so, for the most part. Settlerism, in time, merges quite well with an imperial consciousness that placed the U.S. worker in opposition to the interests of workers in other countries. I will address this a bit later.

The linking of race and class is clearly understood by DuBois. His historic claim that the central problem of the twentieth century would be the color line speaks volumes to this.[4] In offering this suggestion, DuBois was not eliminating other contradictions. He was, however, placing his finger on the pulse of global and domestic capitalism. In an obvious sense, DuBois was noting the central importance of what came to be known as the independence or national liberation movements in the colonial and semicolonial world. He was also recognizing the important force that the African American freedom struggle, the Chicano struggle, and other domestic national freedom struggles would be.

I believe that DuBois was also offering an important note on class. As can be derived from a reading of his monumental work *Black Reconstruction in America*,[5] the extent to which so-called white workers saw their interests as linked with their respective colonial powers, or, in the United States, with the white establishment, was the extent to which the class struggle—as such—was muted. DuBois saw, in the smashing of Reconstruction, the construction of what came to be known as Jim Crow segregation, as well as the rise of modern colonialism, a system that ensured that the white worker would be, if not a partner, then a hear-no-evil, see-no-evil, say-no-evil observer in the dynamics of global capitalism.

Thus, race and settlerism *deformed* class struggle in the United States (and, indeed, I would suggest, race and colonialism deformed class struggle in the advanced capitalist world as a whole) in ways that help explain the peculiarity of consciousness of the U.S. working class as a whole, and white workers in particular. There are certain examples that I like to reference because of the paradoxes that they demonstrate. The International Seamen's Union (ISU) of the nineteenth century is an interesting case in point. Here was a union that could be described as militant, if not in some respects radical. Yet at the same time, it was thoroughly white supremacist. The politics of this union suggested that the interests of white workers needed to be protected against the interests of the hordes of Asia. What compounds this paradox is that, at one point in the nineteenth century, approximately one-third of U.S. sailors were black, but this was in no way reflected in the vision and actions of the ISU. The ISU saw the working class as *white*.

From a similar period came the Workingman's Party of California. This political initiative was, as well, white supremacist, focusing on the issue of Asian immigration. The question of who was in the working class was clearly answered in both race and gender terms; the working class was made up of men (and women only based on their relationship to their husbands and/or fathers), and white men (and women) in particular.

In the context of World War I, and indeed until his death, Lenin focused a great deal of attention on the splits in the international working class. To a great extent this focus was born out of what he saw as the betrayal of social democratic parties in their endorsement of the war. In his study of capitalist imperialism he focused on the notion of a "labor aristocracy" created as a result of the great riches that the major capitalist powers accumulated through colonialism.

Many theorists on the political Left have focused a great deal on this question of a labor aristocracy as being the principal split in the working class and the brake on class consciousness. While I would agree that the question of empire is very important in serving as a brake on consciousness, I believe that the economic benefits derived from colonial expansion exist as only one part of the larger problem. The conclusion at which many on the Left have arrived based on a *particular* reading of Lenin is that, in the absence of the economic benefits of colonialism or empire, a more recognizable and progressive class consciousness would emerge. I believe that such thinking is in error.

The construction of the "white working class" and its relationship to those deemed nonwhite have little to do with the temporary success or failure of the economy. The problem is far more deeply rooted. In the Great Depression, for instance, black workers were removed from jobs that they had previously occupied and replaced by whites—*earning the wages that black workers had been earning.* In other words, what was constituted was a *privileged situation,* or a *relative differential in treatment,* that was not based on the strength or weakness of the economy. Interestingly enough, Lenin himself discussed such a relationship when he wrote about the question of *national privilege,* though this has not received the same level of attention as the theory of the labor aristocracy.

With regard to privilege or relative differential, "Compared to what?" can be answered: whoever or whatever group is perceived to be at the bottom. This privileged position turns *whiteness* not only into an ideological category but into a practical, everyday category of life as well. Class, in any real sense that transcends or supersedes race or ethnicity, becomes more difficult to see because the lens through which one looks at it is racial. It is only through an understanding of this racial dimension that a class consciousness and a practice that attacks the reality of racist oppression can surface. I would draw similar conclusions about gender, by the way, though its history is quite different and I don't want to collapse one into the other.

Given this split in the working class and the factors that obscure class consciousness, traditional trade unionism faces objective limitations, a point that one can see time and again throughout U.S. labor history. What does working class unity mean, for instance, when the perception of that class and its interests are obscured by race, ethnicity, and gender? How can the South and the Southwest be unionized if key to organizing in these regions is the mobilization of African Americans, Latino immigrants, and Chicanos?

In fact, the obscuring of class by race almost ensures that the limits of trade unionism will be various forms of what is usually referred to as business unionism—sometimes more, sometimes less progressive. In either case, the dominance of a racial framework ensures that the most sophisticated form of class collaboration by most white workers vis-à-vis white capitalists dominates, even when coated with militancy. I would suggest to you that *this* is what lies behind the statement by Ben Fletcher, quoted earlier.

None of this means that there cannot be a certain form of operational unity. Clearly trade unions have been built, and in many cases they are multiracial and multiethnic. Nevertheless, the limitations of these organizations are displayed when the "racial trip wire" of U.S. social movements is breached. In the trade union movement this might mean coming up against internal issues such as job segregation, seniority systems, affirmative action, and hiring policies. Externally, it might mean encountering issues such as housing segregation and availability, school quality and segregation, and police violence. It should be noted here that issues such as these are not divided simply along the lines of a black-white dichotomy. The changing demographics of the United States have been felt deeply in the working class specifically, and the workforce generally. Thus, job competition has intensified between African American workers and Latino immigrants in many sectors. The manner in which this competition is viewed and interpreted has often undermined the possibility of developing an approach toward class and class struggle that builds unity rather than promotes interethnic rivalry.

The layer of "empire" or "imperial consciousness" exacerbates these contradictions. Returning to DuBois, to the extent to which workers in the global North, particularly but not exclusively white workers, see their interests linked with multinational capital and the political forces that support it, the possibility of building a sense of consciousness that crosses borders is foreclosed, except perhaps on a very tactical or nonpolitical basis. Let me use a provocative example. During the presidency of the late George Meany, the difficulty with the AFL-CIO's approach to foreign policy was not simply or solely a matter of what the leaders did or did not do. The fact of the matter is that these policies had social support in significant sections of the membership. That support was open and blatant, as well as being silent and acquiescent. Thus, AFL-CIO involvement in covert operations overseas to overthrow duly elected governments; participation in covert operations to undermine legitimate trade union movements; active support of the U.S. involvement in the Indochina War . . . these practices were at the least accepted or tolerated by a constituency in the membership. There was little in the work of the AFL-CIO, its affiliates, or most unions generally that addressed real international working class solidarity that may have challenged U.S. foreign policy. Again, such support of empire need not be very public; it can be support by omission—the omission of struggle.

The contemporary situation in the global North takes this matter of imperial consciousness a step further. While the living standard for the bulk of U.S. workers declined between 1973 and roughly 1996, and there were similar patterns in other parts of the global North, a sense of betrayal began to emerge as a major *political* force in the working class. This betrayal has often taken on a racial overtone and provided the necessary foundation for the growth of right-wing populism. One can see this in France, Italy, Austria, Germany, and Britain, just to name a few countries in the global North. In the United States one can see it as well, whether in the more extreme populism of Timothy McVeigh and the right-wing militias, or the more "credible" right-wing populism of politicians such as Patrick Buchanan. What is particularly interesting about this phenomenon, a phenomenon to which I have given a good deal of attention, is that it combines elements of a class analysis with right-wing irrationalism and racism. Parts of its message are anticorporate and appear to speak to the interests of the working class—or at least a segment of the working class—but then draw a whole set of conclusions that are antithetical to working class unity and progressive politics.

This right-wing populism reasserts the basic notion that under the white working class there should be a cushion. This cushion should be workers of color. In some cases, this cushion is determined by gender, particularly when it is asserted that women are taking "men's jobs." At the international level, there is also this notion of a cushion. Rather than accepting an analysis of capitalism that suggests that capital will move— or threaten to move—wherever it can in order to increase its own profitability, the right-wing populist message advances the view that it is the workers outside of the United States that are the threat. These workers are trying to take "our jobs." Thus, it should not surprise us that many foreign workers are deeply suspicious of our intentions, when it appears that the U.S. trade union movement is attempting to stop trade or the inflow of jobs that might help to alleviate their desperate situations. To the extent to which we articulate an anticorporate message that sounds protectionist, we will not be building solidarity, nor will we be promoting an advanced form of class consciousness here in the United States.

Given both the competition that is engendered by capitalism and the matter of social control that has been introduced over several hundred years, what does one do? What are the implications? Let me offer a few thoughts by way of conclusion.

I am fond of using a movie metaphor to describe a larger task. Back in the 1980s John Carpenter directed a film called *They Live.* It is a science fiction story about aliens that turn Earth into a neocolony, operating through human collaborators as well as with their own people who are made to look human. An underground group discovers that by wearing a certain type of sunglasses one can see not only what the aliens look like but also the subliminal written messages that they have placed all around us.

In a critical scene, one homeless man who has joined the underground tries to convince another homeless man to put on the glasses and see what is actually going on. There is a lengthy fight scene, since the second man refuses to put the glasses on. He keeps saying that he does not want to see. Eventually he does put on the glasses.

So, the first thing that is critical in our own adventure is that people must comprehend the truth about racial capitalism. They must put on the glasses, so to speak. There is great resistance to this, because in uncovering the little secret about social control in the United States, one is confronted with a whole new set of challenges. One can no longer rest comfortably, which is what the second homeless man in *They Live* realizes without saying it.

"Putting on the glasses" is not solely a matter of developing an intellectual knowledge of racial capitalism. There must be a practical knowledge of how the system works that only comes about through a fusion of intellectual knowledge and practical experience in struggle. I thought about this the other day when I was in a conference with someone who told us that while he was in college, years ago, he was in many discussions with white students about racism that were tearjerkers. Supposedly everyone was coming to a more advanced understanding of racism. This man's roommate—one Jerry Seinfeld—was allegedly one of those students. Yet Seinfeld would go on to make one of the most popular TV series of all time, which takes place in New York City, but in which people of color are all but invisible. In other words, "getting it" about racist oppression is not simply about talk.

An additional necessary step is the introduction of a new paradigm for trade unionism. My colleague and friend Fernando Gapasin calls it *social justice unionism*. I realize that there are all sorts of semantics involved in identifying a new sort of trade unionism and I don't want to engage in a frivolous discussion. Nevertheless, what we are attempting to identify is that trade unionism must be about more than rebuilding a movement. It must be more than a coalition. It must be more than organizing and militancy. *It must be transformative*. The trade unionism we need is one that builds a class consciousness that does not construct class so narrowly that we limit ourselves to either common economic demands or the fight for immediate rights and issues in the workplace. The fact that workers live in several dimensions simultaneously is what leads to a particular construction of class. This must be recognized in the approach that we take in organizing ourselves and moving forward.

Social justice unionism must challenge racial capitalism, and in that regard it treads on very dangerous ground. There are examples of unions, such as the Packinghouse Workers, that took on racism in the workplace, as well as encouraged their staff and stewards to engage in community organizing. This seems to approach a social justice trade unionism. Few unions have been willing to take such risks. Social justice unionism must engage in struggling against the actual divisions in the working class, whether in the workplace or in communities. This can take place only on the basis of an educational program that seeks to build solid support in the membership for such an advance. This is not about the simple passing of resolutions.

Let us consider one of the most formidable problems we face in the working class. Opinion poll after opinion poll indicates that white people generally believe that racist discrimination no longer exists as a systemic problem. In many cases they believe that African Americans are doing better than whites! Such a view makes working class consciousness in any real sense impossible. This reality became very clear during the O. J. Simpson case. Consider, for a moment, the evolution of that case. When O. J. was first arrested he had an entire following of white men who saw this case as an unfair attack on a man. The misogynist character of this support was blatant. As the trial progressed, it became a racial conflict, despite the fact that O. J. was never one to advance the black freedom struggle. At few points was the matter raised that O. J. got the best justice that money could buy. On top of this, the fact that blacks and whites experience U.S. so-called justice in such different ways led to a grand canyon in terms of understandings and assessments. One cannot have a progressive class understanding when such a canyon exists.

Consider also the question of immigrants. Across the racial divide in the United States, anti-immigrant views and practices are common. Rarely is there a discussion about why immigrants, particularly from the global South, come to the United States (or, for that matter, to the global North generally). I believe that the U.S. trade union movement has done a great disservice in not taking up this question, but it cannot unless it is prepared to tackle the implications of U.S. foreign policy and the implications of empire. We are not dealing with everyone wanting to come to the United States to live out their dreams, as a Jamaican immigrant character said on the TV show *Girlfriends*, but rather we are living with the implications of colonialism and imperialism and the destruction of economies and ecologies. As a British immigrant rights group says: "We are here because you were there."

There is no shortcut in the reconstruction of class and class consciousness that bypasses the reality of racial capitalism in the United States. Class consciousness, let alone class unity, will not be built by simply understanding that there are masses of people who have similar relations to the means of production, distribution, and exchange and thus have a common basis for unity. Unless the racial trip wire is defused, the closest we may ever come to working class consciousness is tactical unity on economic issues among all workers, and right-wing populism among a significant segment of white workers.

THE TANGLED KNOT OF RACE AND CLASS IN AMERICA

R. Jeffrey Lustig

A paradox haunts current considerations of class in America. Signs of class society appear all around us but the militant working class foreseen by traditional social critics is missing in action.

The living conditions of working men and working women deteriorate, on one hand, as companies downsize; low-paying, dead-end jobs proliferate; union rights are thwarted; the ranks of the poor expand; and the gap between rich and poor widens. One percent of the U.S. population now owns 42 percent of the nation's wealth and enjoys the power that comes with it.[1] Business exploits not only its workers but our environment and areas of social life—health care, schooling, the news media, even local government—that used to be protected from the profit motive.

On the other hand, the working class as an organized force and champion of other oppressed groups in society is absent from national politics. If class forces are those that challenge the basic structures of corporate production, then many doubt that even organized labor fills the bill. Activists and social critics in recent years have located the major social cleavages on lines of race, ethnicity, gender, or attitudes toward the environment, not class.

Already by the 1950s, many social scientists had begun to deny that America was any longer a class society. Struck by the absence of cutthroat individualists like Rockefeller or Carnegie, distracted by midcentury prosperity, and oblivious to new methods of corporate capitalism, they announced that the two-party system had given a "democratic translation [to] the class struggle"; workers were now integrated into the system as a nascent middle class; and interest-group competition now "guarantee[d] that the products of the society will not accumulate in the hands of a few power-holders."[2] Mirroring the old socialists' belief that class societies produce revolutionary struggle, these observers took the absence of struggle to signal the disappearance of classes. They mistook the absence of the cure for the passing of the disease.

But class remains a stubborn presence, as Michael Zweig shows in this book's introduction. What obscures this fact and produces the paradox are two things: Americans' famous social mobility and their identification of themselves in unexpected terms. Geographical mobility and job shifts alter people's lives and confuse their understanding of their situations; but they do not usually produce a real shift in class position.[3] More central in explaining the absence of an organized class movement is the unexpected self-identification of a major part of the workforce. This is clear, for example, in the support a majority of white working men have given the party that leads the fight against their interests *as* workers since the 1980s, the Republicans. Why do they do this? The answer is revealed by incidents like the Willie Horton ad in the 1988 presidential campaign, appealing to race prejudice while appearing to address crime, or California's Proposition 187 (discussed below), which coded race as illegal immigration. A majority of white workers currently identify themselves by race rather than class. And that has serious consequences not only for blacks, Hispanics, and other minorities but also for the white workers themselves and their efforts to achieve economic security.

Race and class are the "tangled knot" of American history.[4] This chapter traces how those two forces have interacted to constrict the lives of working people and choke off the long-term struggle for democracy in the country as a whole. We need to examine that knot to understand how class works in America and how the idea of class might be rethought so that we can regain its power as a tool of social analysis. Examining that knot will also help us to understand how race works in America and, in particular, why the two most favored remedies for racism today, the goals of colorblindness, on one hand, and of recognizing "diversity," on the other, have proven so ineffective. The first of those remedies attempts to deny race, while the second seeks to accentuate it, but neither addresses the class basis of minority oppression. Neither acknowledges that ending racism requires neither affirming nor denying blackness but, as Joel Olson puts it, "abolish[ing] whiteness"—dismantling a peculiar permutation of class and social power.[5] First, let's be clear about what we mean by "class."

TRADITIONAL CLASS THEORY

The language of class first emerged in England and France at the end of the eighteenth century to describe the new groups collecting around the emergent factories.[6] Those groups contrasted with the previous ranks, castes, and estates of the feudal era in that the earlier castes and estates had been parts of an organic hierarchical whole, defined by law and legitimated by custom. The new "classes," by contrast, were made up of atomized individuals, gathered by the accident of employment and bereft of customary rights and claims. The bourgeois fiction that everyone was an equal citizen released public officials from any obligations to or responsibility for the misery and degradation of these people, many of whom worked seventy-two-hour weeks in the brutal conditions described by Charles Dickens, Emile Zola, and, later, Upton Sinclair.

The socialists took the plight of the new working classes seriously, and their keenest analyst, Karl Marx, discerned that the workers' misery was due to the fact they were exploited and the products of their labor taken for the new factory owners' profits. The production of wealth in the new capitalist system, he saw, was also a simultaneous production of poverty. The capitalists' wealth did not come from clever trading in the marketplace (the realm of exchange), as they claimed, but from oppressing their workers in the factories (the realm of production). Because the new workers lived under economic conditions "that separate[d] their modes of life, their interests and their culture from those of other classes," Marx predicted in *The Eighteenth Brumaire*, they would develop different social values, create alternative institutions, and organize politically against those others to create a society in which no one had the power to systematically exploit others, and the wealth modern production provided could be enjoyed by all.[7]

Many societies have been divided into the haves and the have-nots. It was the contribution of class theorists to note that in capitalism the haves have because they take from the have-nots. Owners of production wealth have the power to determine what the society will and will not produce, and how it will produce it, and what will be left to the workers for their survival. Employees put up with this only because they have to in order to survive, their "labor contracts" disguising as voluntary agreement what is actually a form of coercion. Class analysts also saw that modern democracy harbors a system of domination at its heart, because the Bill of Rights stops at the plant gates. The wealth gained by capitalists through exploitation, finally, confers on them a private power that will rival, and eventually exceed, the public's power to govern itself.

The early class analysts thought that intermediate strata (farmers, small businessmen, artisans) would disappear as capitalism developed, and a homogeneous, unified working class would appear.[8] They thought that the major social contradiction would acquire visible expression as the two major class formations became arrayed against each other: exploiters versus exploited, capitalists versus workers.

Most students of race relations and writers on economic development agreed. They viewed racism as an obsolete holdover from the past, an epiphenomenon that would lose its force with time. In the 1940s, a decade before the civil rights movement, the sociologist Gunnar Myrdal concluded, "In principle, the Negro problem was solved long ago."[9] Race seemed like a cultural accident, whereas class was structurally generated and fundamental.

Marx and others saw the working class emerging in the society's mines, mills, and factories, in short, as a social force that would put an end to exploitation, racism, and other forms of social oppression. Workers, coming to understand their exploitation, would become a "class-for-itself" and then transform the structures of their work and life in fulfillment of the communitarian values they had incubated on the shop floor and in their local institutions. They would prove to be a "universal class," "a class which did not claim *particular redress,* because the wrong which has been done to it is not a *particular wrong* but *wrong in general,*" a class that would be "the dissolution of all classes" because it was in its interests to lay the groundwork for all people's liberation.[10] Working people's values would lead them to spurn bourgeois selfishness in favor of solidarity and economic anarchy in favor of rational social organization. This would give rise to the demand not simply for higher wages but for a qualitatively different way of life,[11] not simply for a bigger piece of the pie but for a different pie altogether.

In this view workers were not only poor and not only kept poor despite their efforts but, more positively, were also the creators of social wealth, holders of strategic leverage, agents of collective action, and champions of general emancipation. In contrast to the recent notion of class that reduces it to a step on an income or status ladder, this larger theory saw class position as determined by ownership of *wealth*—producer (not consumer) wealth. Wealth confers individual power over life chances and social power over workers' lives, the nation's priorities, and the society's paths of development. ("Lack of income means you don't get by; lack of . . . [wealth] means you [also] don't get ahead.")[12] That class is a matter of power escapes those who focus attention on income gradients without taking time to examine the causes of the gradation.

In contrast to the view that reduces class to an income or status group, the broader theory also sees the relationship between classes as inherently conflictual. Businessmen concentrate their holdings and are constantly forced by the need for capital accumulation to try to cut wages and curtail workers' political rights in the effort to reduce them to the status of commodities. Workers, seeking stability and greater freedom for themselves and their families, are forced to resist. The antagonism and contradiction between the two survives even periods of quiescence and apparent truce.

Despite the accuracy of many of the older analysts' predictions, class formation and political organization in America have not occurred in the manner predicted. The political scientists Donald Kinder and Lynn Sanders found that class division was "fading . . . as a force in politics"— and in contrast, intriguingly, to the growing importance of race. By the 1990s, one Marxist scholar was forced to admit, "Class struggle . . . has disappeared from the scene." And the historian David Brion Davis concludes, "We have entered another era when race has preempted class."[13]

To see how this has come about and what it reveals about the shortcomings of traditional class theory it helps to look at what recent scholarship has revealed about the interconnected historical evolution of race and class in America.

THE LEGACY OF RACISM

When an emigrant population from a "multiracial" Europe goes to North America . . . and there, by constitutional fiat, incorporates itself as the "white race," that is no part of genetic evolution. It is . . . a political act."
— Theodore Allen, The Invention of the White Race

The first point to understand is that race and ethnicity affected class formation in America from the beginning. Already by the 1840s, organized "workers split themselves along ethno-religious lines. American-born Protestant workers participated in broad evangelical reform movements or more nativist groups, while immigrant Roman Catholic workers withdrew into insular ethnic communities. . . . Workers fractured politically."[14]

Capitalist employers exploited those ethno-religious distinctions in their efforts to break strikes and periodically cut wages. But it was the workers themselves who "fractured politically." The early craft unions often operated as protectionist guilds, for example, to exclude new immigrants from Ireland and southern Europe (who were not yet "white") from apprenticeships, jobs, and political influence.

The second point is that, from the beginning, worker identity in America included a racial identification. Coming to consciousness of their standing in a society that preserved racialized chattel slavery, members of the new working class often drew the distinction between themselves and the slaves more sharply than that between themselves and their bosses. Whiteness became an integral part of the new identity, "worker." This identification was particularly important given that the workers, aspiring to dignity and independence, were constantly threatened with status demotion by common law master-servant precedents that treated them as less than full citizens.[15] Membership in the "white race" provided status and recognition and a shoring up against this threatened derogation. In the South, as W. E. B. DuBois famously noted, poor whites were paid "a sort of public and psychological wage" in social standing in return for helping police and coerce blacks, offsetting the sense of their own inferiority and distracting them from their own degrading job conditions.[16]

The subsequent struggle to create unions and workers' political associations in the late nineteenth century became in important ways a racial project, as Saxton has shown. The workers' clubs and political parties did not simply attract like-minded people; they *created* a propensity in their members for racializing those, like the Chinese in California, who looked different.[17] Not incidentally, this helped create a sense of belonging among people who themselves were strangers in a strange land. Part of learning to be a "worker" for dominant sectors of the American workforce became learning to seek group advantage by racializing fellow workers and scapegoating them for problems not of their making. That assured access not only to scarce jobs but also to increasingly scarce dignity in the context of emerging class antagonisms.[18]

This history, thirdly, reveals something important about whiteness. It reveals that that quality did not derive from a common ancestry, for there was none. French, Germans, Irish, and Eastern Europeans all eventually became "white" along with English people. Nor did whiteness refer to a common physiognomy, for the same reason. Nor, despite many people's claims, did it denote a common culture, there being little to unite Irish Catholics with Scandinavian Lutherans (or with Hungarian Catholics, for that matter), or impoverished sharecroppers with plantation bourgeoisie. What it did denote was membership in the white race, a sociological group that was "neither a biological nor a cultural category, but . . . a *cross-class alliance* between the capitalist class and a section of the working class."[19]

The precondition for membership in that race was what people were *not*—they were not black, the hue of the now-paradigmatic Other. "Without the presence of black people in America, European-Americans would not be 'white,'" Cornel West observes; "they would be only Irish, Italian, Poles, Welsh, and others."[20]

Blackness for its part drew its meaning, Chief Justice Tawney candidly admitted in his notorious *Dred Scott* opinion, from the fact that whites had "stigmatized them . . . with deep and enduring marks of inferiority and degradation."[21] It had become a "badge of servitude" not, that is, because

of anything intrinsic to African heritage but because of the physical oppression to which African Americans had been subjected for economic
purposes. Negroes wound up not just as noncitizens but as "*anticiti-
zens*,"[22] the Other against whom citizenship defined itself. And race, since
its origins, has thus been an artifact of economic oppression and political
decision (like the *Dred Scott* decision itself). Guinier and Torres acknowledge this with their idea of "political race."[23]

Fourth, the creation of the white race alliance critically affected working class formation in America. Class distinctions among whites were not
ended "but secured by it," as Olson notes.[24] The fact that in the years after Reconstruction the dominant sectors of the working class were defined in racial terms served to blunt white workers' efforts to plumb the
real sources of their degradation on the job and before the law, discour-
aging them, in contrast to Europeans, from taking their own *wage* slavery
seriously.[25] This is not to say that the period lacked for class struggle. The
Haymarket, Homestead, and Pullman strikes epitomized a long series of
conflicts that shook the country at the end of the century. But the reluctance of workers to acknowledge the real character of their subordination
prevented them, on balance, from analyzing their working conditions in
a way that transcended traditional terms. "The chains that bound the
African-American thus also held down the standards of the Irish-Amer-
ican slum-dweller and canal-digger as well."[26]

Fifth and last, racism would became part of the institutional reality of
American society. The segmentation of the labor market epitomized by
slavery continued in other forms and for other subordinated peoples. By
mid–twentieth century, even social scientists who ostensibly denied the
significance of class inadvertently acknowledged that "there are two
working classes in America today," a white one and a Negro, Puerto Rican, and Mexican one—the former of which "benefit[s] economically and
socially from the existence of these 'lower castes' within their midst."[27]
Segments of organized labor unfortunately played a role in maintaining
this situation.[28]

This labor market segmentation is the keystone in an arch of institutions—economic, educational, legal, and political—that function systematically to disadvantage racialized groups and to advantage the
racializers. The processes in different social sectors interact so as to create
a system of institutionalized racism. It is not difficult to see how this
works. To consider a simplified model: we know that a bad job pays poor
wages; poor wages can pay for only cheap lodgings; areas of cheap housing offer poor schooling; poor schooling in turn prepares people for only
bad jobs; bad jobs pay poor wages . . . and the cycle continues.[29]

Racism, then, is part of the institutional and material, not simply the attitudinal, reality of the society. Differential racial opportunities are churned out as part of the society's normal workings, and are not simply residues of an unfortunate past. Nor are they dependent on overt acts of prejudice.[30] Without having asked for special favors, white people acquire what George Lipsitz terms a "possessive investment in whiteness"—an accumulation of assets gained from unequal educational access, job access, housing advantages, eligibility for bank loans, and access to insider networks.[31] While most may not be conscious racists, in the absence of a larger vision or shared purpose they oppose any effort to devalue those investments. Ending racism in America would require a breaking up of that cycle and enactment of broad social-structural reforms, something more substantial than an appeal to tolerance or weekend "diversity" retreats.

RACE, CLASS, AND AMERICAN POLITICS

The Struggle for Social Citizenship

The knot of race and class has left its permanent mark on American politics, blocking the path toward democracy. Democracy requires formal rights, like those enumerated in the Bill of Rights to free speech, free conscience, free association, trial by jury, and so forth. But beyond the formal statement it also requires that those rights be actually usable. And for people to have rights that are usable and *effective*, certain material preconditions have to be secured—a job, physical safety, an education, adequate housing, medical care. Without those preconditions the formal rights are a dead letter. They can't be exercised. This struggle for substantive (not merely formal) democracy is a struggle for *social* (not merely political) citizenship.[32] For a brief period after the Civil War, white and black workers both expected to secure this citizenship. Blacks looked to enforcement of the new Thirteenth, Fourteenth, and Fifteenth Amendments and the promise of "forty acres and a mule" (i.e., the acquisition of producer wealth). White workers hoped that the labor movement, the Homestead Act, and other measures would give them a starting stake. The betrayal of Reconstruction, however—the gutting of the Fourteenth Amendment and defeat of a divided labor movement—ended such hopes for sixty years.[33] A solid South resting on that cross-class alliance, the white race, providing only minimal security for poor whites, was permitted to consolidate itself.

Sixty years after Reconstruction this bloc came back during the New Deal to thwart poor whites' renewed effort to attain the material preconditions for equality and citizenship. The southern elites, constituting the hidden power in the Democratic Party, made up the "reactionary core . . . at the heart of the New Deal coalition" that stopped the New Deal in its tracks and "prevented all Americans from securing the boon of social citizenship." The southern Bourbons successfully weakened the efforts to provide national unemployment and full old-age insurance, erect labor protections for all (including agricultural and domestic workers), fashion an effective Fair Labor Standards Act, and put teeth into the Employment Act of 1946.[34] While the civil rights struggles of the 1950s and 1960s succeeded in ending legal segregation and overt discrimination, they did not return to this older struggle for substantive democracy.

As we enter the twenty-first century American society still reveals the disregard for working people's interests (opposition to their right to organize, for example, or absence of low-cost housing), the subordination of their needs to the interests of capital (as with plant closures and job loss), the failure to provide decent wages or unemployment insurance, and the depleted public services (deteriorating schools and mass transit, shuttered libraries) characteristic of a class society. But the anxiety and dismay produced by such dislocations expresses itself in other than directly economic terms. Pain travels.

And American racism endures and evolves. It continues to justify the displacement of capitalism's human costs onto the weak. It provides a way for whites still suffering insecurity and poverty to shore up scarce status and dignity. And by providing a lightning rod for ultimately class-based fears and worries, it masks the major causes of social inequality and makes it seem "natural." It, of course, does other things as well. Race in America has always had its own character, dynamics, psychologies, and approach to social control—along with the positive beauty and richness of ghetto and barrio cultures. It would be a mistake to reduce race *to* class. But it would also be a mistake, we see, to try to understand it *without* class.[35] Race is a political and economic, and not just a cultural and psychological, phenomenon.

Further Twists in the Knot

Understanding the knot of race and class makes it possible to also understand the outbreak of race and immigration politics during the 1990s that heralded a distinctly undemocratic turn in national politics.

California is often regarded as the bellwether of developments in the rest of the country, and events in that state are instructive about this turn in national politics. A new punitive mood had become apparent in the Golden State already back in 1986, when voters, ignoring their state's bilingual origins and booming immigration rate, passed an initiative

(Proposition 63) that declared English to be the state's official language.[36] That mood took on breadth and force during the economic downturn of the early 1990s, as voters, blaming the scarcity of jobs and state monies on an alleged generosity toward immigrants and prisoners and on affirmative action benefits for minorities and women, passed further retributive measures.

Proposition 184, the "three-strikes" law that mandated prison sentences of twenty-five years to life for criminals convicted of a third felony, passed in 1994. Considering the demographics of those convicted and sentenced, many saw it as part of a coded racial agenda. Proposition 187, passed in the same election, sought, more importantly, to annul the rights of undocumented immigrants (now construed as criminals) to social services, nonemergency health care, and public schooling. The measure, which also required social service providers to report suspicious applicants to authorities, inadvertently created a new Insider in the process of fashioning a new Outsider—the citizen as informer to match the noncitizen as criminal welfare cheat. The sentiments kindled during its controversial passage helped persuade the federal government to later cut benefits for *legal* immigrants in the welfare reductions of 1996.

A spate of antiminority measures followed. The Regents of the University of California banned racial preferences in college admissions in 1995. By spring of that year ten anti–affirmative action bills moved through the state legislature. These were lumped into Proposition 209, prohibiting the use of race, ethnicity, or gender in public university admissions and public sector hiring and contracting. This proposition became a constitutional amendment in 1996, also effectively outlawing any voluntary public-sector efforts to break up the mechanisms of institutional racism unless ordered to do so by the court as remedy for past discrimination.[37]

In 1997 the state's Industrial Welfare Commission also abolished a rule dating back to the Progressive Era requiring most nonfarm workers who put in more than an eight-hour day to be paid overtime. And in 1998, state voters passed Proposition 227, drafted and financed by a Silicon Valley executive, outlawing bilingual education and requiring that foreign students be immersed in English-speaking classes.

These were serious measures, rekindling xenophobic and exclusionist sentiments and recasting the terms of social membership, even if key provisions of Proposition 187 were later overturned by the courts. A physical wall began to be built through a binational society at the Mexico–United States border at the same time walls were being torn down in Berlin and South Africa. Such drastic measures were defended by only the flimsiest of pretexts. The half-billion dollars spent on social services for people without papers hardly accounted for the massive $14.3 billion state budget shortfall of 1991–1992 and multibillion dollar deficits thereafter. Many studies indicated that the newcomers actually made a net contribution to the state's finances.[38] In fact, undocumented immigration had long been part of the state's policy for precisely that reason, to fuel profits for agribusiness and for marginal firms in Los Angeles. Nor had affirmative action or bilingual classes provided significant preferences given the institutionalized pattern of advantage and disadvantage noted above.

The fears about jobs and personal stability were real enough, but their causes lay elsewhere. They lay in a national recession, cutbacks in defense spending, job loss as capital encouraged by tax laws sought super profits in other nations, and a frayed public safety net caused by the *structural* budget crisis that began to appear after Proposition 13's tax cuts of 1978.[39] In the era of corporate capital, wealth wrested from workers in factories is no longer enough. Wealth must also be siphoned away from public programs and the limited reforms of the New Deal dismantled. Public controls on capital must also be removed to increase its freedom of maneuver (as with Enron), and convert the state into a vehicle of *corporate* welfare. The causes, that is, were largely class causes.

Affirmative action is essentially a rationing system that attempts to offset the operation of the nation's primary system, which is rationing by wealth and the cultural literacy wealth provides. It seeks to make up for minorities' lack of a real starting stake and to make genuine equality of opportunity possible. Wealth, cultural literacy, and the economic patterns described above, not some pristine "merit," are what allocate scarce education, health care, housing, and legal resources in our society. (That's why one researcher can say, "Tell me the zip code of a child, and I will predict her chances of college completion.")[40]

But the real question posed in the 1990s had less to do with methods of rationing than with why rationing is necessary in the first place. It had to do with that preexisting scarcity. Why should the material conditions of citizenship be scarce? Why in the wealthiest nation in the world *are* jobs and housing and health care hard to get? Given the record salaries of the biggest CEOs and increases in wealth of the richest citizens in the 1990s at the same time that massive reductions caused a *dis*investment in education, hospitals, and social infrastructure, this is a question about the power of private profit to work its will against social needs. It is a class question.

It cannot be recognized as such, however, and class questions cannot be raised politically as long as people stick to the racial terms in which issues and social conditions are currently presented. Nor can the power of business to siphon off more jobs and degrade working conditions be checked, nor the public's power to rebuild higher education and public health facilities be restored. Nor, finally, can white workers and their families see that they too will suffer from the continuing fragmentation of popular power.

Class questions cannot be raised because the groups that might raise them remain divided between racializers and racialized, fighting in a box without questioning the existence of the box itself. And despite the hopes of many, those divisions are not diminishing. All too many blacks "are more deeply mired in poverty and despair than they were during the 'separate but equal' era."[41] And the difference between blacks and whites on many public issues is "greater today than in any other period for which we have data," political scientists Kinder and Sanders report.[42]

The social construct of "whiteness" also remains intact. Indeed, California's politics in the 1990s are to be understood not primarily as expressions of nativism or exclusionism but as efforts to hang on to the privileges of whiteness in unstable times. Whiteness remains, first, in those socially conferred privileges noted above. Even the poorest whites can avail themselves of at least some "wages" of status and opportunity. Whiteness remains, second, as an assumed commonality with the powerful, a fictional likeness that blinds people to the fragility of their own hold on economic security and the ways the game is rigged against them. Whiteness remains, finally, as that most basic of benefits enjoyed by a dominant order, the privilege of thinking oneself normal, of taking one's own position for granted and not having to reflect on one's relations with or responsibilities to others. The color of power is white.

The tangled knot remains. In order to deal with class we will have to overcome race. But in order to deal with race, as David Brion Davis suggests, Americans will have "to confront the underlying reality of class division in America and the destructive myth of a classless society."[43]

CLASS RECONSIDERED

It will help in clarifying this underlying reality if we understand that the ordeal of race in America not only disproves the predictions of older class theorists but also identifies elements of class theory that need to be rethought and reformulated if we are to comprehend the character of social power and the plight of other groups in addition to African Americans. We can summarize these points before concluding this chapter.

First and most obviously, the continued salience of race disproves the prediction that working people would develop a single homogeneous identity and that the social structure would become simplified over time.[44] Working people in all industrial societies remain differentiated beyond race by skill level, urban or rural location, industrial sector (white collar versus blue collar), and divisions based on new job categories (e.g., new technologists versus high-tech workers). These factors provide different bases for group identification and rivalry.

Second, then, the experience of racism warns against assuming that people's interests can be deduced directly from their positions in the economic structure and that objective laws can be deduced about them. Human beings are not physical objects or stimulus/response mechanisms about whom scientific laws can be formulated. Between stimulus and human response, consciousness intervenes; and consciousness is a product of history and politics.[45] This is where America's famed social mobility plays a role—not disposing of class, but constantly disrupting the cultures that might help us to understand class situations and roles over time. Without this focus many workers may, on the basis of their histories or of current politics, choose, as we have seen, to trace their troubles to workers of color, or immigrants, or even the government.

Third, in light of these different social divisions, the very idea of "identity," with its implications of singularity, may be misleading. People possess multiple, overlapping self-conceptions. They may simultaneously identify with their job, their region, their ethnic group, the nation (as patriots), the middle class (as consumers), or the working class (as producers). "Class," Aronowitz writes, "never appears in pure form."[46] Which of these aspects acquires priority depends on the issues at hand and how they are framed. Rather than objective positions producing "interests," the way a political struggle is defined and explained often determines how people identify themselves.

Thus, fourth, we need to reimagine the sort of body that can give voice to class issues. A class-for-itself is not an objectively given entity. Nor will future class issues be formulated or struggles undertaken on the lines traditionally predicted. Class issues will most probably be raised by an alliance or bloc of forces, the elements of which experience class in different ways. And class issues will become politically significant only to the extent that working people reforge the connection with the community severed by modern industry, and remember that class consciousness is not an exclusive product of the shop floor or the union movement. That consciousness, as Thompson emphasized, is also a product of larger community institutions engaged in struggle. (The success of the Justice for Janitors' and hotel employees' struggles in Los Angeles in the late 1990s was due to their appreciation of this fact. They understood the threats posed by Proposition 187 and other measures and successfully recruited their larger communities to their struggles.)

The variability of group identification warns us, lastly, against assuming the automatic leadership or universal role of any group in the broader community institutions. Different oppressed groups face different forms of injustice, and they seek different remedies. Ridding the society of systematic economic exploitation is a necessary condition for overcoming racism, and ethnic prejudice, and sexism, and neocolonial pretensions; but it is not the only condition. It is perfectly legitimate and desirable that different groups will give different issues priority. The cultures of such groups may even provide the qualitatively different values and communal forms that traditional class analysis recognized as necessary for real social change.

Creating unity between different subordinated groups, developing different forms of class consciousness in each, and framing an alternative vision that can unite them will not be achieved by any preexisting "universal class." These are tasks that can only be accomplished through political struggle. And such a vision, to truly appeal to a majority of people, would have to be built up out of their current identities and the different ways they live class now.

CONCLUSION

After three centuries of bond labor, Jim Crow laws, and segmented labor markets, race is an established part of American life, part of its "material" reality and not just a cultural epiphenomenon. It is the social formation that openly manifests among other things the society's class contradictions.

That's why the struggle against it holds a central place in the larger struggle for democracy and against the concentration of power and the suppression of human possibility characteristic of class societies. The class character of American race also explains why it is that the current remedies for racism have been so ineffective in their results. One of these remedies, we noted, seeks to achieve colorblindness. It attempts to attain equality before the law, but without acknowledging that lacking the material conditions of citizenship, this will not provide equality of opportunity or any other meaningful parity. It fails to recognize the truth of Justice Blackmun's dissenting opinion in *Bakke:* "In order to get beyond racism, we must first take account of race. . . . In order to treat some persons equally, we must treat them differently."[47]

The contrasting appeal, to "diversity," takes its cues from identity politics and our differences rather than any underlying commonality. The proponents of black (or brown, or feminist, or gay) politics have made genuine contributions to our understanding of social injustice and identified forms of exclusion formerly denied by both mainstream and radical politics. But in recent years they have moved away from broad social critiques and ceased to look for the deeper causes of their inequalities. And they have ceased to present qualitative alternatives to current arrangements and a larger social vision that could unite their struggles with others'.[48] They therefore risk reducing the call for diversity to a call only to get more members from their own groups in corporate headquarters and state legislatures. They risk limiting themselves to the call for a larger share of the spoils of a game still rigged to exclude the majority of their fellow-citizens.

Neither of these approaches addresses the reality of institutional racism or its deeper class character. Neither addresses the need to confront the class conditions of racial minorities' lives. And neither acknowledges that whiteness, as the visible sign and mask of a system of power, is not something to be emulated or treated on par with other ethnicities. It is the sign of a cross-class bloc of power that needs to be dismantled. And that can only be done by creating a cross-*racial* alliance among working people.

It will help in this if white workingmen and workingwomen remember two truths learned by our forbears in earlier struggles. The first is that democracy is not provided by official documents or large armies sent overseas but by political activity on the part of all, having secured the material bases for a citizen's life. Racializing minorities and scapegoating outsiders does nothing to accomplish this, and raises barriers against it instead. The second is that freedom is ultimately a matter of mutual care and social solidarity, not of private possessions and separate group fortunes. We are dependent on each other, "members one of another," as the old Puritan phrase put it. Social obligations precede political rights.

At the beginning of a new century things look worrisome for both the racializing and racialized sectors of the workforce. Both are on thin ice in their job rights and living standards. We are entering another period in which white workers will be divested of gains they thought they'd won, and minorities cheated of advances they thought were coming their way. Security in the job is gone, public services are starved, the quality of life is declining. We know from understanding how capital works that pressures to deprive workers of decent job conditions and social rights will increase. We also know that the political party on which both groups depended in the past is no longer seriously interested in their plight. There is nothing, then, to prevent the pressures from breaking through the thinning ice in the next decade.

Nothing, that is, except working people's own political struggle. Will we react to coming reverses by fracturing again on racial lines, whites and would-be whites turning on the weak, as anticipated by California's Proposition 187? Or will we get out of this historical rut, attempt a cross-race alliance, and resume a common struggle for democracy? The answer will depend not on outside forces, economic trends, or national leaders but on the character of our own political leadership and organizing.

PART II
CLASS IN A GLOBAL ECONOMY

In part 1 Bill Fletcher warned that an "imperial consciousness" among American workers is an obstacle to resolving the tensions between race and class in the United States. Globalization has enmeshed every country in an increasingly integrated network of economic and political relationships. The chapters in part 2 look more closely at the global economy, using class analysis to understand its rules and implications.

WILLIAM K. TABB begins with the observation that class operates in the global economy very much as it does within individual capitalist countries. Globalization is a process through which the United States seeks to extend the economic power of its capitalist elite. The economic freedom that comes with the spread of the free market is the freedom for capitalists to gain from trade and, especially, from the flow of capital across borders. Tabb shows us how this works to the detriment of workers and the environment everywhere. He demonstrates that globalization is not simply an economic process but a deeply political one in which the power relations of class play out. He suggests that the antiglobalization movement that has arisen on the basis of the 1999 protests against the WTO in Seattle should recast itself as a global justice movement that demands a *different kind* of global economy, and national economies as well.

LEO PANITCH also stresses the political aspects of class and the economy. He documents the continuing importance of the nation-state as a central institution of globalization. He argues that effective power is not in the hands of a new and coherent transnational capitalist class. Rather, the superpower United States has become the world's first global capitalist empire. Panitch adds one more element to the context for September 11: the systematic destruction of left-wing secular opposition to capitalism and empire in recent decades. In the absence of viable secular nationalist or communist parties, fundamentalist religious parties have

often filled the vacuum to deliver organized opposition to the injustices
and suffering that global capitalism spreads. The U.S. response has been
to try to consolidate its empire. It has extended its military power farther
and more permanently across the globe and pressured other countries to
apply their own military resources to support U.S. political and economic
goals. Panitch suggests that the conflicts this process engenders in Third
World and advanced countries alike can best be understood with a class
analysis of those countries and the global economy.

KATIE QUAN brings the discussion back to the United States. She describes the impact of globalization on workers in the garment industry
and shows that the international mobility of capital threatens the jobs of
workers in Thailand and other Third World low-wage countries as much
as in America. Yet Quan has found that international labor solidarity is
difficult to sustain, especially in the absence of class understanding. She
traces the history of the AFL-CIO's attitudes toward immigrants and foreign workers and reports that the new policies under the leadership of
John Sweeney provide an important opening for more class-based organizing.

NEOLIBERALISM AND ANTICORPORATE GLOBALIZATION AS CLASS STRUGGLE

William K. Tabb

How class works in a global economy is not so different from how class works in individual nation-states, although it is complicated by a number of factors: the increasing globalization both of labor markets and of corporate investment, production, and sales; the reorganization and reconstitution of the capitalist class caused by increased international economic penetration; and the corresponding reorganization and reconstitution of the capitalist class, whose members, despite their diverse locations and cultural identities, now more than ever need to unite. So far the capitalists, through mediating tools such as the World Economic Forum and the International Monetary Fund, have done far better than the working class in recognizing and acting on their class interests to restructure the way the economic, political, and social spheres function. But, increasingly, workers, too, via trade unions and social movements, have developed their consciousness and organizing capacities in pursuit of their class interests.

Corporate globalization's political agenda is the acceptance of what are euphemistically called "free markets" and "free trade"—providing freedom for capital to further dominate labor by structuring exchange in such a way that nonmarket criteria of fairness and equity are inapplicable, and democratic control and social regulation are beyond the pale. Labor is cast as a special interest, the state is seen as inherently totalitarian, and public fulfillment of basic social needs is claimed to be unaffordable. Thus do the most internationalized sectors of capital seek to remake the world closer to their own desire, a world in which all wants are satisfied by markets and markets appear to be part of the natural order.

Those of us who believe that a fundamentally different mode of production and social relations can be achieved on a global level need to interrogate these developments with care, for a coherent theoretical understanding of class must embrace not only global developments but the specific dynamics of how globalization phenomena are experienced in diverse locations. Having been assigned this gargantuan task, I shall proceed in what is, of course, only an introduction to such a project by first saying something about the meaning of "globalization," that over-worked keyword of our time,[1] focusing on the class nature of neoliberal-ism and what is called the Washington Consensus; then I will consider class itself as a theoretical construct; and finally I will deal with the work-ings of class in the global economy.

GLOBALIZATION

We can identify key determinants of the world system as it has evolved since the early 1970s, the period we distinguish as the era of globaliza-tion, which is still ongoing. The first measures are the increases in trade, foreign investment, and capital flows. The last of these deserves special emphasis, because the growing dominance of finance over production is a key characteristic of the era—as was also the case at the beginning of the last century, when finance capital reorganized regional producers and economic units into national capitalisms in a process known in the United States as "Morganization," after the role played by J. P. Morgan in re-structuring the economy of that time.

The growing dominance of finance also warrants using the term "forces of accumulation" rather than the more limited "forces of produc-tion." "Forces of accumulation" signals the importance of the redistribu-tion of surplus through the exercise of monopolistic and monopsonistic market power—power deriving from control over such pressure points as marketing, extraction of technological rents through enforceable claims to intellectual property rights, and the nexus of debt creation and collection. In the eras of colonialism and classic imperialism, the redistri-bution of surplus was achieved by governments of the core though mili-tary conquest; in the current period, the use of force (as in Iraq) and threat of violence, still evident, are powerfully supplemented by the imposi-tions of international institutions such as the International Monetary Fund and the World Trade Organization, which reinforce unequal ex-change.

The conventional view, with which I disagree, is that as the world mar-ket emerges liberalization brings more rapid growth, that efficient capi-tal markets match the best use of investment with funding sources, and that new work relations, team production, and the premium on knowl-edge as a factor of production not only increase worker autonomy but also privilege skill and creativity over the mere ownership of capital. These new phenomena promise economic growth for all, it is said. If only this were true. Instead, what we have is a process of uneven and combined development in which income and power inequalities grow apace in a pattern of redistribution that is ecologically damaging and socially irresponsible. This pattern of redistributive growth plays out in three ways. First, there is redistribution from labor to capital as the newer forms of organization, like the old, allow surplus labor to be extracted from the producers, whose bargaining position is weakened by the greater mobility of capital. Second, there is continued exploitation of the poorer economies, not only via forced lower wages and workers' inability to organize or to bargain collectively but also via the debt peonage of the poorer countries, a condition created by their own elites, foreign financiers, and global state economic governance institutions, especially the International Monetary Fund. Third, there are interclass and intergenerational redistributions, manifest as well in the environmental destruction of irreplaceable natural resources in a wholesale plundering of the collective riches of the planet.

The conventional view of globalism suggests that national borders are obsolete and that state-imposed market rigidities are counterproductive. Ancillary arguments claim that the idea of class conflict is harmful, since raising living standards in an era of rapid technological change depends on labor-market flexibility. These are hardly new messages, being, rather, the reformulation of an all-too-familiar orthodoxy. But as we live through massive, fundamental change in the location and structure of work, and corresponding changes in social relations (including the undermining of traditional industrial unionism in the advanced economies), working people—in different ways and to different degrees, to be sure—discover commonalty in the consequences of a globalized capitalism. The time-space compression of globalized capitalism's operation increases what people everywhere know about what is happening elsewhere; everyone is in a position to see that the reorganization of production, distribution, and consumption makes working people's life conditions more similar, their jobs less secure, their future more uncertain—markets are free, people are not.

In the post–World War II era, the core states required National Keynesianism and its welfare state protections to preserve the system, given the crisis of legitimacy represented by the Great Depression as well as the prestige of the Left in Europe and Japan after World War II. In the periphery, state populism provided relative (only relative) gains for the urban working classes when the rising industrial elites needed them as allies against traditional landed oligarchies. These strategies in the core and the periphery have now been replaced by global neoliberalism, which offers a punishing austerity both to urban workers and to rural populations. Agencies of transnational capitalism and finance such as the World Trade Organization (WTO) and the International Monetary Fund (IMF), which I characterize as global state economic governance institutions,[2] present, in embryonic form, the features of a global state, a governance capacity that represents an extension of the imperial power of the leading core states, above all of the United States and the dominant sectors of the capitalist class that so profoundly influence the U.S. government's international activities.

A concomitant feature of contemporary globalization, alluded to earlier, is the development of a culture of resistance and an understanding of the ways that globalization pervades all local realities. Many millions of people are indeed learning to think globally and act locally, and many rivulets of resistance are increasingly coming together. Naomi Klein,[3] writing of the situation in Argentina, tells of a group of Buenos Aires residents who barricaded themselves inside their building to prevent eviction and refused to leave. On the building facade a hand-painted sign read "IMF GO TO HELL." The connection between the IMF, their own predicament, and that of their nation was very obvious and real to them. They have learned to think globally and act locally, to target globalist agencies and theorize how the global pervades the local everywhere. Unemployed and underpaid workers and those denied public services because of structural adjustment and conditions imposed by global state economic governance institutions make the same connections. The impact of disciplinary neoliberalism and the new constitutionalism of a repressive globalism—that is, capitalism reorganized beyond its national borders—is creating a new regulatory regime. Local government leaders are paid-off coconspirators—given a cut as junior partners, administrators of a new global order that is a more organic, single world political economy dominated by transnational capital. Those who refuse to cooperate are subject to regime change.

Of a piece with this broader design are the WTO's refusal to accept labor rights as a legitimate demand and the IMF's insistence on contractionary policies that produce starvation, increasing marginalization, loss of already inadequate public services, rising unemployment, and the forcing down of wages. The same results are being experienced in the lives of millions of Americans as our domestic institutions intensify class rule and extract ever more surplus from the poorest and most oppressed segments of the population, as each new tax "cut" sold as a job creation program only redistributes more once public funds to the already megawealthy.

Translating the so-called Washington Consensus—the demand for privatization, contracting out, cutting wages and government services, all of which add up to a punishing austerity—into class terms helps make clear that these policies are not mistakes, not merely bad choices in terms of development prospects, but effective impositions by the dominant class to further subjugate the working people of the world and to strengthen class rule in the service of long-term control and accumulation by the most powerful fractions of the ruling class.

If we take the frame of working class studies seriously, it should be possible to talk about the capitalist class in such structural and systemic terms. At the start of the twenty-first century, when tens of thousands of demonstrators are willing to brave violent police repression of their right to free speech and assembly, the placards they carry—"THEY ARE ENRON, WE ARE ARGENTINA"—resonate widely. The widespread revulsion against those who benefit from the political venality, criminal accountancy, corporate self-dealing, and the debt collector role of global state economic governance institutions means that a more fundamental rejection of actually existing capitalism is possible. "Free markets" have been shown to have exceedingly high social costs, and neoliberalism has not achieved its announced goals. To the contrary, it has produced slower growth, greater inequality, greater instability, and massive popular suffering.[4] Yet, while widely discredited, the Washington Consensus policies are rational, for they have achieved their unannounced goals: forcing open national economies to core transnational corporations, collecting debt for international financiers, and in other ways changing the balance of power to further favor the most influential fractions of capital.

THE WASHINGTON CONSENSUS

By now, the elements of the Washington Consensus are clear. Codified by John Williamson in a frequently cited 1990 paper,[5] and named after the city that headquarters the IMF and World Bank (located close to each other and conveniently not far from the U.S. Treasury), this consensus includes agreement on the need for trade and financial liberalization, competitive exchange rates, openness of foreign direct investment, privatization, deregulation, fiscal discipline, and secure property rights. All of these remove protections the working class had previously enjoyed, increase their risks of unemployment, sharpen the harshness of the conditions under which they are forced to live, and favor the most powerful fractions of capital. The consensus denies the social sphere as a shared space of caring and community, demands further commodification of the public realm, and disallows any decision-making role to agencies or organizations of civil society that oppose or limit the activities of capital.

Within such a framework, the "failure" of the Washington Consensus (to take its purposes for the moment as unproblematic) is that it seeks to explain a given country's economic and social trends exclusively as a result of government ineptitude, rather than as the effect of global political-economic constraints, in which external coercion plays a central role. Not only is this normative nationalism[6] an ideological reading, but the impact of deregulation, enhanced capital flows, privatization, and other features of market fundamentalism on stability and growth has been disappointing, to say the least.[7] Of course, if the real agenda is to promote crisis to force greater external control and resource transfer to transnational capital and international financiers, then the verdict must be that the Washington Consensus has been a great success.

This return to state-enforced laissez-faire is presented as the obvious wisdom of the ages by an aggressive ruling class and its policy-maker technician shills. Intellectually most insidious is the assertion of an arrogant and ideological claim. Williamson[8] writes that the precepts of the Washington Consensus are "the common core of wisdom embraced by all serious economists." He dismisses those who challenge the consensus as "cranks." "The proof," he writes, "may not be quite as conclusive as the proof that the earth is not flat, but it is sufficiently well established as to give sensible people better things to do with their time than to challenge its veracity." A decade after he wrote those pompous words, nearly everybody[9] questions the veracity of the Washington Consensus, except perhaps those who gain from the pain it inflicts, along with some free-market ideologues. A counterhegemonic understanding that another world is possible is now widely in evidence.

As governments that have adopted these policies have continued to suffer slow or no growth or have endured economic crises and collapse, the power of capital has asserted itself in the so-called augmented Washington Consensus, which, to the original set of policies, has added detailed demands for greater labor-market flexibility, anticorruption measures, financial regulation, legal and political reform, WTO agreements, and—in a bid for some shred of legitimacy—the promise of social safety nets and poverty reduction. The latter goals are to be achieved by having client states draw up poverty-reduction strategy papers as part of the expanded conditions for rolling over loans. The idea that adherence to these new demands will produce a reduction in poverty or sustainable development does not inspire great confidence. But adoption of reforms, a willingness to dialogue on the part of the discredited global state economic governance institutions, and the eagerness of some NGOs to accommodate to the new rules make this a particularly tricky time for activist movements.

At the heart of such differences lie basic questions about the nature of capitalism and the role of nation-states as the locus of power in the world system, indeed about the world capitalist system as the proper unit of analysis and struggle. When global state economic governance institutions focus attention on the nation-state as the agency in need of reform, calling attention to alleged policy errors and ill-suited regulatory frameworks, they are asking that what little is left of national sovereignty be surrendered to the priorities of transnational capital, the hegemonic fraction of the capitalist class. The Left, and indeed the populist Right, is inclined to respond with a defense of nationalist priorities. This is a losing game, as the failure of social democracies and the Right's misbegotten nostalgia for a nonexistent past should suggest. What is called for is internationalist solidarity.

The social democratic position was easier to maintain during the era of National Keynesianism, those postwar years to about 1973, which can be contrasted with the period of global neoliberalism we then entered. National Keynesianism was the strategy of capitalist recovery in which the government played a central role by creating demand through direct spending and judicious use of tax cuts. National Keynesianism represented, as well, a new class balance based on a coalition that included organized labor and involved social protections and automatic stabilizers. Higher spending meant larger markets and greater opportunity for profit and economic growth. In Europe, after the devastation of the Second World War, with right-wing parties discredited for siding with the Nazis and Fascists, and socialists and communists enjoying high prestige for leading the resistance, the need for national recovery permitted adoption of a social democratic corporatist model, a welfare state in which the demands of organized labor and the power of Left parties set the tone for much of what happened in the larger efforts to rebuild. In the United States, a liberal-labor coalition around the Democratic Party, with its New Frontier and Great Society programs, set the terms for domestic policy making. In Latin America, populism, a coalition of emergent industrial and urban business interests, relied on working class support to wrest control from the long-dominant landed interests; an import-substitution industrialization strategy protected domestic industry to the advantage of the emergent capitalist class and organized urban workers.

The emergence of what is called the New Economy—the rise of new sectors to the commanding heights of the economy, so that the firms that dominate are no longer the steel companies and other basic industries so important through most of the twentieth century but software giants like Microsoft, providers of computer chips like Intel, and new media giants like Time Warner—was supposed to show that free-market capitalism would bring prosperity if only markets were left to do their magic. The deflating of the hype surrounding the high-tech sector, to say nothing of the stock market that was inflated by these false promises, shows these developments in a different light. These companies do have the capacity to reorganize the now Internetted world and to disseminate a unifying culture from the United States—Hollywood, McDonald's, and Coca-Cola commodity lifestyles beyond the imagination of earlier generations. In the United States since the late 1940s, and now globally, consumerism has become an element of personal identity; consumer culture takes on new power, cloaking the working conditions pioneered by the dominant firms, with their use of factory technologies in the service sector and their massive use of part-time labor and low pay in a decisively nonunionized environment. The same labor policies, combined with the same use of information technology to control inventory and to foster just-in-time production and delivery systems, allowed Wal-Mart to restructure retailing and force competitors to follow, in much the same way Henry Ford once did. And as with Henry Ford's repressive labor policies, the technological possibilities are guided into channels that foster accumulation and the oppression of working people, so that technology's promise is compromised in the way it is controlled by capital.

Globalization destroyed the material base of the cross-class alliances of the liberal-labor coalition in the United States and of peripheral populism, as transnational capital reorganized production on a world scale, playing groups of workers in one country against others elsewhere, increasing insecurities everywhere. The globalization of financial markets led to a dramatic expansion of debt, as OPEC raised its prices and many nations had to borrow to pay for oil; at the same time, the oil-price spike created a surplus in OPEC funds, which banks needed to recycle. The inflation unleashed by higher energy costs produced monetary tightening, and the resultant higher interest rates made Third World debt unsustainable, primarily, but hardly exclusively, in Latin America. The Washington Consensus "solution" to the Third World debt crisis, as noted earlier, involved austerity measures, devaluation, privatization, and the abandonment of nationalistic economic development strategies. This general pattern of conditions for aid was extended to the transitional economies in Russia and Eastern Europe, where, guided by foreign advisers, a new class of capitalists was created through the appropriation of state property and through the control of debt to undercut the remaining vestiges of Soviet-style socialism while increasing Western control. The East Asian financial crisis toward the end of the 1990s replayed the same elements, as countries caught in liquidity crises were forced to open their economies to Western investors on most favorable terms. Out of such developments, globalization emerges as a new form of capitalist domination, a new imperialism that enforces rules demanded by transnational corporations and international financiers.

Resistance must still function in national political space even if it is—that is, should be—addressed to a broader, global understanding of class solidarity. The long-standing questions about what the working class is and how the workers of the world will unite at the start of the twenty-first century remain as complex as they are important. Further, they must now be related to how we theorize capitalist development, the role of global governance institutions, and capital's structural power. And all this must be seen as part of a transformative project that addresses the different understandings of disparate communities in struggle in a great variety of places.

John Williamson and others become upset at those who would "politicize" the Washington Consensus, which they continue to present as a "technocratic policy agenda."[10] This has become a laughable claim, as political consciousness of the class nature of real existing globalization has developed. Whose interests are served by the Washington Consensus is clear enough, given the social costs of policies ranging from freeing short-term speculative capital movements to redefining intellectual property. To allow discussion only at the level of market efficiency obscures central motivations and impacts.

The monopoly of that perspective has effectively been broken. The importance of this change in popular consciousness must not be underestimated. For a quarter of a century, the conventional wisdom was that the neoliberal policies that had governed the global economy were a great success; the transitional costs were considered to be relatively minor and well worth the gains that would soon be enjoyed by anyone not already benefiting from the investments by rich countries in capital-deficient economies. The gap between rich and poor was closing, thanks to developing countries' embrace of an export orientation and of international trade in a liberal world marketplace. There is now overwhelming evidence that little or none of this is true. On the contrary, savings move from poor to rich countries not because "efficiency market theory" is logically inconsistent with the model's assumptions but because the assumptions, and thus the model, are not accurate descriptors or the real world to which they are promiscuously applied. The model used by the global state economic governance bodies is misleading, and simply wrong about how the world capitalist system works, and the policies for which the model provides the rationale are irrelevant at best and, more typically, harmful, as is the case most prominently at this writing in Argentina.[11]

The freedom of capital movements in a system of freely floating exchange rates has meant that small economies are overwhelmed by speculative capital inflows. This bidding-up of assets produces domestic inflation and a bubble that, as it deflates, leaves misery in its wake along with a huge debt in foreign currency, leading to long-lasting deflationary pressures and social suffering. Liberalization has not lowered the cost of borrowing, again not because the abstractions of efficient market theory are logically incorrect but because they do not describe actually existing market relations. The fact is that the cost of borrowing has risen, as the high risks of a liberalized global economy have led investors to demand a higher risk premium. Economic theory properly done easily explains such developments, but was, and to a significant extent still is, ignored by ideologically rigid free-market analysis. The Washington Consensus, which was to have increased global economic stability and growth rates, has done neither.[12]

CLASS

I have presented the policies of global state economic governance institutions as favoring the most powerful and internationalized sectors of the capitalist class, but I have not yet said what class is. Given both the general confusion about what is meant by class and how older understandings need to be extended and revised in the current conjuncture, the era of globalization, this omission must be repaired.

I understand class not as a structure nor even as a category but as something that in fact happens, and can be shown to have happened, in human relations. In the tradition of E. P. Thompson,[13] we can say that class "happens" when some men and some women, as a result of common experiences, both inherited and shared, feel and are able to articulate an identity of interests among themselves, and as against others whose interests are different from (and usually opposed to) theirs. Class experience is determined by the productive relations into which people are born or enter, and class consciousness is the way in which they handle these experiences in cultural terms. Consciousness is embodied in value systems, ideas, and institutions. There is a common logic in the response of similarly situated groups undergoing similar experience, but no binding law determines an individual's specific response, because personality, individual history, and sense of group belonging (among other identity characteristics) can dominate over awareness of class.

Further, consciousness of class can arise in similar ways in different periods, but never in just the same way. If history is "stopped" at a particular point, then there are no classes but simply a multitude of individuals with a multitude of experiences. But if we watch these men and women over a period of social change, we observe patterns in their relationships, their ideas, and their institutions. Class is defined by men and women as they live their own history, and, in the end, this is its only definition, a definition embedded in the lives of real people as we (and they) come to understand them. If we take such an approach as our entry to class, what is called globalization is obviously re-forming structures within nation-states and, in terms of class consciousness, on an international level.

The coming into being of a single global economy at the present stage of capitalist development is not a one-time discrete event but a continuing flux that over time will refigure the borders of classes. Within national-state formations, these borders are being redefined by the international force of migration and by foreign investment organized globally in transnational enterprises. Moreover, as state functions also become globalized, hundreds of millions, perhaps billions, of people are enrolled in a global labor market, as the new forces of production are enmeshed more widely and inclusively in the old relations of production. Formerly peasant communities become proletarianized, and the international division of labor is reorganized along new lines: the industrial center is no longer at the core, with production of raw materials taking place in the periphery; instead we have the industrialization of significant parts of the non-Western world, and commodity chains of a new sort controlled from afar, albeit more directly, through high-tech information generation, communication, and processing. Thus not only is production reshaped but social consciousness as well.

In the new world order of growing income inequality, of the undermining of welfare states and the dismantling of progressive regulation, a world of forced givebacks and economic insecurity, the hegemonic ideology is psychologically imbibed through the pleasures of consumption—the overpriced cup of coffee at Starbucks, or the family visit to Wal-Mart. For some workers a symbolic means of participating in the make-believe world they wish they had comes from Disneyland's Main Street, while McDonald's commercials create sentimentalized pseudo-memories of a conflict-free America ruled by patriarchal values. Disneyland and McDonald's both offer a nostalgia for a world that never was, in which all good comes as the gift of benign corporations that make profits in a nonobjectionable manner by offering consumers what they want. The same transnationals that create low-wage, regimented jobs and use their power to foster neoliberal social Darwinism also produce a dream world of hollow fulfillment, which, like any other addiction, requires a frequent "fix." Your job and the life it allows may be pretty lousy, but you deserve a break today. Escape from reality is as close as the nearest McDonald's.

Historically, some people injured by the oppressive structures of the world have found in religion an inspiration to defend the weak and to enact God's prophetic justice on earth. Others have used religion to dull their pain, or to deflect their anger, in some cases claiming an otherworldly authority as justification for striking out. Religion remains a potent force in today's world. However, for many people in this era of corporate globalization, the heart of a heartless world is the commodified form of love and self-respect offered by merchants of fast food and status through logos. Consumer society's internalized ideology of commodified pleasure poisons body and mind. It has not gone unnoticed that Coke rots your teeth and makes you hyper, and that Burger King makes people obese and promotes heart disease and a host of other health problems. The social movements that make connections between the exploitation of McJobs and the harm done to people and the planet augur, at least potentially, the integration of justice campaigns and organizational alliances.

The immense impact of the importance we give to commodities as a source of our identity in an image-rich world is subject to both manipulation and controversy. As we pursue our investigations, we are aware that group identities—ethnic, religious, racial, and others—are socially created phenomena and that transnational corporations are fundamental actors, along with all of us as individuals and as members of social resistance movements, in shaping identity and consciousness.

The global economy makes more evident the connectedness of capitalism as a worldwide mode of production. Moreover, globalization takes place not only through the movement of foreign investment to sites of exploitable labor but through the movement of people—through immigration. Imperialist intervention, capital restructuring, and imperially sponsored or aggravated wars make parts of the world less livable and force their inhabitants to come to the countries of the core to survive. The older suburbs of our large metropolitan areas are servants' quarters for the immigrant day laborers who work off the books at construction, landscaping, and other poorly paid jobs, risking brutalization by local patriots who challenge their right to be here. In these suburbs we see not only the ghettoes of twenty-first-century racist America but also the scene of immigrant dreams and achievements and the terrain of a renewed class struggle.

In North America and Western Europe, the migrant stock has grown far more rapidly than the indigenous populations. At the start of the twenty-first century, more than 130 million people are estimated to live outside the country of their birth, and that number is rising at a minimum of 2 percent a year. While the numbers are uncertain, the phenomenon is undeniably crucial to understanding globalization in our time. Further, while attention has generally been focused on low-wage immigrants, to a remarkable degree knowledge workers are crossing borders as well and are recomposing segments of labor markets around the world. The absorption of millions of new immigrants in numbers about equal to the size of the black population in the U.S. workforce has affected not only African Americans but all workers. It is an important part of employers' efforts to create what is called labor-market flexibility by avoiding labor protection laws, thus making it easier to hire and fire at will and to use more temporary and contract workers in the broader economy. For reasons of self-interest, if not for more principled ones, international labor solidarity, like globalization, exists not only "out there" but also here at home.

CLASS IN THE GLOBAL POLITICAL ECONOMY

The dynamism of the forces comprising what is called the antiglobalization movement comes from the rejection of capitalist norms. In a profound sense, this movement goes beyond the reformist impulses of older working class movements that take trade union and electoral forms (even though it has attracted support and enthusiastic participation from members of these formations). The new movement is distant from political parties and, in its core belief that another world is possible, represents a return to the utopian impulse that historically has often inspired revolutionary movements. The antiglobalization forces reject amelioration limited to existing institutional channels. Their leadership style is not the vertical one typical of the Left in the past. They privilege personal witness and cultural responses in contesting and redefining the meaning of symbols and identities, from corporate logos to entitlements of citizenship.

Today's antiglobalization movement should be called the global social justice movement, I believe, since it is not against being part of the global economy. Indeed, international solidarity is what the movement is about. It is about fair inclusion, honest and equitable opportunity for all, and protection of the common spaceship. It is predominantly radically democratic and anticorporate, but not yet anticapitalist. For it underestimates both the power of capital as a class and capital's ability to command the state; it sees evil or greedy men as its targets, rather than a structurally oppressive system whose leading figures serve the needs of accumulation and whose institutions support exploitation. Thus the movement, trying to convince the powerful that reform is in everybody's interest, tends to accommodate rather than oppose class power.

Theorizing these rapid historical changes collectively called globalization has lagged behind our experience of them. Capital has become internationalized and, as noted, local elites have moved from being members of nationalistic coalitions in the immediate postwar period of National Keynesianism, peripheral populism, and national liberation unity to become junior partners of globalized capital and enforcers of neoliberalism. In the countries of the core, social democratic leaders have lost leverage to bargain with capital, which no longer needs to make concessions and can insist on a continuing flow of givebacks and new sacrifices.

But no changes of such dramatic moment occur without resistance. While the shock of globalization at first paralyzed Left forces shaken by the speed and extent of the changes, movements of civil society emerged into broad public awareness in the 1990s and continue to challenge corporate globalization, and while turtle-Teamster alliances are far more tenuous than the euphoria in Seattle reflected, awareness of the costs of corporate globalization is spreading. An anticorporate consciousness is being fed by events such as the corruption and collapse of Enron, WorldCom and the rest, and perhaps by an overreaching by the confident forces of reaction represented by George W. Bush and his administration. The expansion and maturity of the movement will be greatly strengthened if progressive intellectuals (not to be equated with academics) and activists—that is, thinking, class-conscious Americans and others around the world—do more to expose the logic of the system, its structures of oppression and relations of coercion. These tasks are served by an understanding of how class works today and how a counterhegemonic class consciousness can be produced not only in church basements, union halls, and the odd classroom but more generally in linking up separate agendas and demonstrating the historical capacity of class awareness, organization, and solidarity.

SEPTEMBER 11 AND ITS AFTERMATH THROUGH THE LENS OF CLASS

Leo Panitch

Class does matter: the proper question is not *whether* class matters but *how* it matters. The attention that has had to be focused in recent years on *whether* class matters, at least in part as a product of class analysis having become so unfashionable in the academic world, has diverted us from developing better analyses of *how* class matters, which should be the continuing goal of those who do class analysis and engage in class struggle.

Of course, class is certainly not everything. Class politics, which was never the central fulcrum of party division and electoral mobilization in the United States, has in recent decades faded even in Europe. But we need to insist that even if class is not everything, that hardly makes it nothing. Especially in this era of so-called globalization—which is really another word for the spread of capitalist social relations to every corner of the globe and every facet of our lives—the world can't be understood without some sort of framework that incorporates class analysis. Indeed, globalization is best understood as mobile capital having an increasing number of proletariats around the world to land on:

> The tendency of much contemporary scholarship and political discourse to treat globalization as simply a matter of the increased mobility of capital . . . is to make three linked mistakes. It is to think of capital in a fetishized form, to forget that capital is necessarily always a social relationship, and to ignore the way in which the growth of capital in general is possible only through the expanding extraction of value from labor power. Capital is not suddenly more globally mobile because of the revolution in information technology or the deregulation of financial markets; capital is more geographically diversified than it used to be because it now has more working classes to exploit. Those who declare that we live in an age without classes need to count the growing numbers of those sections of the world's producers who now—directly or indirectly—de-

pend on the sale of their labor power for their own daily reproduction. The World Bank in 1995 put that number at 2.5 billion. The global proletariat is not vanishing but expanding at a rate that has doubled its numbers since 1975.[1]

Alongside the classic process of proletarianization taking place in most countries in the so-called Third World, we can also witness in the advanced capitalist countries, where there has been a decline in the proportion of the labor force engaged in industrial production, an unmistakable process of proletarianization taking place among service and professional occupations, alongside the casualization of work in general. None of these developments can be properly comprehended without a renewal and reinvigoration of class analysis, which, we may hope, will also help lay the basis for some new strategies for moving class struggle beyond the limits of the old class politics.

I would like to relate class to September 11. Since I don't want to be accused of being reductionist, the stress here must be on the verb "relate"—which emphatically does not mean "reduce." I have no inclination to reduce the horror of September 11 and its aftermath to a simplistic class analysis. It would be all too easy to fall into such a reduction, for, as with almost anything else you look at that matters, and especially with as traumatic an event as September 11, class pops up everywhere—not in terms that convey profound meaning, but at a superficial, immediately visible level. The simplistic class analysis that has occurred is not just a matter of the focus on the fate of the firefighters, or of the role of Bruce Springsteen, or of the general way working class symbols were used to represent the disaster so as to link working class identity with patriotism. It is even a matter of news reportage that reflected, in some measure, a critical class perspective on the effects of September 11. Take, for instance, a story in the New York Times that reported that the largest corporations that had offices in lower Manhattan were getting in compensation over $6,000 for each employee for the interruption of their business, while small entrepreneurs in Chinatown were getting less than half of what the large corporations were getting per employee; and people who lived in expensive apartments were getting far more compensation than people who lived on the Lower East Side or in Chinatown.[2] Notably, this account in the Times went on to ask whether the financial service worker is more valuable to the city than the owner of the dumpling shop and whether the owner of a million-dollar loft is worthy of more aid than an immigrant in a tiny apartment. The answer to this ought to be obvious. In the definition of worth given by capitalist society, the answer can only be yes. Whether that should be so is another question, and if the New York Times is serious about that one, we may conclude that socialists are finding allies in strange places these days. In asking these questions one is raising very profound moral and analytic issues about the class society that is the United States of America.

We should also be extremely wary of attempts to reduce September 11 and its aftermath to a simplistic and immediate class *effect*. Certainly in the days after September 11, I had no patience whatsoever with the one or two people—and they were indeed only one or two—who in comments I read on the Internet shrugged off the horror of the events with some offhand comment that, after all, this happened on Wall Street and the victims were stock brokers, and so on. Apart from the incorrect assessment of the class position of most of those who were killed, the disgustingly unethical stance that this implies with regard to human life—whether a stockbroker's or anybody else's—is not to be tolerated.

That cavalier attitude toward human life was not common on the Left. Rather more common, indeed seen virtually everywhere in the American progressive media, was the citation of statistics to show how wrong it is, in the context of the war on terrorism, that Bush's tax cut package should be giving more to the wealthy than to the ordinary working class family.[3] We normally read in the progressive media that the top 1 percent of tax payers get one-third of the total tax cut benefit; that the top 1.3 million of the richest Americans therefore benefit as much as the poorest 78 million from the tax cut; that the $46 billion increase in military spending is more than all primary and secondary vocational expenditure of the federal government combined; that this is taking place at the same time that food subsidies are still being cut, and so on

This kind of analysis is facile if not dangerous. It implies that there is nothing wrong with the American state's response to September 11 through an apparently unlimited "war on terrorism" except that it is not funded equally through more progressive taxes; it also implies that more military spending is fine but ought to be matched by more social spending (as in, "Please, can we have more guns *and* more butter?"). This approach to the aftermath of September 11, which is presented as though it were a critical class analysis, at least implicitly—and sometimes explicitly—legitimizes the orientation to wage war as a proper response to September 11.

Moreover, insofar as it meant especially to appeal to workers and the poor, it treats them far too economistically. It is not the crude cost-benefit calculus of the notional "taxpayer" that determines patriotism. Not only American workers but the working classes in Canada and Europe generally initially showed a remarkably patriotic attitude toward the United States in the face of September 11. To understand this—and why it didn't last—we need to avoid economistic class analyses: we need a political class analysis.

No serious class analysis of September 11 and its aftermath is possible unless it is put in the context of the two defining features of the last quarter of the twentieth century. The first of these is the emergence of the United States as the world's sole superpower, or, properly speaking, the first really global capitalist empire. The second is the historic defeat of the Left in the same period. The communist, social democratic, and progressive nationalist movements of the twentieth century were all founded on attempts to make class the central pivot of discourse, organization, mobilization, and transformation in national and international politics. Even if they did not very often apply this consistently, the class foundation of their politics lent it a rational, purposive, strategic outlook. With the defeat of that Left, of course, the opposition to capitalism and imperialism did not go away. Capitalism and imperialism will always bring forth opposition. But the atavistic form that it took on September 11 needs to be understood in relation to the defeat of the political forces that took class as the basis of their strategic orientation. The American imperium, of course, contributed a great deal to that defeat, although there were many self-inflicted failures that played a role as well.

Most people who have looked at September 11 at all seriously through the eyes of class have begun with the distributive inequalities between North and South. A recent article in the *Economic Journal* by Branko Milanovic is probably now the best source available for this.[4] On the basis of a study of 85 percent of the world's population from ninety-one countries around the globe, it shows that the richest fifty million people have the income equivalent of the poorest 2.7 billion or, put another way, that the top 1 percent of income earners have an income equivalent to the bottom 57 percent of the world's population. This represents a staggering increase in inequality over the past decade. But these kinds of statistics can be made sense of only in terms of growing inequality within each social formation—and here is where class really comes in. As Milanovic shows, the main factors here include stagnant incomes in the countries of South Asia and Africa, the growing divide between rural China and urban China, and the polarization of incomes in Eastern Europe and the former Soviet Union. Of course one cannot ignore the polarization that has occurred in the rich capitalist countries either. This has taken place to such a degree that some want to recast the concept of the Third World so it bears less a spatial than a social meaning, in the sense of the Third World conditions existing in the First World. Nevertheless, there can be no ignoring the fact that even the poorest 10 percent of Americans are better off than two-thirds of the world's population, as Milanovic shows, and that four-fifths of the world's population live below what is defined as the poverty line in the rich capitalist countries. Recent estimates by the United Nations and the World Resources Institute indicate that twelve to thirteen million children a year are dying unnecessarily by virtue of economic policies that force their countries to remove tariffs and subsidies for local production, policies imposed by countries that remain closed to their exports.[5]

Dismissing the relevance of this kind of data to the meaning of September 11 was common on the Right, which pointed out that middle class young men from Saudi Arabia did the evil deed. This argument operates on the truly reductionist premise that a person's immediate class membership and immediate thoughts and actions are directly related to one another without any impact on them from the society and the world in which that person lives. This kind of simple-mindedness would, for instance, have denied the working class nature of the Swedish Labor Party because Olaf Palme had a middle class background. Yet I think it is true that the kind of analysis that attempts to locate September 11 directly in terms of global income and wealth inequalities doesn't tell us all that much. It doesn't tell us why it was the United States that was targeted, and why it was by these particular people from their part of the world. Understanding these factors requires a much finer-tuned class analysis.

That said, the kind of statistics I just cited are certainly relevant for putting the way the word "terror" is used in some perspective. To make this clear, I'd like to quote, directly in this context, one of America's greatest nineteenth-century writers, Mark Twain, who, in *A Connecticut Yankee in King Arthur's Court*, wrote the following, well over a century ago:

> There were two "Reigns of Terror," if we would but remember it and consider it; the one wrought murder in hot passion, the other in heartless cold blood; the one lasted mere months, the other had lasted a thousand years; the one inflicted death upon ten thousand persons, the other upon a hundred millions; but our shudders are all for the "horrors" of the minor Terror, the momentary Terror, so to speak; whereas, what is the horror of swift death by the ax compared with lifelong death from hunger, cold, insult, cruelty, and heartbreak? What is swift death by lightning compared with death by slow fire at the stake? A city cemetery could contain the coffins filled by that brief Terror which we have all been so diligently taught to shiver at and mourn over; but all France could hardly contain the coffins filled by that older and real Terror—that unspeakably bitter and awful Terror which none of us has been taught to see in its vastness or pity as it deserves.[6]

Twain was writing this on the centenary of the French Revolution. And the kind of reasoning he was employing regarding the two regimes of terror helps us, I think, understand why the overwhelming balance of world public opinion moved against the American war on terrorism, as it was conducted first in Afghanistan and then especially in Iraq. This was revealed in a remarkable series of global opinion surveys undertaken by the Ipsos-Reid polling organization, which demonstrated that, whereas 85 percent of Americans and between 58 percent and 66 percent of people in the other Group of Seven rich capitalist countries supported the war in Afghanistan, it was opposed by 70 to 75 percent of the populations of the world's poor countries, including those in Latin America in this hemisphere.[7] In these countries most people still experience firsthand what Twain meant by "long death from hunger, cold, insult, cruelty, and heartbreak." And they are not entirely wrong to think that the role of the American state as a guarantor of the wealth of North America and Europe may have something to do with this.

If the majority of the world's population, as the polls showed, were unsympathetic to the momentary terror wrought by the September 11 acts, this may well have to do with their recognition of the purely symbolic and atavistic nature of the attacks. It is recognized, in other words, not only that these acts were immoral from the point of view of the innocent people they killed, but also—unlike the terror of the French Revolution, which Twain was talking about—that they were driven by a reactionary and futile impulse. Moreover, the French Revolution, whatever the horrors of the transitional terror, did, after all, overthrow the old regime; but the kind of political action that September 11 represented can only be counterproductive and ineffective. The inevitable outcome of September 11 could only be that of stoking the self-righteous aims of imperial power, fueling their spread.

The reason that most people in the rich countries even outside the United States originally looked on the war on terrorism so differently than most of the world's population has, of course, something to do with the complicity of their own states in the American imperium, in its cultural as well as its economic, if not so much in its military, dimensions. I'll return to what this amounts to in the context of the rich countries' opposition to the U.S. invasion of Iraq later, but first I'd like to introduce a note of justification for the use of the word "empire" here. I don't use it polemically, but rather descriptively. We clearly need some concept to capture the fundamentally different role the American state plays in the world. The word "superpower" fails to capture this precisely because it implies merely greater power than others. It thereby elides the fact that American power is different because of the way it penetrates and structures other states. It is for this reason that the concept of empire—which used to be quite unfashionable, even more unfashionable than class, not very long ago—is now making a comeback among political scientists (including among many on the right of the political spectrum). Even one of Tony Blair's advisers has recently made a positive case for the reemergence of empire in the twenty-first century, preferably of a kind that would be humanitarian and liberal, but essentially playing the same "white man's burden" role of nineteenth-century empires in the sense, as he put it, that the weak still need the strong and the strong still need an orderly world.[8]

Of course, the American empire is quite different from the old colonial empires. It would be, in my view, a very serious mistake to revive Hobson's or Lenin's notion of imperialism, as a stage of capitalism marked by interimperial rivalry and war among the leading imperial countries. Nor should we think that narrow domestic interests abroad drive every American intervention, as too many crude class analyses of American policy suggest. On the contrary, in my view, it may be more accurate to see the American state today as burdened by the function, which it alone can play, of maintaining world order in today's global capitalism. A great Canadian political economist, Harold Innis, once observed "that American imperialism has been made plausible and attractive in part by its insistence that it is not imperialistic."[9] He recognized that what has made this new type of imperialism particularly effective has been its internalization in the Canadian state and economy. And it can now be said of a great many states around the world that they have internalized American imperialism.

What made this imperialism "plausible and attractive" since World War II had also to do, of course, with the legitimacy that liberal democratic institutions at home lent to the deployment of violence by the American state worldwide. Max Weber's definition of the modern Western state in terms of the legitimacy that is claimed for the monopoly over the means of violence rather than in terms of its goals or range of activities remains fundamental to social science. But this legitimacy, as Weber also understood, is bound up—albeit by no means to the exclusion of all kinds of irrational, charismatic, and traditionalist elements—with the rule of law, representative of a responsible government, competitive elections, and the liberal freedoms of speech, association, and assembly that comprise the liberal democratic form of the capitalist state. Globalization entails not only the spread of global capitalism but the legitimation of the American state's role in policing global order, including by remaking the world's states in the image of the United States. It was precisely this that lent some credence to the claim that American-led wars in Iraq, Yugoslavia, and Afghanistan were all about human rights, democracy, and freedom.

This is not really as new a development as it is sometimes thought to be. Ever since World War II the determination of what was in the American national interest continued to reflect the particularity of the American state and social formation, but it was increasingly inflected toward a conception of the American state's role as that of ensuring the survival of "free enterprise" in the United States itself through its promotion of free enterprise and free trade internationally. This was classically articulated in President Truman's famous speech against isolationism at Baylor University in March 1947: "Now, as in the year 1920, we have reached a turning point in history. National economies have been disrupted by the war. The future is uncertain everywhere. Economic policies are in a state of flux. In this atmosphere of doubt and hesitation, the decisive factor will be the type of leadership that the United States gives the world. We are the giant of the economic world. Whether we like it or not, the future pattern of economic relations depends upon us. . . . Our foreign relations, political and economic, are indivisible."[10] The "internationalization" of the American state that this implied was encapsulated in the National Security Council document NSC-68 of 1950, which (although it remained "Top Secret" until 1975) Gabriel Kolko calls "the most important of all postwar policy documents." It articulated most clearly the goal of constructing a "world environment in which the American system can survive and flourish. . . . Even if there were no Soviet Union we would face the great problem . . . [that] the absence of order among nations is becoming less and less tolerable."[11]

So what is the nature of the American imperial system, precisely? Is it best defined in terms of democracy and freedom, or in terms of capitalism and class? It must be said in this respect that there is a staggering amount of self-delusion in the view of the Bush administration that terrorists hate America because "we elect our leaders." Osama bin Laden, we may be sure, could not have cared less whether Americans elected their governments or not; the same could be said of many more people in the world than liberal democrats care to admit. The global deployment of American military power even when narrow American interests and security are not foremost in mind, and even when the interventions are legitimated and sometimes invited by international human rights advocates and agencies, does not of course necessarily lead to the spread of human rights and liberal democracy, let alone greater economic equality. And this poses a real problem of legitimacy. The dubiousness of the war on terrorism to much of the world's population stems no doubt partly from this. But it also stems from long memories of the major role played by the American imperium in cynically suppressing progressive forces, in the name of spreading democracy and freedom.

September 11 was "blow-back" from this, with such a vengeance as could only have been stoked up over half a century of political resentment in Islamic countries. The term "blow-back" was first coined in Washington, DC, in 1954, as CIA and Pentagon bureaucrats mulled over the consequences of their decision to overthrow the left nationalist Mossadeq government in Iran. The Iranian revolution in 1979 had its roots in that moment, and the hijacking of that revolution by political Islam produced a regime that was as anti-American as it was antisocialist, and unleashed a chain of events that led to the American backing of Iraq in the Iraq-Iran war through the 1980s. Given the backing he had secured from the United States in the 1980s, Saddam Hussein came to believe he could get away with absorbing the state of Kuwait, which had emerged from the artificial borders of the region drawn by the British in the interwar period. He was wrong, but the placement of American military bases throughout the Persian Gulf, and especially in Saudi Arabia, inflamed political Islam all the more and attracted to Islamic fundamentalism a great many bright, young, middle class students who a generation before would have been attracted to left nationalist or communist parties. Robin Blackburn has made the argument that the defeats and failures of a secular left in the Arabic and Muslim countries mired them in a socioeconomic condition not unlike the hybrid between feudalism and capitalism that produced Puritan fundamentalism in colonial America. Drawing on an analysis by Michael Walzer of the Puritans (although taking a very different position than Walzer on the war on terrorism), Blackburn has argued that political Islam (or "Islamic fundamentalism," as it is now called) is much like Puritanism, not least in its similar political use of the symbols of the devil and the infidel.[12]

Be that as it may, there can be no doubt that political Islam's version of "propaganda of the deed" produced the most spectacular act of terrorism against an imperial power in world history, just as there can be doubt that the empire's response to this has to do with strategic imperial concerns that go far beyond al Qaeda or even political Islam more broadly. The new American bases that have been established in post-Soviet central Asia will not be dismantled now that the war in Afghanistan is over. American military bases will now circle the world from Japan to China's western border. The Russian resistance to the building of the National Missile Defense Shield (with all this implies that the militarization of space) has been definitively broken, or should we say bribed away, even while we are told that the Pentagon is seriously entertaining the use of conventional nuclear weapons as a contingency against even non-nuclear states, the ultimate means of terror in the maintenance of global order.

Moreover, the coalition against terrorism that the United States built after September 11 was explicitly designed to legitimate and sustain every state's repression of internal separatist and other dissident groups. Less well known than the free hand that was given after September 11 to the Russians in Chechnya is the free hand given to the Chinese Communist-capitalist elite to act against the Muslim separatists in the country's westernmost province. It was made clear to the Chinese elite that their treatment of the separatists would not be used against them by the Americans in ongoing negotiations over the terms of Chinese integration into the capitalist world economy. Consistency, of course, need not be a principle of imperial strategy. And this was never more evident than in the stunningly quick about-face the United States made after the war in Yugoslavia, when the justification for that war was the right of self-determination in the old communist world for every ethno-nationalist group that demanded it.

The United States is now requiring all states to restructure their coercive apparatuses to fit America's strategic concerns. This would seem to reinforce the earlier requirement set by the imperium that all states restructure their economic apparatuses to fit with what has become known as neoliberalism. The possibilities of blow-back are visible everywhere, albeit nowhere more graphically than in Pakistan. This is a country where up to 90 percent of the state's budget is devoted to paying interest on the debt and to the military and coercive apparatus—over 40 percent goes to maintaining the military apparatus, 40 percent goes to paying the foreign debt. Almost nothing is left for anything else. Little wonder, with no public education system to speak of, that the poor in Pakistan, who do not vote for fundamentalist parties in any great number, have nevertheless been sending their boys to religious schools where the boys are fed as well as indoctrinated in fundamentalism. And little wonder that the imperium now worries about Pakistan losing control of its nuclear arsenal.

The consequences are incalculable precisely because the imperium, even if it has military bases everywhere, cannot rule except with and through the other states of the world. Ellen Meiksins Wood puts this particularly well:

> The very detachment of economic domination from political rule that makes it possible for capital to extend its reach beyond the capacity of any other imperial power in history is also the source of a fundamental weakness. . . . National states implement and enforce the global economy, and they remain the most effective means of intervening in it. This means that the state is also the point at which global capital is most vulnerable, both as a target of opposition in the dominant economies and as a lever of resistance elsewhere. It also means that now more than ever, much depends

on the particular class forces embodied in the state, and that now more than ever, there is scope, as well as need, for class struggle.[13]

The perspective I have presented here of empire and globalization clearly calls for the kind of class analysis that attempts to understand each state, including the imperial state, in terms of the balance of class forces within that state. There are other class analyses that see globalization in terms of either reemerging rivalries between national bourgeoisies or, at the other extreme, a cross-national class formation, led by an already emergent transnational capitalist class, but these miss, in my view, the central role of states, and especially the American state, in making globalization happen.[14] The strategic response of the American ruling class to the crisis of the international economic order that emerged in the 1970s (itself a product of a worldwide class struggle against that order) was crucial to the formation of the neoliberal, imperial strategic capacities with which we have grown so familiar over the past two decades. But we should be very wary of trying to understand American imperial policy in terms of the narrow interests of domestic capitalist class fractions. Those who see a relationship between oil interests and today's militarism in the Middle East are not wrong, but oil is only a factor in combination with the management of world order with which the American state has become burdened. The structural relationship that America's capitalist class has to the state in this project is important, but so is the specific role and nature of what can only properly be called the "warrior class," which has been spawned by the American capitalist state's coercive structures over the course of the past half century.

Just as neoliberalism at home has not meant a smaller or weaker state, but rather one in which coercive apparatuses flourish (as welfare offices have emptied out, the prisons have filled up), so has neoliberalism led to the enhancement of the coercive apparatus the imperial state needs to police social order around the world. The American military and security apparatus was transformed through the 1990s in such a way as to facilitate global policing. Its role as the coercive apparatus of the imperial state was already apparent in the responses to "rogue states" under the first Bush and the Clinton administrations. The United States did work hard to win the UN's support for the 1990–1991 Gulf War and oversaw the long regime of sanctions against Iraq that the American state insisted on through the 1990s. But other governments sensed a growing unilateralism on the part of the United States that made them increasingly nervous, if only in terms of maintaining their own states' legitimacy. The Gulf War had shown that the United Nations could be made to serve "as an imprimatur for a policy that the United States wanted to follow and either persuaded or coerced everybody else to support," as the Canadian ambassador to the UN put it at the time. And this playing "fast and loose with the provisions of the UN Charter" unnerved "a lot of developing countries, which were privately outraged by what was going on but felt utterly impotent to do anything—a demonstration of the enormous U.S. power and influence when it is unleashed."[15] At the same time, the Gulf War made American strategists aware just how little they could rely on the UN if they had to go to such trouble to get their way.

Perhaps the most important change in the administrative structure of the American empire in the transition from the Clinton administration to the second Bush administration has been the displacement of the Treasury from its position at the pinnacle of the state apparatus. Those branches of the American state controlling the means of violence are now in the driver's seat; in an administration representing a Republican Party that has always been made up of a coalition of free marketeers, social conservatives, and military hawks, the balance has been tilted decisively by September 11 toward the military hawks. But the unconcealed imperial face that the American state is now prepared to show to the world above all pertains to the increasing difficulty of managing a truly global informal empire—a problem that goes well beyond any change from administration to administration.

The trouble for the American empire as it inclines in this strategic direction is that very few of the world's "non-core" states today, given their economic and political structures and social forces, could be reconstructed along the lines of postwar Japan and Germany, even if (indeed especially if) they were occupied by the U.S. military, and even if they were penetrated rather than marginalized by globalization. What is more, an American imperialism that is so blatantly imperialistic risks losing the appearance of not being imperialist—the appearance that historically made it plausible and attractive.

The old question of whether an extended empire can be consistent with republican liberty—posed at the founding of the American state, and again and again over the subsequent two centuries by those at home who stood up against American imperialism—is back on the agenda. The need to sustain intervention abroad by mobilizing support and limiting opposition, which in turn is accomplished through instilling fear and repression at home, raises the prospect of the American state's becoming much more authoritarian internally while becoming more blatantly aggressive externally. But the unattractiveness of an empire whose coercive nature at home and abroad is no longer concealed suggests that anti-imperialist struggles—in the rich capitalist states at the heart of the empire as well as in the poor ones at its extremities—will have enormous resonance.

The ability of the American imperial state to impose both military and economic discipline on the world relates to the failures and defeats of the Left class politics that I spoke of earlier. But the story is not over. New working class and peasant movements with a new politics influenced by liberation theology and libertarian Marxism have emerged, as has, of course, the antiglobalization movement. That anarchism plays a significant role in the latter movement is hardly surprising—so did it at the end of the nineteenth century, when working class parties were barely emerging, and when a democratic transformation of state power seemed most unlikely. Anarchism is sustained today, moreover, by a suspicion of the working class itself—not for being white and male (this image is now so out of date as to be persuasive to hardly anyone), but rather for being overly chauvinist and statist in its orientation, and too prone to engage in class collaboration. This class collaboration is thought to result from the construction of working class interests as bettering the conditions of wage labor rather than breaking the capital-labor relationship and the subordinate position of the working class in it.

A good example of this is the way in which the AFL-CIO made a mockery of the spirit of Seattle protests against the World Trade Organization (WTO) in December 1999. By the time of the protests against the International Monetary Fund (IMF) and World Bank in Washington, DC, four months later, the American union leadership had narrowed the terms of debate down to whether or not the U.S. Congress should endorse China's inclusion in the WTO. The problem is not one of "protectionism" per se (any serious attempt to challenge globalization entails "protection" for local and national communities); it is rather what can only be called the *chauvinist* protectionism and *imperial* condescension that lay behind the demand that the American state not give the Chinese masses the "benefit" of access to its markets until "labor rights" were enforced in China. The whole discourse was framed as an appeal to the American state to play its "proper" world role as a democratic and benevolent good guy against the Chinese state. The absence of a strong alternative vision, and the danger of not having one, was revealed in the astonishing support that key American nongovernmental organization (NGO) leaders gave to the AFL-CIO's narrowly conceived campaign against China's inclusion in the WTO. These NGO leaders thus joined the AFL-CIO in legitimating the WTO as something really worth getting into, even as they mobilized for the Washington, DC, demonstration against the other institutions of globalization, the IMF and World Bank.

Lost in the rhetoric in the debate on China after Seattle were two main things: first, the enormous concessions China is making to foreign capital to get into the WTO; and second, the fact that the struggle for labor rights is not external to China but is being conducted within it (as it is in all developing countries), including by the millions of Chinese workers who, by official estimates, undertook over 120,000 strikes in 1999 alone. If the AFL-CIO really wants to help Chinese workers, it will campaign for the exclusion of those provisions of the WTO that would rob public enterprises of their "subsidies," resulting in tens of millions of Chinese workers' losing their jobs. It will take direct action itself by providing the level of resources and support to those struggling to build independent trade unions in China that it once provided to Solidarity in Poland (of course the AFL-CIO was encouraged in this at the time by the American state—as it will not be regarding Chinese independent unions now).

But can much better be said of those Third World elites who themselves employ the charge of imperialism against those who call for labor rights to be included in the WTO? We should have no illusions, either, about Third World leaders and their technocratic advisers, who are ready and willing to set aside labor rights in their anxiety to ensure at all costs that foreign capital comes their way rather than leaves them marginalized in the new world capitalist order. It is misleading to speak, as Samir Amin has done occasionally, of the "political authorities in the active peripheries—and behind them all of society (including the contradictions within society itself)—hav[ing] a project and a strategy" for national economic development that stands in "confrontation with globally dominant imperialism."[16] He included in the "active peripheries" China, Korea, and India, as well as unnamed others in Southeast Asia and Latin America, and contrasted these with "marginalized peripheries" that are "the passive subjects of globalization." But while the political elites of India, Korea, and especially China are definitely not merely the passive subjects of globalization as they actively maneuver for a place in the new global order, it is also patently clear that only a major transformation in class relations in each of these countries will lead to anything like a "confrontation with globally dominant imperialism." For Third World state elites who really want to take an anti-imperial stand, a good place to start would be to stop their repression of domestic class struggle and their denial of freedom of association.

One of the promising aspects of the antiglobalization movement, compared with the antiwar movement of the 1960s, is that it has increasingly designated itself as anticapitalist. This is an important advance from its self-designation as an "antifree-trade" or "anticorporate" movement through much of the 1990s. But, despite its visions of a decentralized and participatory order, the primary objective of that movement has still all too often been to protest the international economic and financial institutions of globalization—behind which stands the imperial state itself and the multitude of large and small, rich and poor states through which and with which it rules, or seeks to rule, the globe. So long as the international agencies continue to be the main focus of attention, the institutions of globalization will be legitimized by many labor, NGO, and Third World leaders who see no practical alternative to them, and therefore seek a seat at the table of the international meetings, where they might win some concessions from elites who, for their part, have certainly been chastened enough by the swarm of protests to look for interlocutors from the movement.

There is considerable suspicion among antiglobalization direct-action militants of those who would seek a seat at the table. But there is also a growing sense that protest is not enough. If the Internet has been an asset in unleashing the capacity to organize dissent and resistance on the global stage, it has proved no substitute for the hard work of class formation and political organization that the landless movement in Brazil and the Zapatistas in Chiapas had to engage in on their own ground. The Internet may have been indispensable as way of bringing together hundred of thousands of activists from around the world to attend the World Social Forum in Porto Alegre and the many regional social forums that have grown out of it to discuss the various meanings of "another world is possible." The Internet may have been no less important in informing and mobilizing the fifteen million who took the streets around the world before the invasion of Iraq in the largest antiwar protest in history. But it is no substitute for building in each country new class-based parties, post-communist and post–social democratic, capable of developing new structures of popular democracy as a prelude to and an effect of competing for state power. In an essay that extols the Internet as the key to a new form of political organizing, Naomi Klein admits:

> There is no question that the communications culture that reigns on the Net is better at speed and volume than it is at synthesis. It is capable of getting tens of thousands of people to meet on the same street corner, placards in hand, but it is far less adept at helping those same people to agree on what they are really asking for before they get to the barricades—or after they leave. Perhaps that's why a certain repetitive quality has set in at these large demonstrations; from smashing McDonald's windows to giant puppets, they can begin to look like McProtests. The Net made them possible, but it's not proving particularly helpful in taking them to a new stage. . . . Now the police have subscribed to all the e-mail lists and have used the supposed threat posed by anarchists as giant fundraising schemes, allowing them to buy up all manner of new toys, from surveil-

lance equipment to water cannons. More substantively, . . . the movement, no manner how decentralized, [is] in grave danger of seeming re-
mote, cut off from the issues that affect people's daily lives.[17]

On my way to the 2002 World Social Forum in Porto Alegre, I stopped in
Santiago, Chile, to speak at a labor summer school. I met there two brothers whose parents had been involved in the movement of armed struggle
in the early 1970s and who had escaped to Cuba after the Pinochet coup
against Allende and the mass murder of the Chilean Left that ensued. The
brothers returned to Chile as young men, having rejected their parents'
armed struggle politics, with a determined orientation, very much in tune
with that of the new generation of activists in the North, toward working
with people in their neighborhood associations as much as in their workplaces on a broad agenda of social, ecological, and cultural, as well as economic, issues to begin anew the difficult process of class formation and
political organization. As we traveled from Santiago to Porto Alegre together I asked them to give me one concrete example of the kind of organizing on the ground they were doing to bring this about. The example
they gave me certainly qualifies as direct action. It involved organizing
workers in the construction sector, in which trade unions and collective
bargaining have been completely wiped out, and in which all workers are
casual and contract labor. The brothers led an occupation by the workers
of a building site where an Italian multinational construction company
was developing the largest planetarium in Latin America. When the police massed outside to break the occupation, the Italian engineers on the
project, locked up inside but sympathetic to the protest, insisted that the
minister of interior negotiate with the workers. A seventy-two-hour cell-
phone negotiation ensued, ending in a collective agreement, with minimum wages and standards specified.

This is the kind of direct action that may well come more and more
onto the agenda of activists in Europe and North America. As the new
generation on the Left seeks to ground its protest against the global structures of oppression and exploitation, building as it will on both the
antiglobalization movement and the new antiwar movement, it will increasingly engage itself in addressing, including through direct action,
the immediate troubles facing people in their own societies, helping in
this way to begin anew the long-term process of class formation and political organization in the countries of the North. If this process is going
to be repressed by the state as violent activity, indeed as terrorist activity,
we are in for some very ugly times.

Though new class formation will always be locally rooted, as in the example above, it also will have to be connected with a much larger strate-

gic vision that involves inviting working people to think ambitiously again about their role in changing the world. Given that there are no national bourgeoisies any longer that see their role as accumulating on the terrain of a single state, class collaboration is much less plausible as a working class strategy than at any point in the past. Nor will neoliberal states be long able to effectively incorporate labor movements to which they give so few benefits and legal protections. But there will be no new transformative politics emanating from the working classes until existing labor movements transform themselves or are succeeded by new ones better suited to the task. The goal must be to make unions and other working class organizations more inclusive not only in terms of their members' racial, ethnic, and gender identities but also in terms of their members' full life experiences as more than "just workers." This will need to be reflected in collective bargaining priorities and workplace struggles, but it will also mean thinking hard about the limits of unions in relation to all the places working people currently interact outside of work, and interrogating the degree of democracy and developmental capacity building that they might enjoy if such centers of working class life could be appropriately restructured. For all these reasons, working class socialist parties are more than ever needed, and could still have enormous potential to change the world that brought us September 11.[18]

GLOBAL STRATEGIES FOR WORKERS
HOW CLASS ANALYSIS CLARIFIES <u>US</u> AND <u>THEM</u>
AND WHAT WE NEED TO DO

Katie Quan

INTRODUCTION

As images of "Teamsters and Turtles" joining forces to protest the 1999 World Trade Organization (WTO) meetings in Seattle flashed across television screens worldwide, globalization and antiglobalization became household terms. Many activists anticipated that this would be the beginning of a new partnership among the world's populist forces, in which environmentalists and labor unions would lead a heightened level of struggle against corporate greed. However, since Seattle, although stronger relationships have been built among many labor and environmental activists, unions have not sustained the same high level of participation in subsequent antiglobalization protests. Part of the reason for this may be doubt about the relationship of global issues to the central mission of labor unions.

What is the relationship of American workers to workers and their allies in other countries? Historically the position of American unions has varied widely on this question; in some periods we have accused foreign workers of being the enemy for "stealing our jobs," and at other times we have viewed them as victims of sweatshop superexploitation. But rarely have we viewed them as strategic allies with whom we share common goals and targets, as part of a big-picture analysis of power in the global economy. That perspective would lead us to organize ourselves differently than we do now, to place a much stronger priority on building a multinational labor movement in response to multinational capital and ally with other groups that are moving in the same direction.

One tool that helps us understand this relationship is class analysis. During the past twenty-five years, little has been heard about the explicit conceptualization of workers as a "class." Either people actually do not perceive reality as a matter of working class versus capitalist class, or they may avoid using the term "class" to disassociate themselves from unsuccessful Marxist governments of the last century. However, not to think in terms of class is unfortunate, since no matter what our ideological persuasion may be, class analysis gives us a way of viewing the world that identifies power relationships. It clarifies who has power among the global corporate ruling elite and how they are using it against the worldwide working class. It helps us see that if the working class wants to defend its interests and gain more power, it has to build strength among certain allies and target those who do hold power. Without class analysis, workers and unions have no tool for navigating complex situations that challenge us as to where our interests lie, or for formulating strategies that advance our interests. Instead, we often fall victim to pragmatic approaches, doing what seems best at the moment, or, worse yet, adopting beliefs and policies that are not in our interests.

In this chapter, I will talk about class and the global economy from the point of view of a labor activist. I will relate my experiences as a garment worker and union leader to the need for global labor strategies. I will argue that one of the reasons our labor movement has been unable to respond effectively to the need for global labor strategies has been a lack of class analysis. This situation has led us to view foreign workers as not part of "us" but part of "them," and has divided the global working class and made us weak. Examples of this division can be seen in historical and current debates over international trade, as well as in the low priority given to this subject in an era of capital consolidation in global trade and finance. I conclude by arguing that the struggle between the forces in the global economy is the most important class struggle of our time, and that worker power cannot be achieved without class analysis, strategy, and organization.

THE GLOBAL INDUSTRY: BASIC US AND THEM

In the 1970s, I was a garment worker in New York City, sewing zippers and waistbands into hundreds of pants each day on piece rate. Piece rate is that wretched system whereby each sewing operation has a price, and the more pieces you sew, the more money you earn. The piece rate might be twenty-five cents for a zipper, and if you sewed one hundred zippers you would earn $25. I call this the system of being both the slave and the slave driver. You're the slave because you're the one who is working at a furious pace hour after hour, often straight through rest breaks and lunchtimes. And you're also the slave driver—because you are your own taskmaster, spurring yourself on to work faster and faster. In those days, piece rates in union shops were regulated by our union contract, and since I was young and worked fast, it wasn't unusual for me to make $18 an hour. That didn't mean that the other workers and I were well-off though, because the industry is seasonal, and there were many days and weeks when we lived off unemployment checks. Still, we didn't consider ourselves to be sweatshop workers—we believed that our path to freedom was to sew fast enough to beat the slave system and actually earn a decent living.

But the system beat us. We worked so hard and made so much money that our employers closed down our shops. "*We can't compete.* Labor costs are too high," they claimed. "We can't pay minimum wages and union benefits." So they laid us off and moved to areas where labor costs were lower. In the 1950s many employers ran away from the heavily unionized Northeast to the American South, and the textile and apparel unions followed the work to the southern states and organized workers there. Soon the workers in the South were told the same thing that workers in the Northeast had been told—"*We can't compete*"—and the employers went even farther south to Puerto Rico, the Caribbean, and Latin America. By the 1970s, apparel production had expanded to Asia, and by the 1990s, Asia had become the world's largest apparel-exporting region.[1]

As our jobs left, employers told us that the next group of workers were "*stealing our jobs*" from us, and many workers believed them. I'll never forget the time a white woman from Pennsylvania came up to me and pointed her finger in my face, saying, "*You. You Chinatown immigrants are taking our jobs!*" I was stunned. Here I was busting my behind in the "slave and slave driver" system, barely making ends meet, and someone comes along and says I took her job. I would have told her that if she felt so strongly about it she and her co-workers could have our jobs, except that we had nowhere else to go. As immigrant women workers with poor English and few marketable skills, we had few job options, and the employers took advantage of this by forcing us to accept lower piece rates than the Pennsylvania workers.

The Pennsylvania woman and I were in a workshop together, and eventually, through discussion of piece rate dispute settlement and other workplace issues, we found that we actually had much in common. But this incident shows how an employer's message can affect workers' thinking and pit workers against each other. It leads people to believe that the problem is us, Pennsylvania workers and employers, versus them, Chinatown workers and employers—rather than us, Pennsylvania and Chinatown workers who are being exploited, versus them, employers who are moving production from place to place to find even lower labor costs. And absent a strong message from unions or other political leadership that "us" is working class people who have interests in common, no matter whether we work in Pennsylvania, Chinatown, or Latin America, workers may easily believe what the employers tell us.

In 1994, on a visit to Thailand's largest garment factory, Thai Iryo, I met with the plant manager, who railed on endlessly about how the Indonesians were undercutting him by paying lower wages. He said that whereas he was paying $8 a day to his workers for making Wrangler jeans, London Fog raincoats, and Liz Claiborne sportswear, Indonesian factory owners were only paying $1 a day! *I can't compete,* he said, and he claimed that he would have to close his factory in the next twenty-four months. His complaints about the Indonesians undercutting him sounded just like what the American employers said about him. Undoubtedly the Indonesian employers in turn had a scapegoat in another country to blame for undercutting their competitive advantage. It was clear that we were all caught in a worldwide race to the bottom, and that what was driving this was competition to find lower labor costs, because the greatest cost in manufacturing garments is the labor.

Also clear from what the Thai Iryo manager said was that he was being pressured by those who gave him work contracts. The garment industry is like a chain of sweating, with multiple tiers of employers (them) who are trying to get rich off the workers (us). The owner of Thai Iryo was definitely a rich contractor—she owned a factory that employed several thousand workers, and she made much more than $8 a day, so on one level she was part of them. But she was making peanuts compared to Wrangler, London Fog, and Liz Claiborne, the manufacturers who were selling those raincoats and jeans to department stores for perhaps three times what they paid Thai Iryo; these manufacturers were also part of them. But even beyond the manufacturers, retailers like Macy's and Bloomingdale's, which sold those garments for more than twice what they paid the manufacturers, were also profiting hugely from the labor of the Thai Iryo workers, and thus were also part of them. The retailers compete for profits by squeezing the manufacturers and paying them less. The manufacturers make up for this loss and compete with other manufacturers by squeezing the contractors and paying them less. The contractors make up for their loss and compete with other contractors by squeezing the workers and paying them lower piece rates. The workers at the bottom of the chain have no one to squeeze.

If we look at the power relationships in this chain of sweating, "them" are the retailers, manufacturers, and contractors who profit from the garment workers' labor, and who also can control their profit by squeezing those on the next lower link in the chain. The workers are "us" because we have no way of squeezing someone else's prices to benefit ourselves. It doesn't matter whether we're working in New York, Pennsylvania, or Bangkok; we're in the same boat. Our class interests are the same. The only way that we can increase piece rates is to form strong unions that can bargain collectively with our employers.

Indeed, Thai Iryo workers had fought for higher wages and better conditions through their union. Eight dollars a day was twice the Thai minimum wage at the time, and twice the wage rate of most other garment workers in Thailand. Dormitory accommodations consisted of a six-by-ten-foot space of floor, where workers slept for eight hours in rotation with two other sets of women on two other shifts. These working and living conditions weren't great, but they were considered better than most, and many of the women workers at Thai Iryo delayed marriage, in defiance of Thai custom, to continue working there. Said the union president to me, "We Thai Iryo workers are known as 'old maids.'"

When I met with the union's core leadership, it was clear to me that this was a group of women to be reckoned with. Featured prominently on the wall of their union office were photos of two women. "Who are these women?" I asked the group. "Martyrs who died for the cause," I was told. During the battle to unionize the plant some years earlier, one had been run over by a truck as she picketed the plant gate, and the other had been found shot dead in a nearby ditch.

As I heard their stories, it made me furious to think that these courageous and strong women who made Wrangler, London Fog, and Liz Claiborne multimillion dollar companies would ultimately face the same threat that we garment workers in the United States faced: lower your hard-won wages and work standards so that the employers can compete—otherwise they'll move to another country. In America, real wages dropped as employers used the threat of outsourcing to force domestic wages down. Whereas I earned $18 an hour in the 1970s, twenty years later garment workers were earning only an average of $9 an hour (*without* adjustment for inflation) for doing exactly the same work. But even $9 an hour could not provide apparel companies with enough savings, compared with wages of $8 a day in Thailand or $1 a day in Indonesia. So eventually our shops closed in spite of the concessions we gave, leaving workers out on the streets.

Plant closures left a swath of destruction and tragedy for untold numbers of workers. In San Francisco, where I had become head of the district office of the International Ladies' Garment Workers' Union (ILGWU) in 1990, thousands of union members were forced out of jobs that they had held for as long as forty years. Most of them were women, and many of them were immigrants from China or Mexico. They had few skills besides sewing, and were terrified at the thought of training for new careers just as they were making plans to retire. The middle-income lifestyle that they had achieved through sweating the piece rates and organizing a strong union was vanishing. Quite a few had trouble making mortgage payments and sending their children to college. Not a single one that I know of got an equal- or better-paying job. Everyone felt angry, defeated, and powerless.

And now this was going to happen to the Thai Iryo workers as well. Globalization has increased the insane level of competition for profit among capitalists, while plunging workers deeper into poverty. It has caused millions of workers to lose their jobs, as corporations race around the globe to find greater profits, and it has effectively disempowered workers who still have jobs by use of the looming threat of plant closures. In September 2000, Thai Iryo and its sister plant finally closed, laying off 1,231 workers, some of whom had worked there for as long as twenty years.[2]

In the face of globalization, garment workers have struggled to organize strong unions, but have found that traditional ways of organizing are no longer effective. In the first part of the twentieth century, the main strategy that unions adopted was to gain power through organizing a significant portion of the market and then to use collective bargaining to improve working conditions over time. They also sometimes used legal and regulatory policies to strengthen their influence on their labor markets. Whenever they needed to press their demands further, they engaged in strikes as an ultimate form of leverage.[3] Now that labor markets are globalized, garment unions no longer represent a significant portion of the workforce, and they do not have the strength to bargain for high wages and good benefits. If they strike, they have to be prepared for the likelihood that the employer will move the work to another country.

Since the 1960s, aside from organizing across the United States–Canada border, there have been other periodic attempts at union organizing across borders; however, most of those attempts were not carried out on a large scale or in a sustained manner. Some examples are the short-lived attempts in the 1970s to form "company councils" of Americans and Europeans who worked for the same multinational employer;[4] the formation of the banana workers' federation in Guatemala, Honduras, and Costa Rica in the 1980s;[5] and the 1991 Treaty of Maastricht, which provided for cross-border collective bargaining in the European Trade Union Council.[6] In the 1990s, several new global labor strategies were tried, and they are briefly outlined below.

The most well-known strategy in the garment industry is the Codes of Conduct movement to get retail and manufacturing corporations like

Nike and the Gap to assume corporate responsibility for working conditions by requiring that their contractors comply with core labor rights such as payment of a living wage, a limit on overtime hours, a ban on child labor and prison labor, and the right to organize unions and bargain collectively. Since the early 1990s, most apparel corporations in the United States have adopted these codes, and many have hired staff or contracted with vendors to monitor compliance with these codes throughout the world. While there is some agreement that working conditions have improved somewhat as a result of this movement, violations of the codes continue to abound, and there are only a few examples of codes of conduct leading to stronger worker organization.[7]

Another strategy has been the adoption of labor standards in trade agreements, the rationale being that where investors have rights to economic development, workers should have rights to organize unions and enjoy other internationally recognized core labor rights. In Cambodia, where labor standards compliance is a condition of expanded trade with the United States, there is some evidence to show that an improved atmosphere of labor compliance has provided opportunities for union organizers.[8] However, in another case, the labor side letter to the North American Free Trade Agreement has not proven to be effective, either in leading to an improved atmosphere of compliance in Mexico or in remedying violations brought through its complaint procedure.[9] In fact, most trade agreements in today's global economy are aimed at deregulating standards for workers and the environment, which is what the WTO protests were about.

As part of this deregulation, one trade agreement called the Multi-Fiber Arrangement (MFA) is of grave concern to garment workers worldwide. For the past forty years, it has limited the import of apparel through the use of quotas, thereby keeping a certain number of jobs in various garment-producing countries. However, the MFA is scheduled to be phased out in 2005, meaning that the price of quotas will be eliminated from the cost of production, and many believe this will lead to dramatic shifts of production to very low-wage countries such as China and Vietnam.[10]

Some economists have suggested that one way of approaching the "race to the bottom" effect is to find a way to increase wages proportionally for workers in all countries at the same time. In the past, when workers in some countries got wage increases through collective bargaining or other means, they lost their wage advantage relative to other countries, leading employers to shift production elsewhere. However, if a mechanism could be adopted to increase wages by the same proportion in every country at the same time, then countries would maintain their relative wage advantage. No such mechanisms have been put into place, but there is some research to show that it can be done.[11]

In the 1990s a few unions experimented with cross-border organizing and collective bargaining. Examples include the Communications Workers union, which formed an alliance with its British counterpart to organize phone workers in anticipation of a merger of British Telecom with MCI;[12] the Teamsters, which formed an international bargaining committee for negotiations with the United Parcel Service;[13] and the United Food and Commercial Workers, which formed company councils for the purpose of bargaining with a couple of large international food corporations.[14] In 1995, the Association of Flight Attendants signed an agreement with United Airlines that gave all 40,000 flight attendants the same wage rate and benefits, regardless of where in the world they worked or what nationality they were.[15] Except for the flight attendants' contract, all of these experiments were short-lived and do not function on an ongoing basis.

All of these examples of cross-border strategies demonstrate that, while there are some creative experiments going on and there are some definite victories, we have far to go in achieving the kind of union power that existed prior to globalization. In retrospect, one has to ask why unions stopped organizing when industries expanded beyond U.S. borders, but more to the point why even today most unions do not view their role as building unions across national borders, except with Canada. Didn't we know that we were going to lose power in our labor markets if we didn't? What was it that kept us from building unity with foreign workers across borders? Part of the answer might be learned from reviewing the history of our labor movement's positions on international trade.

INTERNATIONAL TRADE: CONFUSING US AND THEM

Capitalists believe that international trade is generally a good thing, because it opens up markets to sell products, provides new opportunities for investment, and gives employers access to cheap labor. Generally, capitalists favor "free-trade" policies that allow them the tariff-free, quota-free ability to engage in global trade, so that they can be more competitive. However, when a group of capitalists find themselves unable to gain advantage over their competitors, then true to their opportunistic self-interests, they spurn free trade and instead erect trade barriers.[16] Examples are textile producers who supported tariffs to protect their markets from the 1970s through to the present, and information technology businessmen who vigorously fought for regulation of intellectual property rights in the World Trade Organization.

On the other hand, for the working class, free trade is generally a bad thing. Multinational corporations claim that consumers pay cheaper prices when businesses produce more cheaply. However, if hundreds of thousands of workers lose their jobs, then not many will have the buying power to purchase those goods. And if the workers producing the goods are being paid little, it's unlikely that they will have much buying power either. Moreover, the growth of the economy doesn't necessarily mean that benefits will trickle down to workers. Indeed, in the past twenty years, during a period of increasingly free trade, the gap between the rich and poor has widened to the point at which the richest in the nation are ten times more wealthy than the poorest, a substantial increase in disparity from earlier periods.[17] Without regulation of the impact of capital, such as on worker rights and environmental protection, "free trade" is not a position that is in the interests of workers.

The problem is that, in advocating for trade regulation, the policy position of the American labor movement has sometimes converged with that of capitalists who erect trade barriers to gain a competitive advantage, and in that convergence unions have adopted the rhetoric, and sometimes the ideology, of the capitalist interests as well. The most well-known example of this was "Buy American," a slogan used to champion the protectionist cause. Originally spearheaded by business interests that wanted to protect their markets, its purpose was to unite the American public, both capitalist and working class, around a common policy that was based on national unity. What was originally us, workers, and them, capitalists, became us, Americans, and them, foreigners. Unions then adopted the "Buy American" slogan and rallied their memberships around it.

In *Buy American: The Untold Story of Economic Nationalism*, Dana Frank describes the controversy among unions about whether or not to protect American markets by imposing tariffs on imported commodities. Said AFL President Samuel Gompers of protectionism in 1881, "If it performed what its advocates claim for it, the protection of labor, it is of the greatest importance and should be adopted." Thus was born the legacy of protecting the jobs of American workers by allying with domestic capitalists to impose barriers to trade such as tariffs and quotas. This was not based on a class analysis; it was a pragmatic approach to a problem faced by workers. In contrast, supporters of the rival union group, the Knights of Labor, argued a class analysis, saying that of the $600 million collected from duties in 1889, "not one penny . . . goes into the pockets of the community, of all shades and grades who work for a living, but to swell the ranks of the sensuous rich, and add to the millions of starving poor, whose daily toil becomes worse and worse under the fetish of protection."[18]

Actually, the labor movement's position on trade has varied greatly from one period to another, depending on the near-term interests in view. During the 1930s, unions supported the Buy American campaign led by big businessmen like William Randolph Hearst, claiming that they were protecting the employment of American workers. Considering how antiunion Hearst was, many in the labor movement found it hard to stomach building an alliance with him. However, by the 1950s and 1960s, the Buy American campaign had subsided, the Cold War was at its height, and anticommunism was proving to be a stronger priority than protectionism. At this point, labor's position shifted in favor of unregulated trade, and AFL-CIO President George Meany wrote to a Rubber Workers' shop steward,

> Millions of American workers are dependent for their livelihood on the sale overseas of the goods they produce. . . . We must keep in our minds the necessity to find even more markets for American-made goods overseas. . . . The free nations around the world will either trade with us, or, for lack of such trade, be forced to trade with the Soviet and its satellites. That would help the communist cause. . . . A Buy American campaign . . . would be to run contrary, not only to the policy of the AFL-CIO, but also against the best interests of American workers.[19]

By the late 1960s and 1970s the world had changed again, and the effects of global outsourcing began to be felt keenly in industries such as garment, auto, and steel. Once again unions initiated Buy American campaigns, accusing foreign workers of "*stealing*" their jobs. In the 1970s, when I was a member of the ILGWU, we were told that it was those foreign workers in "Red China" and other countries working for "unconscionably" low wages who were to blame for plant closures and less work. We were led to believe that workers in foreign countries were our enemies—a scapegoating that not only shielded corporations from accountability but also played on racial prejudice by pitting Americans against workers of color.

It was this kind of message that led to the murder of Vincent Chin in Detroit in 1982. In the 1970s, Japanese autos entered the American market, and were quickly favored by consumers who wanted gas-saving, dependable cars. As a result, sales of American autos plummeted, and thousands of autoworkers lost their jobs. In response, the United Auto Workers (UAW) union mounted a major campaign against Japanese autos, calling on legislators to limit imported autos. To dramatize their point, UAW members smashed Japanese autos on the steps of the Capitol and otherwise bashed Japanese products, playing on anti-Japanese sentiment that had its roots not only in racial prejudice against Asians but also in propaganda against our World War II enemy the "Japs."[20]

One evening in 1982, Vincent Chin, a Chinese American man, went to a Detroit bar to celebrate his upcoming wedding. Two unemployed autoworkers started a fight with him, fingering him as a "Jap" and accusing him of taking their jobs. They chased him out to the parking lot and clubbed him to death.[21] The murder that they committed demonstrates that the demagoguery of the union's anti-Japanese campaign had deeply penetrated American workers' psyches, so that they believed that their enemy was a race of people, not the corporate bosses who laid them off. Dana Frank points out that race baiting has often accompanied the protectionist philosophy, from the Chinese Exclusion Act of 1882, which banned immigrant workers from China, to the anti-Japanese rhetoric of the 1970s.

Then, beginning with the debate over the North American Free Trade Agreement (NAFTA) in the 1990s, the official message from the American labor movement changed. Probably because many in the labor movement realized that mistakes had been made in the 1970s and 1980s, and because some unions had important relationships with Mexican unions, during the NAFTA debate unions refrained from blaming foreign workers for stealing our jobs. Instead we became more interested in their concerns, and some unions sent delegations to Mexico to tour factories and build ties with labor activists.[22] Rather than opposing free trade or calling for stricter regulation, unions demanded "Fair Trade" in the form of inclusion of enforceable labor rights in the main body of the agreement.

This new position represented an important advance in working class solidarity, as it no longer pitted workers from one country against workers from another, and instead sought common ground by uniting Canadian, U.S., and Mexican labor movements to press for internationally recognized core labor standards and rights. During the past several years, the demand for labor standards and labor rights has become the rallying cry for the emerging global labor movement that has moved the same policy demands toward multinational corporations and supranational trade and financial institutions such as the WTO, the World Bank, the International Monetary Fund (IMF), and the Multinational Agreement on Investments (MAI). Significantly, the global labor movement has not only pressed the demands of unions, but has linked with environmental and popular movements to jointly voice concerns regarding environmental standards and human rights.

However, just as it seemed that we were progressing with building a multinational working class movement, the 2001 debate over Permanent Normal Trade Relations (PNTR) with China showed that without vigilance we could again lapse into race baiting and the protectionist danger of pitting worker against worker. At union rallies to protest PNTR, top union leaders could be heard threatening that China would see its "last pair of chopsticks," and workers in the crowd could be seen wearing union T-shirts emblazoned with drawings of Chinese workers being lynched.[23]

The tendency of the American labor movement to pit American workers against foreign workers illustrates how strongly workers identify with nationalist interests in comparison to their class interests. We are a movement without a strong working class consciousness based on an analysis that clearly links our class interests with those of workers in other countries. When faced with global issues such as international trade, we have often reacted in ways that have hurt working class solidarity. No wonder few have thought seriously about crossing borders to organize. If we really wanted to mobilize consumers to buy things in the interests of our class, our slogan would have more accurately identified the us and them—we should have said "Buy Union," rather than "Buy American."

THE NEW US AND THEM

As a result of both the reluctance to cross borders to organize and a history of promoting nationalism over class unity, the American working class and its allies around the world are woefully unprepared to meet the challenge of globalized capital in the twenty-first century.

Consider the case of NAFTA's Chapter 11. Many of us predicted that NAFTA would accelerate the movement of production to Mexico, and it did. More than three million net jobs and job opportunities were lost in the United States between 1994 and 2000,[24] and the kind of jobs that were created by export opportunities were likely not filled by workers who lost their jobs because of imports. But what most of us did not realize is that there was an even more dangerous and insidious effect stemming from a provision of NAFTA called Chapter 11, which gives corporations unprecedented new powers to privatize public services and deregulate environmental and labor standards.

Under the terms of Chapter 11, United Parcel Service (UPS) is suing the Canadian government for $230 million, in actual and anticipated losses, because the government is subsidizing its postal system while not giving the same subsidies to UPS. Why? The reason is that Chapter 11 prohibits governments from engaging in "national treatment," or favoring their domestic goods and services over those of foreign competitors. UPS claims that the Canadian government's subsidization of its postal system is favoring its domestic parcel service, which puts UPS at a competitive disadvantage and is therefore a violation of "national treatment." If UPS wins this lawsuit, Canada may be forced to give up all or part of its postal system! In addition, many Canadians may lose any postal service, since there is nothing to stop private companies from eliminating unprofitable service routes once they take over. If UPS can successfully sue the Canadian government for its postal service, it will not be long before all public services become potential targets of similar privatization efforts.

In another Chapter 11 case, a British Columbian chemical company named Methanex is suing the State of California for $970 million, in actual and anticipated losses, for banning the carcinogen MTBE, a fuel additive that is polluting fresh water resources. Methanex claims that the ban keeps them out of the lucrative California market, in violation of the "investors' rights" provision of Chapter 11. This provision allows private corporations to sue governments that enact laws and regulations that restrict free market competition. If Methanex succeeds, then a wide range of laws and regulations that protect workers and the environment could be challenged—ranging from minimum wage laws to health and safety regulations to right-to-organize laws. For the first time in history, it is possible for corporations to legally overturn governments' laws, even when the laws have been established through thoroughly democratic means.[25]

Not only has Chapter 11 given corporations vast powers that they never had before but those who sit in judgment of these lawsuits are not elected by or accountable to citizens. Moreover, when "the people" are the defendant, such as in the Methanex case, in which the people of California are being sued, they are represented by the U.S. trade representative (USTR), an appointee of the president. Since both Democrat and Republican administrations negotiated and supported NAFTA and Chapter 11, it is difficult to imagine that the USTR could be counted on to muster a strong defense against the effects of national treatment and investors' rights.

NAFTA achieved a stunning advance for corporate power that will be multiplied many times over if Chapter 11–type provisions are incorporated into the Free Trade Area of the Americas (FTAA), a free trade treaty being negotiated to cover North and South America (except Cuba). It follows other measures undertaken by the WTO, the IMF, and the World Bank to restructure the world in ways favorable to their own interests—at the expense of the people. No longer are individual multinational corporations the face of global capital; today their individual corporate interests are consolidated into supranational trade and financial institutions that are setting the ground rules in secret and are asserting increasing dominance over the world's governments and citizens.

While capital is consolidating at lightning speed, unions and citizen groups are just beginning to respond. The demonstrations in Seattle, Montreal, Porto Negro, Qatar, and Cancun show a growing network of popular movements, yet the movement overall is still relatively small and lacks sustained cohesion and focused strategy. It has won some skirmishes, such as delaying the implementation of the MAI and contributing to the lack of conclusion of the WTO meetings in Seattle, Genoa, and Cancun. However, it lost the battle to deny "fast track" negotiating authority to the president for the FTAA. Overall the movement has not organized itself to wage an effective struggle to stop capital from its aggressive power grab and project a vision and strategy for the future.

In the twenty-first century, the global economy is the central battleground of class struggle. The world has changed since the 1970s, when "us" was the workers in New York's Chinatown, Pennsylvania, and Bangkok, and "them" was Thai Iryo, Liz Claiborne, and Macy's. A class analysis tells us that "them" is the very powerful forces of global capital that are changing the rules of global trade and finance to suit their corporate interests. And "us" is now defined as everyone who does not benefit from the consolidation of global capital—workers, farmers, environmentalists, and most other people in the world. To be sure, there is still a level of class struggle on the shop floor over piece rates, and there is still a level of class struggle between workers and their various employers up the chain of sweating. But this new level of struggle between the institutions of global capital and the people of the world will define the rules of all other levels of class struggle—everything from whether we will have jobs, to whether a country can have a postal service, to whether we can pass laws to protect our health. It is not just an economic struggle but also a political struggle between, on the one hand, a small group of capitalists who are not accountable to anyone, and, on the other hand, us working people.

Failure to understand this means that we will continue with a myopic vision of what needs to be done, relegating global issues to low priority when they should in fact be central. Rather than appropriating resources to unite workers and grassroots activists across borders, we might easily end up blaming each other for the problems that global capitalists have caused. And, unfortunately, if global issues don't become a central priority, we will continue to lose ground, because our strategies will be designed only to fight skirmishes, not to win the war.

If we're serious about building global labor strategies, we will need to address many questions. How will we organize ourselves? Which other grassroots movements will be our allies? Who will participate in leadership? What issues will we take on? Will we target several issues at the same time, such as labor rights, biogenetic foods, and global warming, and build movements wherever those issues resonate? Or will we target a single issue, such as debt cancellation, and organize all the grassroots movements to concentrate efforts on it? How can working at the policy level complement the organizing? Can laws and regulations be passed that deny the right of private investors to sue governments for unfair competition? Can lawsuits be brought under other international laws that will set favorable precedents? What kinds of research do we need in order to do all of this?

In this context, the American labor movement can play an instrumental role. Since 1995, when John Sweeney became president of the AFL-CIO, significant progress has already been made in improving union-to-union relationships in Latin America and elsewhere, providing technical assistance for cross-border campaigns, and advocating for labor standards conditionality in international economic policies. Just as the AFL-CIO's adoption of a progressive immigration policy in 2000 added tremendous weight to what community activists had been advocating for many years and actually helped bring policy changes to the table, so too could a decision to make global issues a central priority have a significant impact in advancing the people's global movement.

CONCLUSION

Globalization is upon us, and it is unavoidable. Not only is it causing more hardship for workers in many countries but its new rules threaten the core of our democratic values and rights. The challenge for American workers is whether we will be content to watch events unfolding from a distance, or whether we will organize ourselves to unite with global allies to wage an effective response.

In this effort, a class analysis that explains the relationship between us and them is critical. We can't afford to make the mistakes of the past, when workers believed that siding with the bosses to promote the Buy American campaign was in our interests and foreign workers like the "Japs" and immigrants like Vincent Chin were our enemies. We can't formulate strategies that address just our own domestic workforce when in fact labor markets are global—otherwise we will have no power. Class analysis gives us a context for understanding issues that can divide us, such as race, immigration status, and narrow thinking. It makes us ask who is responsible for real wages falling in the garment industry, the closure of Thai Iryo, the takeover threat to the Canadian postal service, and the pollution of the California water supply. It helps us see that "them" is global capital, not just individual Liz Claibornes and Methanexes, but now powerful trade and finance institutions like the WTO that are controlling the world's economy. It leads us to understand that "us" is the rest of the world's citizens, who are being profoundly affected by global capital, and that it is urgent for unions and citizens' groups to organize to implement global strategies.

PART III

CLASS AND WORKING PEOPLE

Poverty is one of the most persistent problems in human history in need of intervention and correction. From biblical times to the present, people have devised various institutions of charity and public policy to alleviate the suffering of the poor.

In the popular vernacular of class in the United States, "the poor," or "the underclass" as they are sometimes known, stand apart from the mainstream of American society, trapped somewhere below the broad "middle class" of stably employed workers and law-abiding citizens. This view of the poor, based on understanding class as a matter of income and life style, confuses the problem.[1] Poverty is rooted in unemployment or low wages for those who do find work. It comes from unstable work histories imposed by the temporary employment practices that mark corporate labor market "flexibility." Poverty comes from lack of childcare and health insurance that forces people, especially women, off the job when problems arise. Poverty comes from bad education and inadequate training. While in any given year 12 to 14 percent of the population is poor, over a ten-year period 40 percent experience poverty in at least one year because most poor people cycle in and out of poverty; they don't stay poor for long periods. Poverty is something that happens to the working class, not some marginal "other" on the fringes of society.

As **FRANCES FOX PIVEN** shows in her chapter, the close intertwining of the poor and the working class played a central role in the "welfare reform" of the mid-1990s, when President Clinton made good on his promise to "end welfare as we know it." The implementation of welfare reform was an integral part of a larger campaign to discipline labor. The passage of welfare reform in 1996 culminated a decades-long campaign by business interests to stigmatize the poor and exercise greater control over the low-wage labor market. Piven shows how the corporate agenda toward the poor became increasingly politicized from the 1970s, through the more widespread deployment of lobbyists and think-tank expertise paid for by corporate endowments. Piven's essay provides evidence that efforts to improve the condition of the poor need links with a working class movement that challenges corporate power in the political realm as well as at the workplace.

MICHAEL YATES assesses the experience of the working class as a whole in the period since the early 1970s. He, too, finds a consistent pattern of corporate power deployed to reduce working class living standards. He documents the broad decline in living standards for working people beginning in 1973. The boom years of the late 1990s supported the first sustained increase in real wages, reaching even to the middle and lower reaches of the working class, but even in those years inequality continued to increase.[2]

Both Yates and Piven address the importance of building a working class social movement to address the problems they describe. Both observe that the patriotism called forth in the war on terror and the assertion of U.S. military power around the world complicate the prospects for such a movement. Yates assesses the prospects for an emerging antiwar, anticorporate working class movement in the context of the leadership John Sweeney has given to the AFL-CIO in the first eight years of his tenure as president. He finds the prospects to be mixed and by no means automatically derived from the suffering workers endure. In these chapters, we see again how the domestic and the international aspects of class power and class experience interact and are inseparable.

NEOLIBERAL SOCIAL POLICY AND LABOR MARKET DISCIPLINE

Frances Fox Piven

Since the 1930s we have had a national program to provide cash assistance to families headed by impoverished mothers. The program is called welfare. By any measure, it has always been small. Even at its peak, in the 1990s, only five million families received assistance; benefit levels were extremely low, averaging less than $400 per month a family (and falling); the program accounted for a mere 1 percent of the federal budget and an additional small percentage of state budgets. But small or not, welfare stimulated a good deal of heated political talk, much of it laced with sexual and racial innuendo. In 1996, amidst a virtual carnival of rhetoric generated by Democrats and Republicans competing for leadership on the issue, welfare was radically overhauled with the passage of the Personal Responsibility and Work Opportunity Reconciliation Act (PRWORA). I think it is difficult to make sense of this development if we focus on welfare alone. In this chapter I show that, while welfare was the subject of most of the political clamor, changes in welfare were related to a broad shift in a series of American social policies that is still unfolding.

Because the overhaul of welfare was freighted with symbolic meaning, both for the Right and the Left, volumes have been written assessing and debating its consequences. I will give short shrift to that literature here, because I want to widen our focus and place changes in welfare policy in the context of a range of other social policy developments that have received considerably less attention. Only when we consider these different policies together does the underlying logic of contemporary American social policy emerge. And that logic is the logic of enforcing low-wage work in a changing and deteriorating labor market. A pattern of neoliberal social policy has thus developed in the United States that meshes with the pattern of stagnant and declining wages and insecure working conditions that characterizes our neoliberal labor market.

After a decades-long campaign against the existing welfare system led by right-wing think tanks, business organizations, and politicians, state entitlements to federal grants-in-aid to provide cash assistance to poor families were ended. The policy put in its place, Temporary Assistance to Needy Families (TANF) provides block grants to the states for cash assistance, but conditions those grants on state policies that establish strict time limits on assistance and require mothers to work in exchange for their benefits. Beyond that, the states have broad discretion in the distribution of aid, and since they can spend that part of their block grant which is not distributed on other programs or even ultimately on tax cuts, state officials have a strong incentive to be very restrictive, as do the private contractors and local governments to whom they often devolve administrative responsibility for the program. This has resulted in the spread of welfare practices that rebuff, deny, or "divert" potential new applicants so they are not allowed to actually apply for cash assistance, and practices that sanction existing applicants with benefit cuts if they transgress any of the detailed rules of the new system, and practices that simply cut families off cash aid.

The argument justifying the new practices, sometimes called "work first," is familiar. The old welfare system presumably made it too easy for men and women to bear children out of wedlock, and then made it too easy for mothers to opt out of wage labor. All sorts of deleterious consequences associated with the "culture of poverty" were said to follow, from dependency to delinquency to school failure. Moreover, because the availability of assistance made it possible for poor mothers to choose not to work, it had the perverse effect of actually increasing the poverty that would exist in the absence of welfare. Social policy experts provided some of the grist for these arguments, but it was politicians, both Democrats and Republicans, who made them a familiar part of our public discourse.

These same politicians have been quick to proclaim the new welfare regime a success and to call for expanding the precedents it introduced. President Bush is calling on Congress to increase the percentage of women on the rolls who are required to work from 50 to 70 percent and to increase the number of hours they are required to work from thirty to forty per week. Ominously, he is also calling for a provision called the "super-waiver" that would allow states to extend the "work first" regime by waiving rules in other programs serving poor people. It is not reassuring that the Heritage Foundation, which played such a large role in crafting the 1996 policy changes, now includes work requirements for public housing tenants and food stamp recipients among its legislative priorities.

Whether the new welfare policy is a success or not depends, of course, on the measure of success. To be sure, the rolls have fallen, by about 60 percent, which is the main thing politicians boast about. And more women who are heads of families are working. But in general their earnings fall far short of what a family requires, and they also have work-related expenses to cope with. Some get help with child care expenses, but most do not. And even the dubious accomplishment of forcing more mothers into low-wage work was made possible by the extraordinary low unemployment rates of the 1990s, which are no more. Meanwhile, women who lost their jobs as the economic slowdown continued were effectively walled off from welfare, which had previously been the real unemployment insurance program for low-wage women earners. Finally, we know very little about the circumstances of the families that were pushed off the rolls but did not find jobs, or were not able to hold onto the jobs they did find, or were turned away when they tried to apply for welfare in the first place. What we do know is that while the overall poverty rate declined slightly, extreme poverty has deepened, and emergency food and shelter providers report a huge increase in the numbers of people they must help.

Even the modest (and temporary) decline in the overall poverty rate reported after the 2000 census, sometimes attributed to welfare reform, is deceptive. For one thing, the boost to low-wage earners from the late-1990s boom was almost surely more important than welfare reform. For another, poverty rates rest on the use of a forty-year-old formula to measure poverty, a formula that fails to take appropriate account of inflated housing, transportation, and medical costs. The Census Bureau claims insuperable technical problems prevent it from adjusting the measure. But Rebecca Blank, dean of the University of Michigan's Gerald Ford School of Public Policy, was surely correct when she told the *Washington Post*, "The politics of this is what has stopped it, not the technical problems."

At first glance, the politics doesn't seem to make much sense. Why would so much political energy and furor be directed against a relatively small program that mainly reaches single mothers and their children? To answer the question I think we need to look beyond welfare itself, and beyond welfare policy discussions, to a range of related changes that have occurred in domestic social policy over the past three decades. Taken together, the changes suggest a large and important set of policy shifts, reflecting a multifaceted campaign, unfolding on many fronts, but sharing a common focus on intensifying labor market discipline, especially in the lower reaches of the workforce. To be sure, the political talk that justifies these policies is often about other things, about restoring civility to our streets and neighborhoods, for example, or shoring up two-parent families, or giving workers a stake in the American dream. But so was the talk that justified the very similar campaign of the late nineteenth century to restore order and tranquility to American cities and restore morality to the poor. With these sorts of justifications, outdoor relief was eliminated or rolled back, and people called "tramps" or "hoboes" were rounded up. In both periods, the talk itself was politics, a politics to make a campaign to discipline working people palatable, even to working people themselves.

So, I turn to a delineation of some of the elements of a larger campaign that I think makes welfare reform comprehensible. It includes a three-decades-long assault on unions, in the workplace and in politics. After World War II, big American employers seemed to have reconciled themselves to unions, and the higher wages and workplace rights they secured, as the price for peace on the shop floor. But waves of strikes in the 1960s, together with pressure on profit margins resulting from rising international competition, changed that. Since the early 1970s, big business has been determined to weaken unions. This new stance first became evident in the 1970s when the head of the AFL-CIO, Lane Kirkland, expressed shock at the intransigence of his corporate colleagues on President Carter's Cost of Living Council, saying that big business had declared class war. Meanwhile, management was digging in its heels in contract negotiations, beginning, for example, to insist on two-tier contracts with sharply lower wages and benefits for new employees, an arrangement that was insidious for its effects on union solidarity. The highlight of this stage of the antiunion war was the standoff between President Reagan and the air traffic controllers' union, which resulted in mass layoffs of the striking workers. In the decades since then, the political assault on organized labor has become less visible (and even subsided under the Clinton administration), but business has continued to lobby for rule changes and probusiness board appointments that have made the National Labor Relations Board, which oversees collective bargaining rights, virtually toothless. As a result, union density has plummeted to pre-1930s levels.

With the ascendance of the Bush administration the campaign against organized labor has again become a war. President Bush has issued a series of antiunion executive orders abolishing labor-management partnerships in federal agencies and halting union recognition agreements on federal construction projects, for example. He pushed through "fast track" trade authority stripped of even mild protections of labor rights, blocked a series of strikes, and insisted on provisions that stripped the 180,000 workers in the new Department of Homeland Security of collective-bargaining rights. In the offing are new union reporting regulations that appear to be an effort to entangle unions in legal problems. Meanwhile, the new Bush budget slashes funds for enforcing workplace health and safety conditions and for investigating business violations of minimum wage, child labor, and family and medical leave mandates.[1]

Or consider contemporary, new style, top-down, educational reform proposals. As usual, the rhetoric is about educational excellence. But the emphasis on standards and testing, on rote teaching methods, on phonics and classroom discipline, suggests something more like the dumbing down of public education. This new pedagogy is far more likely to take root in the schools that educate poor and working class kids than in the affluent suburbs, where, in fact, it is being resisted. In 2003, Mayor Michael Bloomberg of New York City announced a new curriculum for the city's schools, from which better performing schools with generally better-off pupils would be exempted. For the vast majority of minority and poor children there is a program known as "Success for All," which consists of drilling and repetition according to a down-to-the-minute schedule. This style of teaching may mesh with the kind of low-wage work these children are destined to do. It is also reminiscent of late-nineteenth-century pedagogy, with its drills and bells and preoccupation with order, a pedagogy that some analysts thought reflected an effort to shape children for work in the mass-production factories that were emerging.

The cast of characters who are the main educational reformers is also suggestive. Nationally, the Business Roundtable and the testing companies have been at the forefront of educational reform. State and local business coalitions have also emerged as educational reformers,[2] often focusing specifically on achieving economies in school administration, a preoccupation that does not bode well for reducing what Jonathan Kozol calls the "savage inequalities" in spending on schools for poorer minority children.[3] The push for privatization, another aspect of contemporary educational reform, has the added payoff of making public education a new field for profiteering, just as the privatization in many places of the administration of welfare has made it a field for profiteering.

As in the nineteenth century, the criminal justice system is another policy area that has been the focus of reform. "Tough on crime" campaigns over the past three decades have resulted in increased state and federal criminal penalties, mandatory minimum sentencing laws, three-strikes provisions, cutbacks in parole, and more funding for law enforcement and for prisons. City officials also introduced the practice of "sweep-ups" of the homeless or squeegee men, much as nineteenth-century authorities had rounded up tramps and hoboes. The result of course is that there are many more people in prison. State and federal prison populations doubled between 1980 and 1990, and then doubled again between 1990 and 2000, with the result that two million people are now incarcerated, making the United States the new world leader in rates of imprisonment. Ironically, as states confront budget crises compounded of tax cuts and recession, spiraling prison budgets are a problem, and states are contemplating cost-cutting measures. Minnesota, for example, is actually charging prisoners room and board. However, few politicians are proposing prisoner release measures as a solution.

And then there is the growing trend to privatize pensions. As with the privatization of schools, prisons, and welfare, the trend is a measure of the profits that business hopes to gain by expanding the boundaries of the market along these new frontiers. The persistence with which backers of the privatization of Social Security have pressed their cause reflects in part the profits that Wall Street will earn if pension savings are shifted to private accounts. But there is more to pension privatization than that. The rise of 401(k)s is illustrative. Employment-based social benefits, mainly in the form of pensions and health care plans that depend on employers, have always been suspect for the simple reason that they are another way to tie workers who face the risk of illness and the prospect of old age to the firm that employs them, no matter the other conditions of employment. Labor historian Nelson Lichtenstein once said these programs should be understood as a form of serfdom. The increased reliance on 401(k)s underscores Lichtenstein's point. Employers have long understood that just as public income supports undergird a measure of worker independence, so do pension savings invested in the company ensure worker fealty and dependence. But Enron workers lost 1.3 billion of the 2 billion pension dollars they had invested in the company, and other workers' pensions also took big hits as a result of mutual fund investments in Enron stock.

As corporate pension support programs have expanded, the public income support programs initiated in the 1930s and enlarged in the 1960s have been rolled back. Cuts in cash assistance under welfare are an aspect of this, but these cuts are dwarfed by the changes that have occurred in Social Security, unemployment insurance, food stamps, housing, and Medicaid. The great achievement of these programs taken together was that they made working people more secure in the face of the exigencies of old age, unemployment, illness, and disability. Unemployed people who knew they could get unemployment insurance benefits were less terrified, less likely to take any job offered on any terms. In the recession of the mid-1970s nearly two-thirds of the unemployed received these benefits. In the 1990s fewer than 40 percent of the unemployed received benefits,[4] largely because of arcane changes in the formulae determining eligibility. Or consider Old Age Survivors and Dependents Insurance, the program we call Social Security. When the program was inaugurated in 1935, the talk was about removing old people from a crowded labor market in which they did not fare well, and in which they undermined the bargaining power of younger workers. Now, with little fanfare, the age of Social Security eligibility has been raised from sixty-five to sixty-seven years, albeit gently by one month a year so as not to provoke an outcry, and higher earnings by the old are allowed before pension payments are reduced so as to encourage them to take the jobs that fast food restaurants, for example, offer. And not only has eligibility for food stamps been tightened but, because the administration of both the food stamp and Medicaid programs has always been tied to welfare, welfare cutbacks have already resulted in a marked decline in the percentage of eligible people who actually receive these other benefits. The Center for Law and Social Policy recently reported that Medicaid coverage for families in extreme poverty declined by 14 percent, and food stamp coverage for children in extreme poverty fell even more sharply since the implementation of PRWORA.

The Republican budget of 2003 proposed new draconian cuts in the Food Stamp program, in the Child Care and Development Block Grant, in most Workforce Investment Act programs designed to support women who move from welfare to work, in school lunch programs, in Medicaid (a $93 billion cut), and in Medicare, for which new procedural requirements were proposed to make it more difficult for the elderly to appeal benefit denials. (And, patriotic fervor notwithstanding, veterans' benefits were also targeted for big cuts.)

And then there are the cutbacks in cash assistance that follow directly from welfare reform. Between 2.5 and 3 million women have been pushed into the labor market, some to get jobs, others to hunt for them. Quite apart from the impact on family and community well-being, these numbers are significant. Millions of desperate women who otherwise would have been raising their children with welfare grants are scrambling for work. This is roughly equivalent to an increase of 2 to 3 percentage points in the unemployment rate in its impact on worker bargaining power, and, of course, it affects the bargaining power of lower-wage workers most directly. In New York City, where official unemployment rates inched up to 9 percent in the summer of 2003 and real unemployment rates were even higher, the mayor announced a bizarre new effort to push infirm welfare recipients into the work force.

Looming ahead is the impact of the Bush tax cuts and the trillions of dollars in deficits that will result. David Stockman, Ronald Reagan's budget director, famously reported that the creation of deficits through tax cuts under Reagan was in part a deliberate strategy to starve the federal government of the funds on which social spending depends.[5] The strategy appears to be at work again, and the scale of deficits projected over the next decade is ominous. Moreover, not only do workers and the poor bear the burden of contracted social protections but they get comparatively little of the benefit of the tax cuts themselves. The main political motive here is no doubt simply greed. But it is worth pointing to the stubbornness with which Republicans resisted efforts to extend the child tax credit to the poorest families. For these families, the credit would be in effect a government subsidy and therefore, like any public income support, offer some protection from the market. And notice also the discrepancy between the Internal Revenue Service's intensive scrutiny of the tax returns of the working poor and its relatively lax treatment of corporate and well-to-do taxpayers. Those with household incomes of less than $35,000 who claim the Earned Income Tax Credit are subject to intensive examination, and the IRS has announced plans for difficult new document requirements for these families that are sure to discourage many from applying for the credit. Meanwhile, the agency has been scaling back its investigation and prosecution of the returns of the better off and corporations, including those corporations that claim offshore tax havens. The class skew in these policies is important. The rich have more influence, to be sure. But since the revenue gains from scrutinizing the working poor are small relative to the huge estimated losses from tax finagling by businesses and the well-to-do, this IRS policy may also be part of the larger strategy of starving government of the capacity to fund social protections for poor and working people.

There are also cultural dimensions to these initiatives that help make sense of them as a strategy to intensify worker discipline, but before I turn to that I want to say a little about the wider cultural campaign to celebrate markets and reinforce labor market discipline.

American politics has been overtaken by the celebration of markets associated with neoliberalism. One might view this as a renaissance of nineteenth-century laissez-faire and its depiction of markets as operating according to something akin to natural law. This time, however, the deifying of markets gains credibility from the globalization of market exchange, with the result that American goods, and therefore American workers, must now compete in the world marketplace with the goods made by low-wage workers everywhere. Merely national governments are said to be helpless to intervene without putting domestic investment and trade at risk. While international competition has in fact devastated particular industries, for most working people globalization matters more as a rhetorical trope to frighten workers than as a direct cause of their deteriorating condition. However, this is not the occasion to scrutinize the globalization argument carefully, and I will have to be content with asserting that it is wildly exaggerated, especially when it is applied to the United States, since our domestic economy is huge, and our government has great economic and political power in setting the rules of the international economy. The United States is less exposed to international competition than many other rich countries, yet it has experienced larger rollbacks in unionization and in social policy protections, and it scores the highest on inequality measures of any rich country. This is certainly not a result of globalization taken alone. But the argument that it is, pushed to extremes by ideological fanatics, undermines the democratic capacity of working people to press government for protective measures.

Moreover, the ideology of neoliberalism or neo-laissez-faire has been shored up by a campaign to depict Wall Street as a game in which everyone can play and everyone can win. This is part of the meaning of the expansion of 401(k)s. Hoodwinked workers whose pensions are invested in the stock market tie their hopes for a better life to the Dow Jones average. This investment and this illusion allay worker resentments about lagging wages and shrinking public benefits. It turns them away from the old struggles for better wages, better workplace conditions, and better public programs, as they watch the roulette wheel whirl in the vain hope that it will stop at their number.

Welfare reform is part of this cultural transformation. Consider the impact of the campaign against welfare on public opinion, as women on welfare were decried on all sides as dependent, meaning they were addicted to the dole, guilty of sexual excess and license, the contemporary inheritors of nineteenth-century-style moral iniquity. The new welfare regimen itself underlines this form of cultural teaching by stripping recipients of rights and forcing them to perform very public and very demeaning tasks. If farmers who receive federal crop subsidies were subject to the same invasive investigations as welfare recipients, the public understanding of the status of farmers and the meaning of the subsidies would also gradually shift. In 1986, Mickey Kaus, a conservative critic of the old Aid to Families with Dependent Children program, made explicit the purpose of a degrading welfare system when he said that the reason to put Betsy Smith to work sweeping streets and cleaning buildings was not only to deter Betsy Smith from having an illegitimate child but so that the "sight of Betsy Smith sweeping streets after having her illegitimate child will discourage her younger sisters and neighbors from doing as she did."[6] The push to use TANF funds for marriage promotion activities is partly a reflection of the influence of Christian fundamentalists in the conservative coalition. But by underlining the sexual deviance of recipients, it also contributes to their social degradation. And, much as Kaus predicted, these new welfare rituals have an impact on poor women. More important, they have an impact on all low-wage workers, as welfare becomes more demeaning and work—even low-wage and disrespected work—by contrast gains value.

So, who is doing this? And why? I think the campaign to intensify work discipline dates from the early 1970s, when corporate America was grappling with narrowing profit margins. The squeeze on profits resulted partly from intensifying competition from Japan and West Germany—only recall how the auto industry was thrown into disarray by the arrival of small and efficient cars on American markets—and partly from rising raw materials prices, especially rising oil prices. The squeeze also resulted, however, from rising wages and growing expenditures on income support programs that undergirded wages. And business costs had also grown because of the expansion of workplace and environmental regulation. The costs of rising wages, income support programs, and expanded regulation reflected the gains made by the protest movements of the 1960s and the turbulence and electoral upsets they set in motion. No wonder "the Great Society" has become an epithet in the mouths of conservative critics.

The corporate response to these developments has been to try to recover a competitive edge, to enlarge profits, in large part by lowering labor costs, which meant restructuring work and cutting wages and employment-based benefits. More and more jobs became contract or contingent jobs, for example, and wages have lagged sharply behind increases in productivity and profits. However, to effectively lower wage costs, business also had to change the public policies that shored up wages by giving workers a measure of protection and independence. Altogether, this was no small agenda, for it meant rolling back the gains of nearly a century of working class politics. To make headway on it, American business leaders who had grown fat and lazy during the twenty-five years after World War II, when America's economic preeminence was unchallenged, mobilized to do politics. They formed new peak business organizations and revived old business organizations like the National Association of Manufacturers and the Chamber of Commerce, organizations that had become virtually dormant during the heady postwar years of business success. CEOs retooled themselves and became lobbyists, vice presidents for "public affairs" were created, and business became a major Washington presence, as the corporate lobbying offices that line a flourishing K Street demonstrates. Lastly, business money flowed to politicians and their campaigns to buy access and influence.

In the area of social policy, however, business groups acted out their politics cautiously. In effect, they employed front men, the right-wing think tanks funded by business but presenting themselves as class-neutral intellectual arbiters of policy. The names are familiar: the Heritage Foundation, the Cato Institute, the Hudson Institute, the American Enterprise Institute, and the Manhattan Institute. These and other think tanks became the mouthpieces of a business class mobilized to do battle with the social policies inherited from the New Deal and the Great Society. They sponsored public intellectuals like George Gilder and Charles Murray, they wrote and published books, they deluged congressional offices with daily reports giving their take on policies, they promoted their spokespeople on TV talk shows, they flooded the newspapers with op eds. Their agenda was the business agenda of dismantling the social protections painfully developed during the twentieth century. In significant measure, that agenda succeeded.

What then can be done to restore the public policies that brought a measure of security to the lives of working and poor Americans? Some hints at an answer are gained, I think, by sober scrutiny of periods of egalitarian reform in American history. The 1930s gave us federal protection of labor rights and the first national social welfare programs. The 1960s expanded those programs and improved them too, bringing something like the rule of law to the administration of welfare, for example. In both these periods, the poor and their advocates mobilized in protest, raised new demands, made trouble—enough trouble to penetrate electoral politics and threaten dominant electoral coalitions. If we look even further back, into the nineteenth century, we can see a similar pattern in the success of the abolitionists. The abolitionists were despised and harassed for the issues they raised and for the trouble they made, but their issues and their trouble broke up the intersectional national parties and created the conditions for civil war and emancipation.

What about now? Before September 11 there were clear signs that widening inequality in the United States together with corporate abuse of democratic politics was nourishing a new wave of protests. We could see it in the dramatic anticorporate globalization demonstrations, in antisweatshop campaigns on campuses, in the resurgence of the labor movement, in living-wage campaigns in the cities. Those protests have been muffled by the war on terror and the war with Iraq, which, whatever else they may be, have also become a charade to shield from view the public policies that make the rich richer and the poor poorer, in the United States and abroad. Vice President Cheney has said that the war on terror may take fifty years. But it is unlikely to succeed as a diversion from the policies that encourage business greed and enforce labor discipline for fifty years. It may not even work for one election cycle. People do regain their footing, and voices of dissent are important in helping to make that happen.

ECONOMIC CRISIS, THE WORKING CLASS, AND ORGANIZED LABOR

Michael D. Yates

Capitalist economies have always moved in cycles of expansion and contraction. They are crisis prone by their nature. For example, the U.S. economy expanded for ten years, from 1991 until the spring of 2001, and, as is normally the case during such a long expansion, the pundits began to argue that the economy had overcome any tendency to contract and that prosperity could go on forever. Even Alan Greenspan seemed to think that uninterrupted growth was possible, provided, of course, that he remained at the helm of the Federal Reserve. The good times came to an end, however, as they always do. The economy went into a recession in 2001, and while, from a technical point of view (a recession occurs when the gross domestic product, a measure of the economy's total production, falls for two successive quarters), the recession only lasted about a year, the economy has yet to fully recover. It appears to be mired in a jobless recovery, with relatively stable and high unemployment. In May 2003, the unemployment rate nationally was 6 percent, and there were more than five million people either working part-time but preferring full-time work or too discouraged to look for work.

Economic crises always have class dimensions. Workers are inherently more vulnerable than employers, so they suffer more when the economy falters. Let us use the most recent crisis as an example.

What a crisis means for workers depends in part on what they managed to achieve during the boom. A period of economic expansion is ordinarily good for workers. Sustained growth creates an empowering climate for workers by depressing the rate of unemployment, which, in turn, puts upward pressure on wages and increases the security of working people. This growing sense of stability then increases the likelihood that workers will behave more aggressively toward their employers. A falling unemployment rate also narrows the unemployment differential between minority and white workers, and this can facilitate cooperation between them. Rising incomes generate higher revenues for the government without higher tax rates, and this makes it easier to argue in favor of progressive social spending.

Given the long duration of the expansion, one would predict that workers made considerable gains in their life circumstances. The improvements, however, were rather modest and concentrated in the last few years of the expansion. The data show that working people did not benefit much during the first half of the expansion. In fact, real wages (the purchasing power of the workers' actual money wages) for all production and nonsupervisory employees were lower in 1996 than they were in 1991. The unemployment rate actually rose in 1992, the second year of the expansion, and remained relatively high until 1999. Even the low unemployment levels achieved in 1999 and 2000 (4.2 and 4 percent, respectively) were not especially eye-catching when compared to those managed during the post–World War II prosperity.

Still, the workers did make some gains at the end of the boom. For example, hourly wages, adjusted for inflation, for all production and nonsupervisory workers grew by 1.5 percent per year between 1995 and 1999, while they fell by 0.6 percent per year between 1989 and 1995. (By comparison, real hourly wages rose by 2.3 percent per year during the long post–World War II expansion from 1947 to 1967.) Real wages rose more sharply still in 2000. And the large drop in unemployment from 1996 to 2000 broke a decade-by-decade trend of rising unemployment rates from the 1950s through the 1980s. Sharply lower official poverty rates (from 15.1 percent in 1993 to 11.3 percent in 2000) and a slightly more equal distribution of income also marked the last boom years, trends especially helpful to minorities and women.[1]

How well workers fare in an economic expansion depends in part on how well organized workers are. In addition, worker organization should increase during an expansion, and this by itself should improve the lot of working people by more than would have otherwise been the case. It is well known that workers in the United States are not very well organized; union density (the percentage of employed workers in labor unions) in the United States is among the world's lowest.[2] So this helped to limit the gains workers made during the boom.[3] What is more, while the long U.S. expansion was a (modest) boon to workers in general, it was not accompanied by much growth for organized labor. This is important because economic growth in the past has been correlated positively with union membership. Rising union membership in a period of economic growth allows workers to secure more permanent increases in wages and benefits and boosts the power of the working class as a whole.

It had been thought that the 1995 election of John Sweeney and his New Voice slate to the leadership of the AFL-CIO would help to reverse the long decline in union density. Sweeney promised a radical change away from the servicing model of unionism, in which unions were seen primarily as an insurance policy for workers, to an organizing model and a more combative stance against employers.

Sweeney's election corresponded with the acceleration of the expansion, and this by itself should have helped him fulfill his promises. During the remainder of the boom, several unions did shift resources to organizing new members, and some successes were achieved. In 1999, union membership rose by 265,000, the largest gain in twenty years. The victory of the reform-led Teamsters against the United Parcel Service (UPS) in 1997 seemed to be the harbinger of a new day for organized labor. The AFL-CIO even reached out to workers in other countries and to the antiglobalization movement, reversing many years of blind support for U.S. imperialism. Significantly, the AFL-CIO dropped the anticommunist rhetoric that had been a staple for more than fifty years. Unions began to employ and promote political progressives to an extent not seen since the 1930s. However, these achievements could not be sustained. Membership began to fall again in 2000, and today union density is at a meager 13 percent, lower than when Sweeney took office. In the private sector, it is 9 percent, about the same ratio as in 1930. Of the 44 million workers in retail trade, services, and health care, only slightly more than 5 percent are in unions.[4] There have been other successful strikes during the expansion, but none as galvanizing as that at UPS. Worse still, the Teamsters union has been racked by internal crisis. Reform president Ron Carey was stripped of his office because of his participation, perhaps unwitting, in a kickback scheme involving Democratic Party operatives. In his place, the members elected James Hoffa, a man without the experience and savvy of his father Jimmy Hoffa and with close ties to the Republican Party. While many unionists have continued to embrace international solidarity, the AFL-CIO and many member unions devoted an inordinate amount of energy to keeping China out of the World Trade Organization, a strategy that, even if successful, would have done little to improve the lives of workers either here or abroad. And as we shall see, the entire edifice of international solidarity has been gravely threatened by the "war on terrorism."

On average, then, workers made some progress during at least the last half of the long boom. And if the labor movement did not make spectacular gains, it at least reasserted itself on the national stage and regained some of its luster as the champion of the oppressed. It almost prevented the president from winning more "fast track" trade power and it got several relatively progressive congresspersons elected. An unprecedented number of union members ran for political office, and more than two thousand were elected. Yet, neither the working class as a whole nor its organized component made the kind of headway necessary to withstand the antilabor forces unleashed by a prolonged economic slump—certainly nothing comparable to the gains made during the twenty-five years following World War II.

That is, despite the long expansion, workers were not able to reverse the losses inflicted on them during the period of capitalist onslaught that occurred after the end of the post–World War II "golden era." During the period between roughly 1973 and the start of the boom, politics shifted sharply to the right, and corporations embraced "lean production" as they sought to reverse the decline in profit rates that marked the end of the long postwar prosperity. As a consequence of what we can accurately call an employer-government attack on workers, working class living standards plummeted, and organized labor was thoroughly routed.[5]

Workers and unions were helped back on their feet by the ten fat years between 1991 and 2001, but they did not come close to regaining the power they had lost during the eighteen lean years between 1973 and 1991. Unions were not able to make significant wage gains in collective bargaining despite the relatively low unemployment rates in the last part of the expansion. Only in 2000 did the wage gain in collective bargaining agreements rise to the level achieved at the beginning of the boom.[6]

Proof of labor's inadequacies was its inability to pressure the Democratic Party to put up a more progressive candidate than the hapless Al Gore in 2000. It was not even able to prevent the election of the thoroughly reactionary and antilabor George W. Bush. And before the election, labor could not stop the termination of national public assistance, nor could it compel the government to beef up the unemployment insurance system. This means that the impact of the current recession and jobless recovery will not be much moderated by the "automatic stabilizing" mechanisms of welfare and unemployment compensation, both of which in the past would have risen mechanically as the economy worsened. Fewer than 40 percent of the unemployed currently collect benefits, down from nearly three-quarters in the mid-1970s.[7] The limits on receiving public assistance put in place by the 1996 abolition of welfare have been reached, and yet the need for assistance continues to grow. Those forced to work to collect assistance have lost their employment as employers shed jobs. For example, in New York City, welfare recipients were "employed" to clean subway cars. Some had managed to obtain regular employment with the Transit Authority at decent wages. Now the authority has eliminated jobs, including the car-cleaning employment of the welfare recipients. Adding insult to injury, the unemployed may also find it impossible to get public assistance. One of the last acts of the antiworker Rudolph Giuliani administration was to sack thousands of former welfare recipients hired to keep the city's parks clean.

What, then, has happened to workers during the downturn and the anemic recovery? We have just noted how disproportionately affected are the very poor and the unemployed by the current downturn. We have also noted that the unemployment rate, while it did not rise to the levels seen in the crises of the 1970s and 1980s, failed to fall as the economy began to recover. In addition, millions of workers have been able to find only part-time employment or have dropped out of the labor force altogether. Tellingly, the gains made by black and other minority workers have eroded sharply. In May 2003, the unemployment rate for black workers was 10.9 percent (up from 10 percent at the peak of the expansion) and for Hispanics 7.5 percent (the white rate was 5.2 percent). Those who are unemployed are staying out of work longer, unable to find replacement jobs quickly. As would be expected, the weak labor market began to force real wages down. The poverty rate climbed again, passing 12 percent of the population in 2003. In the first two and a half years of the George W. Bush administration, the economy hemorrhaged jobs, more than two million in the private sector.[8] Organized labor was hard hit by the economic crisis, as the economy lost manufacturing jobs to recession and capital flight. (China, with its tens of millions of surplus workers and extremely low wages, has become a manufacturing juggernaut, producing everything from furniture to bicycles to computer chips.)[9] Even though the United States has nearly as many manufacturing jobs as in the early 1970s, many more are poorly paid, as union strongholds have been devastated by decades of concession bargaining.

Each economic crisis is unique, in the sense that it takes place in a unique set of social circumstances. The impact that a particular crisis has on working people will, therefore, be conditioned by whatever special factors surround that crisis. Some of the factors that give the current economic crisis its special character are the September 11 terrorist attacks, the ensuing war on terrorism, and the invasions of Afghanistan and Iraq. It is useful to look at these factors in some detail, not just to show how this economic crisis might differ from previous ones but also because what has happened since September 11 tells us important things about working class experience and class consciousness in the United States.

It is always helpful for employers and their government collaborators to have a scapegoat for what they do to workers in a crisis. Terrorists and terrorism have served very conveniently as such scapegoats. For example, it has been argued that the current economic malaise is due primar-

ily to the attacks on the World Trade Center and the Pentagon and the ensuing war on terrorism, including the run-up to the invasion of Iraq. Let
us look first at this argument.

To put the terrorist attacks in context, let us ask how labor might have
fared during the downturn had the World Trade Center and Pentagon assaults not taken place. (When I speak of "labor," I mean mainly organized
labor. Unorganized workers have little ability to be anything but victims
in an economic crisis.) We know that the U.S. economy was already in recession on September 11, 2001, and the same was true for the economies
of Japan, much of Europe, and most of the poor countries. We also know
a good deal about the state of organized labor just before September 11.
So let us look at the probable impact of both external and internal factors
on labor.

Had the September 11 events not occurred, labor would still have faced
enormous external obstacles as it tried to cope with the downturn. Four
such obstacles come to mind. First, a recession strains union resources
and makes unions less able to cope with the needs of laid-off members.
Had the social safety net been maintained at levels achieved a generation
ago, this strain would have been lessened. Second, the political climate
became more hostile to labor with the election of George W. Bush, which
occurred well before September 11. The few bones thrown to workers by
President Clinton were quickly taken away by Bush, and, even in the absence of the attacks, he would surely have continued to make reactionary
appointments to all of the agencies dealing with working people, such as
the National Labor Relations Board, the courts, the Occupational Safety
and Health Administration, and the Department of Labor. The labor laws
of the United States are already stacked decisively against workers, and
now these laws are being interpreted by those antagonistic to any prolabor provisions remaining in them.[10] For decades, employers have viru-
lently opposed any and all attempts by workers to organize. They have
usually been successful. Now they have an unapologetic friend in the
White House, one who will not give even lip service to working class interests.

Before September 11, organized labor, despite the achievements made
under Sweeney's leadership, faced serious internal problems. The AFL-
CIO and almost all member unions were top-down organizations unwilling or afraid to educate and encourage the rank and file to
self-organize and build up their own unions. Democracy was as little
known in large parts of the labor movement as it was in the boardrooms
of labor's adversaries. It was a rare labor leader who would openly criticize labor's autocrats. Nor could a union democracy movement in any
union count on support from labor officialdom. In addition, only a hand-

ful of unions had made a commitment to organizing, and, of course, the results showed in terms of union membership. The service model of unionism, one in which members are essentially seen as consumers of a union's services, was alive and well.

Organized labor had made overtures to many other progressive groups, both in union struggles and in the larger antiglobalization movement. But it was not close to assuming the leadership role in a broad-based mass movement for social change, much less against capitalism. When push came to shove, organized labor was still firmly tied to the Democratic Party.

Given these external and internal forces, it would have been difficult for the working class not to lose considerable ground even if the episodes of September 11 had not happened. Before September 11, the economic downturn reflected the typical response to the excessive optimism (reflected in runaway stock prices and very large capital investments, especially in information technology) that sometimes accompanies economic expansions. There is no reason to believe that, absent September 11, the economy would have not continued to contract. Corporations would have continued to be plagued by excess capacity and consumers and governments would have continued to be hurt by rapidly falling stock prices.

But September 11 did happen, and the U.S. government did inaugurate a war on terrorism. Both have had and will continue to have an impact on workers that, on the whole, is largely negative. There is no question that September 11 made the crisis immediately worse. For example, the attacks rapidly laid low the New York City economy, still reasonably robust before September 11. After the attacks, the *New York Times* was filled with stories about rising unemployment, failing businesses, increasing poverty, and homelessness, even disappearing bonuses for high-priced lawyers and Wall Street brokers.

Two years after the attacks the *New York Times* and newspapers around the country were still filled with such stories. What happened to New York City spread out to the rest of the nation (and New York City's economic crisis has continued to worsen), so that there is hardly a place on the national map that is not now experiencing recession. States face severe budget shortfalls, and since most states must balance their budgets, they have begun to either raise taxes or, more typically, slash spending. This has resulted in massive layoffs of public employees and sharp cutbacks in everything from public schools to health care to prisons and courts. In Oregon, many public schools have gone on four-day weeks, as have the courts.[11]

While the economy was headed into recession before September 11, it may be that September 11 and the wars in Afghanistan and Iraq have added a new element of uncertainty to the normal calculations of businesses and consumers. Uncertainty can make a crisis deeper and longer lasting than might otherwise have been the case. It can also heighten the economic anxiety brought about by events triggered by the downturn itself, such as the default by Argentina on its debt obligations and the incredible bankruptcy of the Enron Corporation. Again, however, the war on terrorism has been going on for so long that it is very likely that uncertainty has already been built into decisions, and therefore the continuation of slow economic growth cannot plausibly be attributed to the war on terrorism.

It is also possible that an external shock can shorten a crisis, and this may be true for the war on terrorism and the invasion of Iraq. War expenditures did end the Great Depression, but those expenditures were extremely large and lasted for several years. This time around, the relatively small size of the military spending and the already existing gargantuan U.S. arsenal make a repeat performance unlikely. The invasion of Iraq and the subsequent start of the rebuilding of the country have probably had a slight positive impact on the U.S. economy (at least the stock market did well in the aftermath of Iraq), but these will very likely be insufficient to jump-start demand in the United States. It is important to keep in mind that just about the whole world is mired in crisis now. Where, then, will the demand for goods and services necessary for an economic rebound come from?[12]

How have the terrorist attacks, the war on terrorism, and the invasion of Iraq affected labor? Again it is useful to distinguish between external and internal elements. The response of labor unions and their members to the attacks showed us why unions are important. Almost all of the workers at the World Trade Center site were union members, and these unionists uniformly acted in a selfless manner, working tirelessly at the disaster site and assisting union families in need. This was in sharp contrast to the behavior of employers. Their first step was to lobby Congress for bailouts, and none of them entered pleas for aid to their employees, soon to be unemployed. (In fact, employers, especially in the airline industry, have demanded and received enormous concessions from their workers.) The quick and coordinated actions of unions also demonstrated why it is necessary for workers to be part of a collective organization. Without organization, we are on our own, and this is a dangerous place to be in a dog-eat-dog world. Unions give us a kind of family to support us in times of need.

Although union solidarity shined brightly during the immediate aftermath of September 11, it cannot be said that this has redounded to the advantage of organized labor. A lot of words were written about the heroic workers laboring at Ground Zero, but the image presented was one of individual heroes, not of members of collective organizations responding and acting collectively. Newspapers were not filled with editorials urging workers to join unions, nor did politicians tell their constituents to do so. Perhaps when unions try to organize new members, newly sympathetic workers will meet them. Time will tell. However, while it is true that union organizers could have no better illustration of why unions matter than what unions did in the wake of September 11, union leaders do not seem to have done much to spread the word. That is, while they have tried to take care of their own members, they have not done much to build working class solidarity. For an idea of what I mean here, consider the actions of unions in Europe in spring 2003 in response to attempts by governments there to cut pension benefits. Workers took to the streets in the hundreds of thousands, and they engaged in work stoppages that seriously disrupted both local and national economies.[13] Nothing comparable occurred in the United States, even after the government made it clear that it was using the war on terrorism as a cover to attack unions and working people (see below).

Labor's shining image did not do it much good in the White House or the halls of Congress. All of the external difficulties labor faced prior to September 11, Afghanistan, and Iraq are still present; indeed, they are more intractable than ever. Congress immediately passed legislation bailing out the most harmed industries, notably the airlines, while giving affected workers nothing. Congressman Dick Armey intimated that expanded unemployment compensation was not in the spirit of American individualism. In the frenzy of patriotism that followed the terrorist assaults, President Bush rushed draconian restrictions of our civil liberties through a compliant Congress. It is not just that the government has declared a war on terrorism, made life more difficult for noncitizen immigrants, summarily arrested thousands of persons, and prepared to subject suspected terrorists to "trials" before military tribunals. Rather it is that the government has moved the entire political climate much further to the right. As I wrote just after September 11:

> "Terrorism" is a word subject to many meanings. The U.S. government and its allies will define it as broadly as possible, to include for certain rebel forces in Colombia and elsewhere in Latin America and very likely to include as well the Cuban government. Individuals and organizations opposed to their government's actions will be tarred with the terrorist brush and subjected to close surveillance and other more subtle (and not so subtle) forms of harassment. Already some professors and journalists have been fired for criticizing government anti-terrorism actions. We can expect more of this. We will also see more brazen assaults on the anti-glob-

alization and environmental movements. Both will be portrayed as unpatriotic and antagonistic to the economic well being of the majority of people in the rich nations. The "war on terrorism" will prove to be excellent cover for the building of oil pipelines and other destroyers of the earth's ecosystems. "Free trade" will be opposed to the "primitive" economic and cultural views of the "terrorists," and those opposed to it will thereby be linked to the "forces of evil," to use one of President Bush's favorite expressions. The economic and environmental fallout from all of this will be represented as unfortunate but necessary sacrifices we will all have to make to preserve our way of life. . . . It is not farfetched to imagine that strikes and other forms of labor unrest will be smeared as unpatriotic and ultimately supportive of the terrorists.[14]

All types of social legislation have been put on the back burner or taken off the stove completely. And the new political atmosphere has provided excellent camouflage for advancing the right-wing economic agenda. To a certain extent, the antiglobalization movement that had been picking up steam since the events in Seattle in 1999 had put neoliberalism on the defensive. (Neoliberalism is the dogma claiming that the removal of all restrictions on the movement of capital as well as the dismantling of social service programs and the privatization of most public services will lead to maximum economic performance. This has been used to rationalize the assault on workers that has taken place virtually nonstop since the end of post–World War II boom.) But the war on terrorism has given neoliberalism new life. In addition to "fast track" trade legislation (mandating that Congress can vote trade legislation up or down only in its entirety; no amendments can be made), the Right has already pushed for and won regressive tax cuts and further corporate bailouts. The press has already noted the extremely regressive nature of the tax cuts, which somehow managed to exclude millions of poor taxpayers. President Bush and company have quietly placed extreme right-wingers in key administrative posts, abolished some proworker executive orders, prohibited workers in certain Justice Department offices from forming unions (on security grounds), stalled the Department of Labor's comprehensive plan on workplace safety, and eliminated the regional Women's Bureau offices in the Department of Labor.[15]

During the fall of 2002, the federal government actively intervened on the side of employers in the dispute between West Coast dockworkers and the big shipping companies. National security arguments were used to threaten the union into submission, and it was made clear that the government was close to the view that any labor dispute could now be subverted on similar grounds. In this case, the union and the employers ultimately settled on terms beneficial to the workers, but it is critical to note here that the union involved in that dispute, the International Longshore Workers Union (ILWU), is one of the few left-wing and class-conscious unions left in the country.[16]

Organized labor has been shocked by the callousness with which workers have been treated since September 11. Even the Teamsters' Hoffa has begun to criticize Bush's treatment of workers.[17] However, organized labor has not been able to do much about this treatment. The AFL-CIO has proposed no bold initiatives. After Afghanistan, labor leaders strongly condemned the curtailment of civil liberties in the United States and continued to champion rights for immigrant workers (not coincidentally, immigrant workers are among the strongest advocates of unionization), but they also gave nearly unanimous support for the invasion of Afghanistan.[18] By doing this, they gave tacit support for the reactionary underpinnings of the war on terrorism and undercut their liberal protestations. It is naive to support a completely lawless and murderous war, ruinous to the lives of the world's poorest people, and then turn around and say that you hope the government won't target immigrants and will respect civil liberties. In other words, given everything that the war on terrorism has done and will do to harm workers, how can labor leaders be for workers and for the war at the same time? But this is not a question organized labor is prepared to discuss.

September 11 and the war on terrorism and in Iraq confront labor with a dilemma. It has been relatively easy for Sweeney and company to talk about the need for social unionism. And, given the hardships workers have faced for so long and the realities of a greatly strengthened global capitalism, it has not been difficult to argue for a greater commitment to organizing, building alliances with progressive groups, and international labor solidarity. Workers are ready to hear such things. They want to join unions and confront their employers, and they are appalled by the conditions endured by workers in the poor countries. To some extent the AFL-CIO has done the right things. It and some member unions have shown a greater commitment to organizing and showing solidarity. But what is difficult and what Sweeney has not done is develop a firm labor ideology, a class ideology, to serve as the foundation on which a movement could be built. To do this would require a class confrontation, both with employers and with the governments that employers control. Specifically, it would necessitate a confrontation with the U.S. government, the central power in all of the world capitalist system. Too many hard questions would have to be asked, and none harder than why organized labor has actively participated in or supported the most egregiously antilabor international policies and actions of the U.S. government. The oppressive and imperialist power of the U.S. government is the real deal, so to speak—the ultimate enforcer of employer class dominance. If labor does not confront this, it will never get to the root of its problems.[19]

Events since September 11 have brought home how far away labor is from being a movement. With a few notable exceptions, even labor progressives supported the war in Afghanistan, or at least refrained from talking about it. Journalist JoAnn Wypijewski reports "Paul Booth, one-time anti-Vietnam war activist and now International organizing director for AFSCME, warned them [Jobs with Justice, a progressive prolabor and antiglobalization coalition] that there was no benefit in taking a position on the war. JwJ's national office issued a statement of grief that included support for immigrant workers and an admonition against anti-Muslim bigotry but was silent on the war."[20]

Some on the Left seem to think that the economic crisis itself will get workers to question the nature of the system, but this is wishful thinking. I am certain that most working people understand that the system is stacked against them. They can see every day that the economy more and more operates as a gigantic racket, siphoning off the money from their labor and placing it in the hands of the rich. Leaders have to talk about these things, encouraging open debate and discussion. And there have to be democratic organizations in place for such discussions to occur. Most unions are not such organizations, so even when leaders want debate, they do not often get it. The 2002 AFL-CIO convention in Las Vegas passed many progressive resolutions, but there was absolutely no debate among the delegates. And support for the war was more or less taken for granted. What is more, the progressive resolutions were not matched by calls for action, except by the seriously compromised Jesse Jackson.

Wypijewski and others have correctly pointed out that there are hopeful signs in the house of labor.[21] There was not the kind of labor prowar frenzy about Iraq that former AFL-CIO president George Meany demanded about Vietnam. Even in locals directly affected by the terrorist attacks, unionists have generally been respectful of dissenting opinions. Sweeney and his allies have made dissent against war by member unions and union members respectable and have not in any way clamped down on it. Support for what the government is doing is mixed and often contradictory. Most union workers do not want a war on immigrants, nor do they want their civil liberties eliminated and social programs further cut. Several unions are continuing their organizing efforts; immigrants continue to be especially sympathetic to unionization; and some unions and their allies are actively pressing forward international solidarity campaigns. Sweeney's leadership has motivated thousands of prolabor activists, both within and outside of the AFL-CIO, and these ground troops are not going to give up the struggle. Conservative labor leaders may be hard pressed to stifle members' anger when companies keep asking for concessions. As Lee Sustar puts it, "What is more, many union leaders, often local officials, will be unwilling or unable to retreat further without risking the virtual destruction of their unions. . . . And unionized workers—who still haven't made up ground lost in the 1980s—will be much less willing to accept the same old explanations about the need to sacrifice today."[22]

One of the most heartening developments has been the upsurge in antiwar activity on the part of labor unions prior to the invasion of Iraq. As Chris Kutalik and William Johnson reported in early 2003:

> In recent months a growing, if uneven, sense of momentum against an impending war in Iraq has been spreading in the labor movement in the United States and around the world.
>
> Before the fall of 2002, trade union opposition to war plans was mostly isolated into pockets primarily organized in small ad hoc labor antiwar committees in the larger cities, such as New York City Labor against the War and the Labor Committee for Peace and Justice in the San Francisco Bay Area.
>
> As the autumn unfolded an increasing number of antiwar resolutions came from U.S. labor groups. Starting with a few scattered locals, there were important breakthroughs in relatively larger bodies. Early resolutions from larger bodies such as the California Federation of Teachers, SEIU Local 1199, and the Teamsters Local 705 opened space for more unions to sign onto calls. On January 11, 2003, 100 representatives met to set up a national U.S. Labor against the War (USLAW).
>
> By March 2003 roughly 130 locals, 45 central labor councils, 26 regional bodies, 11 national/international unions, and the AFL-CIO Executive Council had passed resolutions condemning the Bush administration's actions around Iraq in varying degrees of criticism. Opposition to war focused on the enormous toll—in workers' lives and tax dollars—and on fears that the Bush administration would use the war as a pretext for even more crackdowns on workers' rights. Public employee unions in particular warned of the inevitable budget cuts that will hurt both the public and their own members.[23]

But against these promising developments must be set some that are less auspicious. Resolutions are one thing; action is another. The huge demonstrations of the weeks before the invasion of Iraq, which did have large labor participation, gave way to much smaller protests, with relatively muted labor participation, once the invasion began. Organized labor had no coherent antiwar response to the invasion itself. Concrete actions such as work stoppages or refusal to ship, unload, or deliver war material, such as occurred in other parts of the world (Scotland and Italy, for example), did not take place in the United States.[24]

In addition, John Sweeney is not a young man, and he has not defeated his enemies. The reactionaries, led by Hoffa and others, are waiting in the wings. Sweeney has likely not built up a progressive constituency strong enough to hold onto power and widen and deepen what he has achieved. It is not at all inconceivable that Sweeney's enemies will win power and move the AFL-CIO back to where it was when the hapless Lane Kirkland was president. And even if Sweeney's allies succeed him, all of the problems discussed above will continue to haunt the labor movement, none moreso than the lack of a class ideology that would allow workers to distinguish between love of country and imperialism.

In connection with this failure of organized labor in the United States to develop class-based ideology, it is important to note the critical connection between this and the issue of race. For most of its history, organized labor in the United States has been a white affair. There was a brief period in the 1930s and 1940s in which some left-led unions pushed for racial equality, but the progressive unions were purged from the CIO in 1949. The so-called post–World War II "accord" between labor and employers benefited mostly white workers. Today this accord is dead, and employers have made it clear that they no longer need an alliance with organized labor. As white workers have come to understand this, they have become susceptible to the right-wing and racist populism of people like Pat Buchanan. Because the leaders of organized labor have never adequately confronted the issue of race, they have found it difficult to counter this right-wing populism, which has the support of many white workers.[25]

I have restricted myself in this chapter to an examination of what I know best—labor in the United States. However, this gives a certain myopia to the piece. If we extend our field of vision to the rest of the world, we see the unfolding of many more encouraging events.[26] Strong and radical workers' movements have been growing in South Korea, South Africa, and especially in the South American countries of Argentina, Ecuador, Colombia, Venezuela, and Brazil. In these places a radical and class-based ideology is more common, as are the actions that follow from such an ideology. It is there that the future course of working class movements may be decided, and it is to them that we must build our bridges. That is, as we fight to rebuild our own unions and reassert a left presence within the larger labor movement, we must at the same time reach out to progressive labor organizations around the world.

We will know that labor in the United States is serious about the emancipation of the working class when our labor leaders openly embrace the highway blockades of the unemployed in Argentina, the takeover of land by peasants in Ecuador, the political campaigns of left-wing leaders like Lula da Silva in Brazil, and a host of similar struggles, including those of Cuba against years of blatant U.S. aggression. Measured against this standard, we can see how many miles we have yet to travel. And at the same time, we can see the difficult struggles that lie ahead.

PART IV

CLASS AND YOUNG ADULTS

Classes exist in relation to one another at any given time, but classes are also reproduced across generations. While some children of working class families enter the middle class or even become capitalists (and some other families experience downward mobility), the single most likely occupation of a child in the United States is that of the parent.[1] Through labor markets and the educational system, our society creates new generations of workers as surely as new generations of capitalists are formed as well.

The experience of class reaches deeply into young people's lives. Patterns of behavior and sets of expectations characteristic of the family's class become second nature as the children absorb them through observation and instruction. As the children grow up, take their places in society, and reflect on their experiences for themselves, what had been automatic can be subject to questioning and reevaluation. Sometimes this happens in the context of work experience, sometimes in college courses. The chapters in part 4 report on the situation of young adults in the labor market and in higher education and give us a sense of the circumstances in which class thinking can take place among the new generation.

GREGORY DEFREITAS and **NIEV DUFFY** find that the wages of young people are of growing importance in total family income. But young workers have been hardest hit by falling wages since the 1980s, even among college graduates. Compared with the rest of the labor force, young people also experience higher rates of unemployment and lower rates of health insurance coverage. Challenging conventional wisdom about apathetic youth, DeFreitas and Duffy find substantial evidence of social activism and a greater sympathy for unions among students and young workers, especially immigrant workers, than among older ones.

A college education is the single most effective means to upward class mobility, to say nothing of its general importance for citizenship and human growth. Yet in 2000 only 26 percent of people aged twenty-five years or older had at least a four-year college degree, and another 8 percent had a two-year associates degree.[2] From this limited base, opportunities for young working class men and women are shrinking as the fiscal crisis, spreading to almost every state, has resulted in higher fees and tuition and less financial aid. The financial strain of attending college is too great for most working class people, even with the availability of loans. In fact, loans have become such a burden to college graduates that many question the wisdom of going to college at all.[3]

Working class students experience more than financial strains when they go to college. In most four-year colleges and universities (as opposed to community colleges), students from the working class are in the minority. As **MICHELLE TOKARCZYK** reports, these students often have difficulty learning in this environment because working class high schools and family expectations undermine their preparation. Immersed in a sea of middle class students and faculty who assume that everyone around them is middle class, working class students may remain invisible when class is not explicitly acknowledged. Based on her own experiences as a student and then as a professor, Tokarczyk explores a number of ways in which colleges and universities might respond institutionally to the needs of their working class students.

Practitioners of working class studies have produced several books that explore the dynamics of teaching working class students, and teaching about class to any student.[4] Many of these writers and others in the field are themselves from working class backgrounds, seeking to make sense of their own histories and trying to smooth the path for young workers coming behind. **BARBARA JENSEN** draws on her own experience and her years of teaching and counseling working class students to describe some of the psychological dynamics young people experience when crossing from one class into the world of another. Among other issues, she explores the conflicts that arise when a person raised in a working class environment of mutual aid and suppression of individual desire in favor of family and community survival arrives in a new environment where individual accomplishment and personal advancement dominate expectations. For these students, the problem is to integrate the college experience with their working class roots. For working class studies, the problem is the same but reversed: to integrate working class experience into the discovery and creation of knowledge.

YOUNG WORKERS, ECONOMIC INEQUALITY, AND COLLECTIVE ACTION

Gregory DeFreitas and Niev Duffy

The American youth population has been growing dramatically since the mid-1990s. Fueled by the "baby boomlet" of huge numbers of baby boom parents and by the mass immigration underway since the early 1970s, the number of 16- to 24-year-olds is projected over this decade to jump 13 percent—faster growth than any other major age group. The impacts will be enormous in all areas of social, political, and economic life.

Certainly, the future American working class will be shaped by the attitudes and job experiences of today's youth. By the year 2010, 16- to 24-year-olds will account for an estimated 16.5 percent of the labor force; and the full 16-to-34 age group will account for nearly *two-fifths* of all workers.[1] Their earnings progress will be crucial to national income and consumption patterns and to funding the massive Social Security needs of baby boom retirees.

This chapter presents new findings on socioeconomic trends among youth and on their attitudes about employers, unions, and class identity. The main questions addressed in the first part are: How much have young workers shared in the economic boom of the past decade? How have the employment, earnings, and health care patterns of youth compared with those of adults? We explore both national and New York data sets. Our findings indicate a general deterioration in most youths' relative socioeconomic status and in their access to affordable higher education and health insurance.

The second part of this chapter asks how young people view their economic status and prospects, and what policy options and forms of organization they would support to improve their job prospects. In addition to analysis of national surveys, we present initial findings from a new poll of Long Island youth. The findings suggest generally *stronger* prounion sympathies and preferences for collective worker action among youth than among adults.[2] And they point to the rising importance to young workers' future jobs and living standards of such contentious public policy issues as: the minimum wage, health insurance costs and coverage, government financial aid for college, job creation programs, union organizing rights, and immigration law reform.

INEQUALITY INDICATORS

Two stereotypes of young people are widespread among adults of all political stripes today. The first is that of *independent, self-centered billionaire wannabes,* intent on dot-com riches. In this view, high school and college-age kids spend their spare time day trading and shopping for nonnecessities. If they bother to take a part-time job, they use the money for more luxuries and completely identify with the management they hope to be part of soon. *Irresponsible slackers* is the other main stereotype: the image of amoral, rudderless teens drifting aimlessly between school and dead-end jobs appears to persist in many quarters. A recent national survey of two thousand adults by the Public Agenda research center found that current adult antagonism toward the young far exceeds the older generation's traditional criticisms. Across demographic lines, whether parents or not, most adults are alarmed by and even fearful of young people: two out of three used the words "rude," "wild," and "irresponsible" to describe teenagers; and only 37 percent think that today's young "will one day make the country a better place."[3]

These stereotypes are as misleading as they are contradictory. Despite their differences, both views have the effect of trivializing young workers and their job experiences. Thus, even progressive supporters of higher minimum wages often stress that only a minority of minimum wage workers are teenagers, thereby implicitly conceding the old conservative refrain that today's teens are too privileged or spoiled by parents to need or deserve higher-paying jobs.

In fact, for millions of low-income households and for increasing numbers of middle-income ones as well, since the 1970s, young peoples' jobs have become relied on as an important component of total income.[4] That may be more difficult for adults to appreciate today because the jobs that *they* held as young workers twenty-five or more years ago generally paid far higher real wages per hour than youth can expect today. And the declining affordability of higher education over this same period has left more and more college-bound students little choice but to hold down jobs, both before and during college.

Falling Relative Wage Rates

Young workers were the hardest hit by the general wage declines of the 1980s and early 1990s. In fact, while the wage gap between youth and adult workers has widened in many advanced countries, it has grown far more in the United States than in any other.[5] Table 1 shows inflation-adjusted wage movements since the early 1970s for youth subdivided by sex and educational attainment. From 1973 to 1995, among 19- to 25-year-old high school grads (with no college), the real wage rate plummeted 30 percent for men and 18.3 percent for women. Only in the late 1990s did youth in this group finally register some wage gains, but not nearly enough to recover their lost ground: by 1999, young men were still over 25 percent and young women over 13 percent below the 1973 wage level.[6]

Young college graduates also were hit by surprising wage declines, though not nearly as large as those affecting the noncollege members of their generation. Over the 1973–1995 period, the hourly wage dropped 11.5 percent for male college grads and 3 percent for women. But both sexes managed to more than recover this lost ground in the late 1990s, capturing 15 percent and 9.4 percent wage increases, respectively. Still, by

Table 1. Changes in hourly wage rates and in wage inequality, 1973–99

Real wage changes	1973–95 (%)	1995–99 (%)	1973–99 (%)
High school grads, 19–25			
Men	−29.8	+6.3	−25.4
Women	−18.3	+6.2	−13.2
College grads, 19–25			
Men	−11.5	+14.9	+3.0
Women	−3.0	+9.4	+6.2
Youth/adult pay ratio	1973 (%)	1995 (%)	1999 (%)
High school grads			
Men	0.70	0.63	0.65
Women	0.87	0.73	0.74
College grads			
Men	0.62	0.61	0.63
Women	0.84	0.75	0.77
High school/college pay ratio			
Men	0.75	0.60	0.55
Women	0.66	0.56	0.54

Source: Analysis of the U.S. Census Bureau's Current Population Survey by Lawrence Mishel, Jared Bernstein, and John Schmitt, *The State of Working America 2000/2001* (Ithaca, NY: Cornell University Press, 2001), 158.

Note: Youth/adult pay ratio is calculated as the average hourly wage of workers aged 19–25 divided by the wage of workers aged 34–40.

1999, the average young college grad's hourly wage was only $0.28 higher than in 1973 for men and just $0.85 higher for women.

The fact that youth and noncollege grads have suffered steeper wage declines than older workers or the college educated has meant a sharp increase in wage inequality by age and education. Young high school grads earned 70 percent as much as older high school grads in 1973, but only 65 percent as much by 1999; among noncollege females, the gap also grew wider: from an 87 percent youth-adult wage ratio in 1973 to 74 percent by 1999. Over this same period, the educational wage differential between high school grads without college and college grads widened by double digits for both sexes. Young noncollege males in 1973 earned about 75 percent as much as young male college grads in 1973, but only 55 percent as much by 1999. For young noncollege women, the ratio dropped from 66 percent to 54 percent.

Mainstream economic theory has had a hard time explaining this trend, and indeed most economists in the early '80s were predicting the exact opposite. After all, they reasoned, the shrinking youth population share of the "baby bust" cohort should improve its job and pay prospects over those of the crowded baby boomer labor market of the 1970s. Industrial shifts toward traditionally "youth-intensive" services and retail trade sectors were also expected to raise employer demand for young workers. And Gen-Xers' higher average schooling levels and familiarity with computers compared to older workers seemed to be additional strong advantages.

One important reason for youths' wage erosion has been the federal government's reluctance to restore the value of the minimum wage to its 1960s levels. One-third of minimum wage workers are teenagers, and they have suffered severe erosion in purchasing power since the 1970s. The inflation-adjusted value of the $5.15 federal minimum by 2002 was 10 percent lower than when it was last increased in 1997, and *19 percent lower than in 1981.*[7] Another factor behind teenagers' earnings decline has been the steep drop in union coverage of youth workers, which we will discuss later. Employers have taken maximum advantage of the low federal wage minimum and shrinking union power by resisting pay increases and restructuring job schedules to increase management flexibility at the expense of workers' pay and nonwork responsibilities. In much of retail and food services, part-time workers are expected to be available full-time to fill in as needed. According to the U.S. Department of Labor these two industries are the worst violators of wage and hours laws.

Moreover, even among unionized youth, the early 1980s saw growing numbers of young entry-level hires become victims of new two-tier wage scales. Many unions, intimidated by Ronald Reagan's 1981 crushing of the air traffic controllers' strike, began conceding to employer demands that new hires be dropped to a lower wage and benefits track than the "core" senior employees. Hence, when the International Brotherhood of Teamsters (IBT) at United Parcel Service accepted a two-tier pay scale in 1982, part-time employees were a small minority of the workforce and averaged wage rates similar to full-timers'. But, from 1982 to 1997, UPS shifted its hiring to mostly part-timers, while holding their average wage flat at $9 per hour. Over this same period, full-timers won a doubling of their hourly wage to nearly $20—at the expense of far worse youth-adult pay inequality.[8]

Rising Unemployment and Underemployment

The end of the 1990s boom threatens to stall, if not roll back, the limited wage recovery that young workers began seeing late in the decade. Young workers are usually first to feel the pinch of a recession, and "last hired, first fired" clearly applies to our recent economic troubles.

According to the U.S. Labor Department's seasonally adjusted estimates, in the first quarter of 2000, the peak of the 1990s expansion, the overall national unemployment rate was 4 percent, and the teenage rate was 13.3 percent, the lowest it had been in years (though still over three times the adult level). As the economy slowed down in the next two years, the overall unemployment rate rose by 1.6 percentage points to 5.6 percent by the first quarter of 2002. But the teenage rate jumped far more, to 16 percent. Among black teens, unemployment rose from 23.9 percent to 29.9 percent over this same period.

Likewise, by an alternative measure, the fraction of the population employed, the recession hit youth harder than others. The overall employment-population ratio fell from 64.6 percent in 2001 to 62.8 percent in early 2002; the youth ratio dropped twice as fast, from 45 percent to 40.4 percent. This likely reflects growing underemployment, caused by a rise in both the officially unemployed (still actively seeking work) and labor force dropouts—jobless persons too discouraged to continue looking for work. The situation is markedly worse in some central cities than national figures can suggest. In New York City, our estimates from unpublished Current Population Survey data indicate that fewer than one in five teenagers have a job![9]

Shrinking Health Insurance Coverage

Young people comprise a unique and vulnerable group in a number of ways. They are beginning the process of establishing independence from their parents both psychologically and financially at a time when they are just learning the skills needed to do so.

On their nineteenth birthday, or even earlier if they leave home, many adolescents lose eligibility for coverage under their parents' health insurance plans. Yet, very few have access to employer-provided health benefits, since they have little or no job experience or training. The lack of access to employer-provided health benefits is worsened by high rates of unemployment, low skill levels, and the fact that young people are far more likely to be limited, involuntarily, to part-time employment. The result is that, in New York State, the rate of uninsurance among adolescents between the ages of 17 and 19 doubled from 15.4 percent to 31.3 percent.[10]

In fact, the loss of "own-employer-provided" health insurance coverage (the health insurance coverage that workers obtain directly through their employer or union) was responsible for the vast majority of the decline in overall private health insurance among older adolescents and young adults in the United States during the 1990s. Since 1989, own-employer-provided health care coverage has declined dramatically for young working adults, particularly for those under the age of 25. Though the decline in employer-provided coverage is often blamed on a rise in part-time and temporary employment, particularly among young people, the bulk of the shrinkage in health insurance benefits among young-adult workers has resulted from *a decline in coverage among full-time year-round workers.* From the early 1990s through the late 1990s, the rate of own-employer-provided coverage among full-time year-round workers dropped markedly, particularly in New York State. Comparison of young workers aged 19–29 with older workers 30–64 during these same years clearly shows a far sharper drop in coverage for younger workers. The result is a serious widening of the gap in coverage between young adults and those over the age of 30 (see figure 1).

Higher Education, Lower Affordability

College education is the most widely accepted solution to unstable jobs and low wages. Far more young people, including more from low-income households, have been able to go to college in recent decades than ever before. However, three out of four Americans over age 25 still do not have a college degree. An increasingly important obstacle to expanding youth access to college training is the fact that college-going costs are rising far faster than government and university financial aid. From 1980 to 2000, tuition and fees at public colleges and universities jumped 107 percent, but average state expenditures per college student crept up just 13 per-

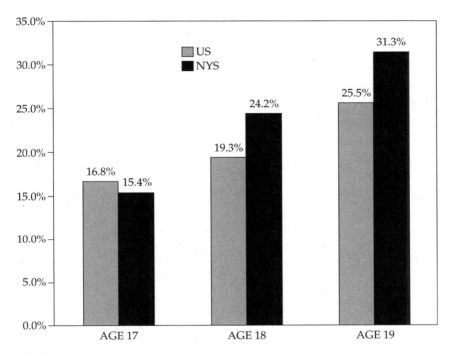

FIG. 1. Lack of private health insurance among adolescents in the late 1990s, United States and New York State

cent. Federal Pell grants, which covered 98 percent of tuition at four-year public colleges in 1986, now cover just 57 percent. And, since 1980, federal aid for students has shifted from mostly outright grants to a loan-based system that has left many lower and working class families fearful of assuming an unsustainable college debt burden.

The result is that higher education has become much less affordable, increasing the importance of class background in determining access to it. One in four high-achievement, low-income students do not enroll in college, compared to only 5 percent of high-achievement students from high-income families.[11] Lower-income students who manage to afford time in college are far more likely to be limited to a two-year program, often training them for no more than skilled working class jobs. Among families in the richest one-fourth of the income pyramid, two out of three high school grads went on to a four-year college, compared to just one-fifth of high school grads from the poorest quarter of families.[12] A recent government study estimates that financial barriers "will produce staggering cumulative losses of 4.4 million college-qualified students unable to enroll in a four-year college and two million who are denied any college at all by the end of this decade."[13] These class differences exacerbate racial and ethnic disparities: among 25- to 29-year-olds in 2001, one-third of whites had obtained a BA or higher degree, but only 18 percent of blacks and 11 percent of Latinos had.[14]

YOUTH AND WORKING CLASS VIEWS

Are the troubling trends facing the rapidly growing youth labor force—growing wage inequality relative to older workers, much higher unemployment and underemployment, falling health insurance coverage, and the declining affordability of higher education—affecting how youth view their socioeconomic prospects and the roles played today by employers and unions? One possible approach to answering this is through class analysis.

Class identification is likely to be more difficult to determine for youth than it is for adults. First, it is by no means clear which is the more relevant class marker: the occupational status of the young worker herself or that of her parents. As the average length of time youth reside with parents has lengthened, identification with parental class loyalties may have become stronger. Next, there are problems posed by much higher job turnover among young workers. The various jobs held by workers in their teens and early twenties may have little relation to their intended career path. So, even if family background is less influential on class identification than a youth's own employment, it may often be far from obvious which of these early jobs to select in drawing a youth's class boundaries. And the handful of national polls that have explicitly asked individuals their class identification cover all ages and seldom distinguish responses by specific age groups.

How do young people identify their class position? As a first pass at this question, we conducted a small survey in late January 2002 of students enrolled at a large private university in Long Island, New York. Questionnaires were distributed the first week of spring term by professors in mostly large introductory courses of several different disciplines. Students were told that this was a completely confidential and voluntary university research survey on "college students' current backgrounds, activities, and attitudes." No names were to be recorded and each professor collected the completed questionnaires by the end of the class period.

The response rate was over 90 percent, and a total of 271 completed questionnaires were collected.

Students enrolled at a private university in a relatively affluent suburban area are likely to have above-average family incomes, which might be expected to generate far more professional and managerial career goals and a stronger identification with upper class and upper middle class views. So, we did not expect our findings to be representative of all youth, much less to come close to the national poll results for all ages and education levels.

More than two out of three students surveyed were employed at the time, and 99 percent were either working at the time or had worked in the past two years. Of these, 93.7 percent were in nonsupervisory "working class" occupations, mostly in retail and service jobs. However, when asked directly "What class are you?" 70.5 percent answered "middle class," compared to 14.3 percent responding "working class" or "lower class." Clearly, given the selective nature of our college student sample, much more research on larger youth samples cutting across educational levels is essential to put these results in proper perspective.

A second, more indirect approach to gauging class identification may be more promising: asking the degree of agreement or disagreement with key behaviors of employers and workers. A series of questions, phrased for comparability with those of other recent surveys, were asked our student sample to judge their "solidaristic sentiments" toward employers and workers.[15] First, students were asked whether employers "do well" or "don't do well enough" in each of the following: sharing of profits, provision of health insurance to workers, provision of family-friendly workplaces, and fair treatment of prounion employees.

Two-thirds of the students said that "employers don't do enough" in sharing profits with their employees. And two-fifths felt that employers don't do enough in three other important areas: providing affordable health care for their employees, treating prounion employees fairly, and providing family-friendly workplaces.

Closer analysis reveals correlations between respondents' jobs, their opinions on employers, and their class identity. For example, health insurance and perceptions of class appear to be linked. Thus, rates of health insurance coverage appear to be higher among those who reported themselves to be "upper class." And perceptions regarding whether or not employers do enough to provide affordable health insurance to employees are also closely linked to class. While a large majority of "upper class" students feel that employers do enough to provide health insurance, only slightly over half of remaining students feel that this is the case. This may reflect the fact that students are more likely to consider themselves upper class if their families own businesses with employees, and among the latter satisfaction with employer provision of health benefits is also somewhat higher. Interestingly, there appears to be no relationship between actually having health insurance coverage and perceptions regarding the responsibility of employers to provide it.

Results from the survey of this somewhat select group of students demonstrate that even in a college setting, patterns of health insurance coverage reflect broader patterns of inequality at the national level. Rates of health insurance coverage are significantly lower among racial and ethnic minorities (with the exception of Asians), among noncitizens, and in households that have experienced marital disruption. Rates of coverage are also somewhat lower among students who are employed, suggesting that economically disadvantaged students are more likely to work while attending school.

Hence, the results reveal that, while only a minority of the college students we questioned explicitly identified themselves as "working class," far larger proportions were critical of employers when asked their opinions in a series of questions about employers' treatment of workers. But, do critical opinions about employers' treatment of workers extend to the point of supporting labor unions?

YOUTH AND UNIONS

Only 5.2 percent of workers aged 16 to 24 today are union members, the lowest rate of any age group. The youth rate has dropped by nearly half, from 9.1 percent in 1983, the first year in which the Bureau of Labor Statistics began collecting annual union membership rates by age group. At the same time, union density has fallen even more among older workers, as the time trends in figure 2 show: it dropped from 19.6 percent in 1983 to 11.5 percent in 2001 among 25- to 34-year-olds, and from 24.8 percent to 15 percent among 35- to 44-year-olds. The gap in union density between youth under 25 and older workers was cut sharply over this period. And, from the mid-1990s on, the youth unionization rate stopped falling, reaching a plateau just above 5 percent. The 1.034 million young workers under 25 who are now union members (over 700,000 fewer than in 1983) account for just over 6 percent of all union members.

Does the low rate of current union membership among young workers reflect weaker prounion and stronger antiunion sentiments among

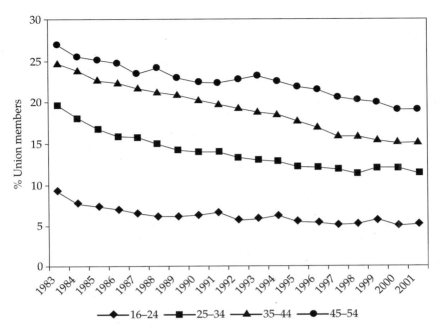

FIG. 2. Union membership rates by age. *Source:* Data from *Employment and Earnings* (U.S. Bureau of Labor Statistics), various issues, 1984–2002.

youth? It does not, according to a number of public opinion surveys, old and new, that asked youth their attitudes toward unions. The nationwide Quality of Employment Survey in 1977 asked nonunion, private sector wage and salary workers: "If an election were held with secret ballots, would you vote for or against having a union or employees' association represent you?" Two-fifths of workers under age 25 responded that they would vote "for" a union, compared to 32 percent of 25- to 44-year-olds and just 26 percent of 45- to 54-year-olds. Even among white-collar employees, 36 percent of youth were prounion, some 10 percentage points higher than in the 25-to-54 age group.[16] Are such sentiments, expressed during the mid-1970s economic stagflation years, similar to those today's youth would express?

Nationwide, a growing majority of Americans, especially youth, tell pollsters that they side with labor unions against employers. In August 2001 the Associated Press polled 1,010 Americans, aged 18 and over, asking them: "In the labor disputes of the last two or three years, have your sympathies, in general, been on the side of the unions or on the side of

the companies?" Of the respondents, 50 percent said that their sympathies were on the side of unions, while just 27 percent sided with companies. This represents a marked rise in prounion sentiment from just a few
years earlier. When the same question was asked in a nationwide Gallup
poll in 1999, just 45 percent of respondents said they sided with unions.

The 2001 poll results in table 2 show that women were more likely than
men to express prounion sympathies: 51 percent to 48 percent. But an especially large gap is evident between young and old. Nearly three out of
every five young people aged 18 to 34 sided with unions, compared to
less than two out of five elderly over age 65.

This is consistent with the findings of another national survey that focused intensively on youth. In the spring of 1999, pollsters Hart Research
Associates (under contract to the AFL-CIO) surveyed 752 nonsupervisory
workers aged 18 to 34. When asked what they would do if given the
chance to vote in a union election at work, 54 percent of the workers said
they would "definitely" or "probably" vote for a union, and only 38 percent said they would not vote for a union. Rising prounion sentiment is
evident from comparison with the responses to a similar question in a
1996 Hart Associates poll, in which the prounion-antiunion split (47 percent yes to 45 percent no) was much narrower (table 3).

In the summer of 2001, public attitudes on unions were the focus of the
Newsday/Stony Brook Poll of Queens, Nassau, and Suffolk counties in
New York. Telephone interviews were conducted with a sample of 1,511
persons, aged 18 and over, using phone numbers generated by random
digit dialing (to cover all possible phone numbers, listed and unlisted).
The sample sizes were 600 in Queens and 911 in Long Island.

The results indicate that 24 percent of Long Islanders were union members at the time, and another nearly 20 percent had been in unions in the
past, but were not members at the time. Regardless of union status, the
majority expressed generally positive attitudes about unions. Only one in
four said that unions were no longer necessary in today's global economy.

Table 2. National AP poll on public sympathies toward unions, 2001

| | All, ages 18 and over (%) | | | | |
	Total	Men	Women	Ages 18–34 (%)	Ages over 65(%)
Side with unions	50	48	51	59	38
Side with companies	27	32	23	24	25
Don't know/no answer	23	20	26	17	37

Source: Associated Press poll, conducted for AP by ICR (Media, PA), August 22–26, 2001. Poll
had an error margin of plus or minus 3 percentage points.

Table 3. National Hart Associates polls on youth attitudes toward unions, 1996, 1997, and 1999

% of young workers who:	1999	1997	1996
Would definitely/probably vote for a union	54	48	47
Would definitely/probably not vote for a union	38	48	45
Don't know/no answer	8	8	8

Source: Research Associates polls of nonsupervisory workers aged 18–34, conducted for AFL-CIO in March 1999, 1997, and 1996. The 1999 sample consisted of 752 workers aged 18–34. Poll had an error margin of plus or minus 3 percentage points. See AFL-CIO, "High Hopes, Little Trust" (1999), www.bctd.workingfamilies.com/articles/high_hopes.

Nine out of ten union members and two out of three nonmembers said that unions "mostly help" their members, and similar proportions agreed that unions are needed to protect job security.

People under age 30, though less likely to have been in unions than workers 30 and over, were even more positive about them. Among nonunion workers, young people were twice as likely as those over age 30 to say that they would be better off in a union.[17]

In our small 2002 survey of students at a Long Island university, we asked how they would vote "if given the chance to vote to have your job covered by a union contract." Overall, nearly one in three students answered that they would "definitely" or "probably" vote for a union at work, compared to just one-fourth of students who would definitely or probably not vote for a union. Of the full sample, 43.1 percent didn't know or checked "no answer."

Breakdowns of voting preferences by various characteristics are shown in table 4. In general, respondents who had jobs at the time, particularly those working over twenty hours weekly, tended to have larger fractions of respondents prounion. Among the 9 percent of students who were union members at the time, nearly two out of three said they would vote for a union, compared to 32.5 percent of nonunion workers. And youth with parents or grandparents who had been or were at the time union members also appear more prounion.

When students were asked their views on various statements about the impacts and value of unions, the results were much more clearly favorable to unions. As shown in table 5, nearly 80 percent agreed with the claim: "Unions usually improve the pay and jobs of union members." The much broader statement "Unions are mostly good for the economy" drew the approval of two out of three students. A smaller proportion, though

Table 4. Survey of New York college students, 2002: Willingess to vote for unions [Question: "If given the chance to vote to have your job covered by a union contract, would you:"]

	Vote for union (%)	Not vote for union (%)	Don't know/ no answer
Total	32.3	24.5	43.1
Now working 1 job	30.9	26.7	42.4
Now working 2 jobs	39.3	14.3	46.4
Work hours/week: 1–20	28.7	16.7	54.6
Work hours/week: 21–34	36.7	23.3	40.0
Work hours/week: 35 or more	38.6	38.6	22.8
Union member	65.2	17.4	17.4
Nonunion	32.5	28.4	39.2
Union family members	41.9	22.3	35.8
No union family members	21.1	26.8	52.0

Source: Survey conducted by Center for the Study of Labor and Democracy, Hofstra University. First- and second-year students at a large private university responded to a written questionaire the first week of classes, January 28–February 1, 2002.

still a majority, disagreed with the statement: "Unions have too much power relative to business." And nearly three out of four students questioned disagreed with the claim: "Unions are no longer needed in today's global economy."

The findings from public opinion polls seem consistent with the research results from studies of actual National Labor Relations Board (NLRB) union elections.[18] If, then, youth have stronger prounion attitudes than adults, what explains their far lower union membership rates? The nature of the jobs that most youth find, and of the firms that hire them, account for a large share of the explanation. First, young people's jobs are more likely to be entry-level, low-skill, and part-time or temporary positions in small businesses—all characteristics long associated with low union density. Second, as Richard Freeman and James Medoff

Table 5. Survey of New York college students, 2002: Attitudes toward unions [Question: "Do you mostly agree or disagree with each of the following statements?"]

	Agree (%)	Disagree (%)
a. Unions usually improve the pay and jobs of union members.	79.0	21.0
b. Unions are mostly good for the economy.	67.9	32.1
c. Unions have too much power relative to business.	44.2	55.8
d. Unions are no longer needed in today's global economy.	26.4	73.2

Source: Survey conducted by Center for the Study of Labor and Democracy, Hofstra University, 2002.

have argued, job creation in growing new firms tends to disproportionately favor youthful hires. Since firms in the traditionally nonunion service sector have increasingly dominated job growth, youth have more
and more found entry jobs only in such nonunion industries.[19] Finally,
large numbers of youth jobs today are with wealthy and notoriously
antiunion employers. Wal-Mart, the world's largest retailer, with $218
billion in annual sales revenue, is also the country's largest private
nonunion employer. Workers' anger over excess work hours, low pay,
and sometimes hazardous conditions at distribution centers did lead to
organizing drives in Missouri in 1971 and in Arkansas in 1976 and 1981.
But all were defeated by a combination of Sam Walton's personal threats
to shut down the stores involved and his use of aggressive union-busting
law firms to train store managers to identify and punish prounion workers.[20] Most other retail chains, and fast-food giants like McDonald's, also
have a long history of devoting enormous resources to bitterly fighting
off any employee efforts to seek union representation. Finally, unions
themselves have too often neglected organizing young workers and advanced senior employees' interests at the expense of youth.

PROSPECTS FOR A NEW LABOR ACTIVISM

The late 1990s witnessed the rise of the largest wave of youth activism in
two decades. Unlike the antiapartheid movement of the early 1980s or the
antiwar demonstrations of the 1960s, the latest wave has been focused on
three sets of related labor issues. First, students at hundreds of campuses
nationwide have protested the sweatshop wages and working conditions
in the foreign factories that produce U.S. college-name clothing. Antisweatshop movements at Brown, Columbia, Cornell, Duke, New York
University, and over 90 other campuses have successfully pressured college administrators to adopt licensing codes of conduct and independent
monitoring of conditions in the overseas plants making campus sweat-
shirts and athletic gear. Student-led antisweatshop organizations, particularly United Students against Sweatshops and the Worker Rights
Consortium, have increasingly been working in coalitions with UNITE,
the largest apparel union.

In the wider campaign for more just global trade and for economic development that promotes higher labor and environmental standards,
young students and workers have also been of central importance. Since
the 1999 Seattle demonstrations against the World Trade Organization
(WTO), young people have been the driving force behind the large-scale
protests against corporate-led global policymaking that have regularly

occurred at meetings of the International Monetary Fund (IMF) and World Bank.[21]

The plight of low-wage workers in the United States has been another labor concern of a number of student movements. In the spring of 2000, students at Johns Hopkins and at Wesleyan occupied their campus administration buildings to demand that their wealthy universities raise the poverty-level pay of their janitors and security guards to a "living-wage" level. The following spring, a widely publicized three-week student sit-in at Harvard demanded that both full-time and temporary, subcontracted, low-paid campus workers be paid a living wage of $15 per hour. The Service Employees International Union (SEIU) and the national AFL-CIO actively supported the sit-in. Harvard has so far agreed to sizable raises (up to an average wage of over $11 per hour) for its lowest-paid workers and to pay parity of subcontracted workers with the university's directly hired workers in similar jobs. Thanks largely to student pressure, four universities now have agreed to living-wage policies for their lowest-paid workers.[22]

There are increasing signs that some American unions are finally beginning to reach out in imaginative ways to young workers. One of the first initiatives of the "New Voice" leadership overhaul of the AFL-CIO was "Union Summer." Over one thousand young students and workers from around the country volunteered for this three-week internship program with unions in twenty-two different cities in the summer of 1996. Sponsoring unions provided housing, transportation, and stipends in return for participants' working on union and community campaigns and taking courses in labor history, organizing strategies, and other subjects. Since then, the program has expanded to four weeks each summer. To date, the number of intern slots has grown slowly and the number of participating unions remains small: thirty AFL-CIO union affiliates have taken part, and twenty-three hundred young people have graduated from the program.[23] But the young people's training and hands-on experience appear to have had lasting effects back on college campuses. According to a leader of the Columbia University antisweatshop campaign: "One of the great untold stories of the '90s is that Union Summer has created, almost from nothing, activism on campus to a point where labor issues are among the leading issues for students today."[24]

A number of promising new union organizing drives are centered on young workers. For example, campaigns for a voice at work are underway across the country among young, low-paid graduate teaching assistants (TAs), who routinely teach classes and grade papers at many universities today. Although universities rely heavily on them for these highly demanding and time-consuming academic tasks, grad assistants are paid a fraction of faculty salaries and are offered no benefits, autonomy, or job security. Teaching assistants at public universities in ten states, including California and New York, won the right to join unions years ago. But the rights of private university TAs to unionize have been more ambiguous. A breakthrough came late in 2000, when seventeen hundred New York University graduate teaching assistants won an NLRB ruling that they were private sector employees, with full rights to representation by their elected union, the United Auto Workers. Since the NYU students' victory, union organizing drives have begun among teaching assistants at Brandeis, Brown, Columbia, and the University of Pennsylvania. In April 2001, Temple University teaching assistants won a lopsided union election for representation by the American Federation of Teachers. That same month, Michigan State grad students also voted for unionization.

A growing portion of this country's youth population is foreign born. Immigrants have long been widely viewed as practically "unorganizable" and as threats to natives' jobs and wages.[25] Some unions, like UNITE, committed themselves years ago to aggressive organizing of all immigrants, regardless of legal status. But many other unions were long unable or unwilling to do the same, and some felt compelled to back restrictive national admissions policies. Today, there are growing signs of a shift toward more inclusive organizing strategies by some unions, inspired in part by the recent AFL-CIO decision to support an amnesty policy toward the millions of undocumented workers now in the United States.

A number of union campaigns have of late been supported by and sometimes led by young immigrant workers. Recent organizing successes range from the SEIU's large-scale victory among tens of thousands of Mexican and Central American home health care aides in California, to small but hard-fought union wins among Asian limousine drivers, Eastern European asbestos removers, and Mexican grocery workers in New York. One of the best-known recent examples is the SEIU "Justice for Janitors" campaign to organize thousands of nonunion building service workers. From its early successes in California and Colorado, the campaign has spread quickly among office cleaners in the New York metropolitan area. Hector Figueroa, a leader of the SEIU's East Coast organizing, has concluded:

I think we need to put the message out there, and match that message with the reality of our commitment and resources, that the new civil rights movement for the 21st century is fighting for low-wage service workers, many of whom are either people of color or immigrants. And that's where the next fight for civil rights needs to happen. And I think that, if we do that, we're going to have much more of an ability to attract young people. Many of these cleaners are very, very young. That message needs to be out there more, not only for J4J [Justice for Janitors], but for other service workers. Look who does the hotel work—it's mostly young workers. Look who cleans buildings—it's mostly young workers too. So we need to have a movement of young people, at work and in the universities.[26]

PROMISES TO KEEP
WORKING CLASS STUDENTS AND HIGHER EDUCATION

Michelle M. Tokarczyk

By now it is widely recognized that, in the words of Michael Bérubé and Cary Nelson, "Where college was once a device for creating tomorrow's leaders, it is now seen as a device for combating socioeconomic inequities."[1] A college education offers the possibility, often the only possibility, that poor youth may escape from poverty and that working class youth may enter the middle class. Indeed, as living-wage union jobs have steadily been replaced by minimum-wage service-industry jobs, a college education is increasingly the only hope young people have for getting work that will support them.[2] College education is important for the working class not only because it gives them entrée into living-wage jobs but also, as important, because it can enable them to become critically thinking adults, which working class primary and secondary schools have often failed to do. Yet there are formidable barriers to working class students' success at colleges at universities. While some barriers are academic, involving college preparedness, many are institutional, resulting from policies and attitudes that are unfriendly to working class students. As a faculty member in a liberal arts college, I have witnessed many of the difficulties working class students experience in this setting. As a working class woman who attended a city university and later worked in city and state universities, I also experienced many of the problems common in these institutions. My own and my students' experiences, coupled with recently published work in the area, illustrate the institutional challenges working class students face. Some innovative programs at a cou-

Special thanks to Goucher's acting dean of students, Gail Edmonds, for sending me to the National Council on Race and Ethnicity Conference in 2000. This chapter also benefited from conversations with my student R. H. A reference librarian at Goucher, Randy Smith, also provided invaluable assistance in helping me track down sources.

ple of colleges suggest ways to enable working class students to succeed in higher education.

Working class students' needs are unmet because their presence in colleges and universities is largely ignored. For example, a series of articles in the *New York Times* described the experiences of three high school seniors applying to colleges.[3] Each of the students applied to and was finally accepted at a competitive liberal arts college or a selective university. Yet as John Alberti notes, "most students in the United States do not attend elite, selective-admissions four-year institutions."[4] College educators often, however, take the relatively elite institutions as the model for higher education: the only real educational environment for faculty and students. What Alberti calls "working-class" colleges and their students are in effect made invisible.

While some faculty resist the notion that an elite institution is the only place where one should teach, some wish that they had positions at these "real" institutions. Certainly there are concrete benefits to teaching at selective colleges and universities: the class sizes and workloads are often more manageable, and at some of the top institutions the pay is certainly better. Yet some faculty who resent their institutions' lack of prestige shift their resentment to their students. Stephen Garger remembers such resentment at the less selective liberal arts college he attended. He especially recalls the faculty member who described his college's mission as "teaching the first generation of immigrant children how to eat with a knife and fork."[5] Some faculty at state and less elite private institutions refuse to acknowledge that their students have unique needs. Rather than try to adapt teaching techniques and school policies to first-generation college students, these faculty behave as though they were indeed teaching in an elite institution. It is thus not surprising that working class students in working class and elite colleges face similar barriers.

A more serious problem for faculty at many state and city colleges is the scarcity of resources. Because schools cannot easily hire more faculty members, they increase the workloads of those they have. Teachers at four-year colleges teach four courses a semester; at community colleges the load is often five courses a semester. Over twenty-five students may be enrolled in a developmental writing class; professional organizations such as the National Council of Teachers of English recommend a cutoff of fifteen in these classes. Content courses are likewise overenrolled. Publication requirements for tenure continue to increase. Given such heavy workloads, it is difficult for faculty to devote much time to mentoring.

As important, there is little time to develop techniques and programs for first-generation students. While many colleges and universities—even the elite ones—offer developmental and study skills classes for under-prepared students, they often do nothing to help working class students adapt to college expectations. College freshmen nationwide are frequently surprised at how much more challenging college courses are than high school ones. Students from mediocre high schools at which little was demanded of them are especially hard hit. In an article on working class students in higher education, one student was paraphrased as saying that college is a very unforgiving place. It is unforgiving not of those who don't learn the rules, but rather of those who did not know the rules before arriving on campus.[6] Faculty at schools with few resources and large numbers of working class students may become exasperated. Rather than teach students the rules of the game—the study habits necessary for success—exasperated faculty sometimes dumb down their courses. In effect, the faculty inadvertently perpetuate the class-based education begun in elementary schools: working class students are taught the basics and given information to absorb, while middle and upper class students are taught critical thinking.[7]

Working class students often have difficulty in their studies partially because many colleges and universities—elite and nonelite—refuse to recognize that many students must work. According to the National Center for Education Studies, "In 1995–96, four out of five undergraduates reported working while they were enrolled in postsecondary education. One half reported that the primary reason they worked was to pay for their education. . . . Students who worked to pay expenses reported working an average of 25 hours per week while enrolled."[8] In addition to working many hours, working class students frequently take heavy course loads in order to graduate early, thereby minimizing tuition costs. At Northern Kentucky University, for example, a semester load of fifteen to eighteen credits, five or six courses, is common. Since working class students do not have the sense of entitlement to a college education that those in upper classes do, and since parents, school personnel, and peers have not continually reinforced their aspirations, when these students' grades suffer, they often do not blame their extraordinary workload, but believe they are just not smart enough to succeed. Not only do students fear failing out, but those who have merit scholarships perpetually worry that their grade point averages will drop below the required level and they will then be unable to afford college.

Often there are no mentors to advise students. Even if mentors are assigned, many do little more than advise on graduation requirements. At the city college I attended I was placed in an honors English program and a selective experimental curricular program. I was assigned advisers, yet none thought to tell me how difficult it would be to complete an honors course of study, with some classes requiring twenty readings, and work sixteen to thirty hours a week. None even asked me if I worked. Perhaps more important, none thought to advise me as to which courses would prepare me for graduate study.

In reading accounts of former working class students, one is repeatedly struck by the number of policies and behaviors that ignore the realities of working class lives. Elizabeth A. Grant tells of having to walk two miles to the Oswego campus during the rough upstate New York winters. When, concerned about her very cold feet, she took off her boots in French class, the teacher ordered her to put them on, get out of class, and not return until she was "civilized." As a freshman in an introductory music history course, I, along with a large proportion of the class, did very poorly on the midterm. It was 1971, the first year of the open enrollment policy at the City University of New York, and my teacher asked how many of us had come in under open enrollment. I wasn't sure how to answer; I had come in that year, but my grades would have gotten me in anyway. Still, I ashamedly raised my hand as the teacher surveyed the raised hands in disgust.

Professors at private colleges, especially liberal arts colleges, rarely show such open disdain for students, mainly because they must recruit students and, to some extent, satisfy them as consumers to ensure that the students will continue to pay the schools' hefty tuitions. Of course, the majority of students at these schools are relatively prepared, middle class students with whom the faculty can identify. The small classes and emphasis on teaching of many liberal arts colleges offer promise to working class students who can manage the tuition there, often through a combination of working, scholarships, and living with family. Yet the fact that working class students are such a minority at these schools poses special challenges.

For one, working class students are often an anomaly to their peers. A working class student at Goucher told me that students did not understand her living at home and working three part-time jobs. Because she did not have a car, she had to continually arrange for rides to and from campus. Students just looked at her as though she were strange, so she stopped talking about her situation, stopped trying to make friends, and kept to herself.

School personnel can be as uncomprehending as undergraduates. Some colleges require internships or other off-campus experiences that can be extremely time consuming, especially for students who do not have cars. At my college now one of the heated debates is whether to require four January programs in which students would go abroad or engage in an intercultural experience, possibly in another locale. Several faculty have pointed out that working class students could not afford the travel costs, and even if the costs were compensated, working class students could not afford to take that much time off from their jobs. It remains to be seen whether the proposed January semester will be designed to meet the needs of all our students.

Many working class students, of course, do succeed. Their success can often be partially traced to a mentor who went out of his or her way to encourage and provide for students. Mike Rose repeatedly praises Jack MacFarland, the high school teacher who encouraged Rose, a boy from south Los Angeles, to attend Loyola College.[9] When Rose was struggling, MacFarland contacted faculty to ensure that Rose got the help he needed. It is difficult to institutionalize such mentoring, because, while people will acknowledge racial or gender difference, they often are only vaguely aware of class inequity. Many unconsciously embrace the American myth that everyone is middle class, that anyone who tries can succeed, and thus may be reluctant to acknowledge the impact of working class status. In her writing Caroline Pari relates the challenges of discussing class at the community college where she teaches.[10] Some students insisted the United States is a classless society; others argued that class was not a meaningful marker, only race was.[11] In my own composition course on class and upward mobility, in any given semester I have one or two students who announce, either to me or to the class, that they have realized they are working class. Such realizations come only after several weeks of learning about the existence of class in this country and the stigma of lower class status. Some students may talk to me or write about their class background but refrain from discussing it publicly. I take care not to out them. Mentoring is crucial to working class students, but it must be part of a program that increases knowledge of class and is attuned to students' needs and fears.

Despite such challenges, some colleges are developing programs to assist first-generation students in their transition to college. The University of La Verne in California has an approach that focuses on "loci of interventions" for students. These involve interactions with the students' families, including some home visits, and institutional adaptations, such as changes in campus processes and structures.[12] The program takes into account that many first-generation students are students of color, so some community intervention may be necessary. For example, college officials met with the local police department to discuss the officers' repeatedly stopping and questioning African American males.[13]

The program at La Verne, sponsored by a James Irvine Foundation grant, recognizes the profound implications of lower socioeconomic class. Not only do students need financial aid for tuition and housing but they also, since they have no cash reserves, need emergency funds to pay

166 Michelle M. Tokarczyk

for unexpected books, delayed checks, and the like.[14] An especially impressive feature of the program at La Verne is its emphasis on continual research to learn how the program is faring and how it can be improved. Thus faculty are learning how mentoring needs vary along race and ethnic lines. When probed about the most important attributes of a mentor, African American students stressed race. Latinos and Latinas emphasized that mentors, regardless of race, should be friends and nurturers. Asian Americans were relatively indifferent to race, and rather than nurturers, they wanted mentors who were older and accomplished in their fields.[15] That the paper reporting these results makes no mention of what white students prefer may reflect the small number of working class white students at this college, or it may reflect a societal assumption that whites are not represented in the lower socioeconomic classes. Nonetheless, the information this college gathered about its students' mentoring preferences undoubtedly enabled it to set up better mentorships.[16]

Mount San Antonio College, a community college also in California, has a similar program for first-generation students that focuses on establishing learning communities consisting of students, faculty, and counselors. These communities not only enable learning but also combat the isolation and alienation many working class students feel when beginning college.

The two institutions I've discussed with programs for first-generation students have significant numbers of students of color, whose class issues are compounded by that of race. Thus these colleges may have felt an acute impetus to develop programs. However, there is no reason why other colleges cannot develop similar programs that would assist working class students—financially, educationally, and socially. The educational effort might begin with faculty and administration. Many colleges have made attempts to enlighten personnel about the specific challenges facing particular ethnic or racial groups, but leave out questions of class. It is striking to me and to many other working class academics that faculty who would never utter a racial slur will casually refer to "trailer trash" or "white trash." Clearly some faculty education is in order.

Similarly, many colleges require first-year students to take a transition-to-college course that includes a component on diversity. Race, ethnicity, sexual orientation, and religion are discussed, but often class is not a part of the curriculum. If such courses had a component on class, upper and middle class students might begin to be more sensitive to economic difference, and working class students might feel less stigmatized.

It is important that colleges acknowledge that the typical student is no longer an eighteen-year-old middle class white male. Students of diverse backgrounds are more likely to be working class, and colleges must work to meet these students' needs. Institutions could begin to do so by considering the implications of policies such as required time abroad or internships for working class students. They could recruit faculty on campus who, often from working class backgrounds themselves, are interested in advising working class students. Institutions could also explore setting aside sums of money for emergency student needs—books, baby-sitting, car repairs, and the like.

In the spring of 2002, Goucher students organized a series of workshops on ethnicity and race. Here a Puerto Rican student complained that minorities are often admitted into colleges, businesses, and other institutions with the provision that they play by white mainstream rules. I would argue that we behave similarly toward working class students of all races and ethnic backgrounds in colleges and universities, admitting them with the tacit understanding that they can and will behave like middle or upper middle class young people. It is time for us to find a way to teach to all students.

My father was a toll collector on first the Whitestone Bridge, then the Henry Hudson Bridge in New York City; my mother worked for about eighteen years in various clerical positions before becoming a homemaker, and she never accumulated more than would fit in the back of a car. I am very grateful that my life is easier than my parents' was. I am further pleased that my work is rewarding. But I am most pleased that I have had the opportunity to hone the critical thinking and verbal skills I saw in my parents. When I was an undergraduate at Lehman College, I heard a student ask a question that has bothered me for years. To paraphrase, "Where do the poor go to get an understanding of themselves and their world? We know where the rich people go; they go to Harvard. Where do the poor go?" Higher education not only promises a chance for upward mobility. It also promises a fuller understanding of and interaction with one's self, community, and society. These are the promises we've made that we must keep, that we can keep, if only we acknowledge to whom we've made the promises.

ACROSS THE GREAT DIVIDE
CROSSING CLASSES AND CLASHING CULTURES

Barbara Jensen

The blonde curls of Shelly's home permanent stuck to the tears on her face as she dashed from the classroom. "Oh God, I'm so sorry," she cried out. Just twenty minutes earlier she had been in the midst of an animated class discussion in a college course she liked, the psychology of women. Shelly had never thought about being a woman much before; she found it exciting and comforting to do so.

The class was having a discussion about relationships between women and men. The subject was intimacy, and the students were discussing some of the different ways men and women understand and express it. Shelly felt she was starting to understand some of the problems in her marriage. Maybe she could make things better. She was eager and animated in the discussion.

But something went wrong. Shelly was talking about the declining intimacy in her marriage and how college "made things really weird" between her and her husband. It wasn't just his complaining about the time she was gone; he was starting to make fun of her studying, saying she was turning into a "geek" and an "egghead." She told the class, "He even picked up a textbook and threw it against the wall, smashing the spine of a $65 book!" Then he hollered, "This shit means more to you than me and the kids!" and stomped out of the house. She said that later, when they "talked it out," he said *she* wasn't any fun anymore, *she* wasn't interested in anything. The class laughed out loud, because in class she was interested in everything. Encouraged, she exclaimed, "I couldn't believe it! That's just what I think about him! He's the one . . . I'm interested in things now that I never even *thought* of before, you know what I mean? I asked him, 'What am I not interested in?' and he said, 'Bowling with Georgie and Bill and watching TV'! Like I have time for that now! Like *he* has shown any interest at all in all the things I've been studying."

Shelly's eyes blurred with tears and she fell silent; her pale skin was flushed. A couple of older women in the class started to talk, gently and with warmth, about how they had had to leave their husbands because they needed to "find themselves" and "get a new start." A forty-something woman offered that her spouse really wanted her to go to school, and that Shelly deserved to have that support. A man, who was on the board of a battered women's shelter, emphasized that she had a *right* to expect that support, that men have to learn to give women the things they have always had. He went on to warn her about "offender psychology" and how "they can't stand for their women to be independent, that's how they keep control." The other women from blue-collar backgrounds were uncharacteristically quiet.

"But that's not it!" Shelly insisted in frustration. "You don't understand . . . ," she trailed off, struggling for words and understanding. "He, he's a good husband, you know. . . . He was my *only* support at first . . . when my family was lecturing me about my duty to him and the kids. He was great, he———"

A woman who had identified herself as a former battered woman and the man who worked for the shelter exchanged glances with each other. Shelly saw this and scrambled to undo the impression she had given: "That's not it! He really doesn't mind me going to school. I know how it must sound . . . he doesn't normally yell and he's never hit me or even thrown anything like that before, you know? My girlfriends always envy me because he's so sweet and he's great with the kids and he's *so* handsome, I mean . . . he always knows what to say to people, I mean, not *college* people, but . . . you know, regular people. And it never really got stale, I mean, I was still crazy about him until . . . until . . . I don't know . . ."

Shelly stumbled to a halt and fell silent. Just when someone else was about to speak she blurted out, "I love him! When I think of losing him . . ." Her eyes teared up and she started shaking her head. "It's like the whole world is turned upside down!" Tears steamed down her red-hot face and she ran from the classroom to the lavatory down the hall.

Shelly is a college student at a small, urban university that mostly serves "returning" older and first-generation college students. She is close to her extended Swedish American and German American farm family and is the first one to go to college. Her husband and friends are all working class. She never really thought about going to college before her boss said she might lose her job if she didn't and that the company would pay for it. To her surprise, she loves it. She eagerly reads the class materials; she finds it surprisingly easy to talk in class, and other people often seem to appreciate what she has to say. She suspects she talks way too much, but she "just get[s] so excited." She wonders how could she not know before that she "loves ideas," as another woman in class put it. She was thirty-two years old and had had two children. "Where was I all those years?" she asked once in class.

After the class had left, Shelly came back in to apologize to me. She assured me that in more than two years of college, she had never behaved so "unprofessional before." She apologized a few more times. Her shoulders sank, deflated. She bowed her head and stared at her shoes. "Maybe he's right, maybe I don't belong here." She was embarrassed, and afraid.

Shelly is experiencing a confusing, exciting, and debilitating situation both in her outer life and within her. She is by turns excited, lost, elated, angry, bewildered, shameful, grateful, and "numb." All of a sudden, her past won't cohere with her present, her future has become uncertain; nothing quite "fits right" anymore. Shelly knows that no one she knew before seems to understand what she is going through, and some even resent it. That night she realized that her new friends don't understand either. She is in the midst of a working class "crossover" experience, something she never expected when she went back to school to "get my piece of paper" so she could keep her job as a legal secretary. She had no idea what she was getting into, she had no idea she would fall in love with a new world. She certainly didn't know that she might actually begin to *become someone else.* Though she is delighted with all the new things she has learned, nothing she has learned in this new world helps explain her situation to her. With no language or concepts to bridge or even explain this experience, she is falling prey to the contradictions within it.

There is suffering in this private passage, unvoiced and unseen, a particularly confused suffering in the midst of outward success. This struggle to figure out "who I am anymore," as Shelly once put it, the crossover's collection of contradictory experiences, emotions, and values are the subject of this chapter. I have come to believe Shelly's struggle constitutes a particular inner and outer (psychological and sociological) constellation that many working class people who enter the middle class experience. The psychological similarities among "upwardly mobile" working class people are striking to me. So is the invisible and "privatized" nature of this potentially painful experience. I am a (counseling and community) psychologist, a teacher of first-generation college students, and a person from the working class who has spent my adult life jostling back and forth between different worlds.

Like me, the people in this chapter have bumped uneasily between professional middle and working class cultures. We engage (or struggle to avoid engaging) with these often opposing world-views. This often creates a state of *cognitive dissonance,* or an inner clashing of values and experiences that create emotional and mental confusion. Common emotional reactions to this are anger, shame, sorrow (loss), "impostor syndrome," and substance abuse. These are often so muffled as to be invisible to crossovers themselves. Common behavioral reactions I have seen are distancing, resisting, and creating/bridging.

I believe that central to the "crossover experience" is an existential dilemma. By "existential" I mean a problem of existence: of living one's life, of how best to live, and of the human need to make meaning in and of our lives. And central to this dilemma, though not its only feature, is the presence of cultural differences between the professional middle class and working class people. There are stories, sacrifices, and secret shame that have no ear and precious little voice. The hearing and seeing of these cultural differences—the ability to see *outside* the cultural biases of the professional middle class—is crucial to any meaningful understanding of working class life. Without this, all the well-meaning "solidarity" one may feel for the working class is ineffective. "I feel like they're always talking down to me," said one of my working class students, who is active in the political Left, "but maybe I *am* stupid, because, honestly, half the time I don't know what the hell they're talking about."

People in or from the professional/managerial class will likely be the vehicle of change for the "upwardly mobile" working class person in higher education, job promotions, marriage, psychotherapy, and other crossover experiences. They can show Shelly how to write and speak in Standard English, how to put her napkin in her lap instead of on the table, and how to negotiate with difficult clients. But they can't tell her where she's been and how it has made her who she is, or where it is she might be going.

In this chapter, I address the less obvious ways that class hurts working class people in higher education (and other avenues of upward mobility). I point toward unfair, unjust advantage and disadvantage that cuts across lines of gender, ethnicity, and "race." In higher education (as elsewhere), this unacknowledged crossover challenge serves to exclude working class people from certain opportunities and privileges, even from their own inner lives. Their counterparts, from the professional middle class, find in higher education the cultural rules, values, language, and community mores that are familiar to them. Working class people must do psychosocial back flips through a maze of new rules, new values, and new language. My concern is twofold: I am worried about the Shellys, and I am worried about the society we all live in that creates, mystifies, and personalizes unequal opportunity and the cultural (as well as economic) domination of one class of people over another. The painful distance between the ideal and the real is felt by those who fall between the cracks; working class crossovers bear it as personal "stupidity," lack of "ambition," "failure," and even psychopathology (depression, substance abuse, and more). These constitute significant invisible costs that working class crossovers are forced to pay. Visibility and voice are the first practical antidotes to this invisible identity crisis.

"SURVIVOR GUILT" AND CULTURAL COLLISION

Working class crossovers are likely to be completely invisible to people from the professional middle class, because middle class people have learned to assume their inner and outer lives are "normal." If you have learned to walk and talk middle class well enough to "fake it," middle class people will assume you have always been one of them, at least if you have white skin. Successful crossovers can't necessarily help you either. As likely as not, they have already been "made safe," as Basil Bernstein points out, via the cultural processes and decisions they have gone through to get where they are.[1]

The *invisibility* and the *unconsciousness* of the crossover experience, in my view, can make it painful, debilitating, even devastating. The dilemma manifests in a multitude of so-called (and genuine) personal problems. If crossovers are not conscious of the cross-class experience, the problems it creates can hide behind many personal perspectives. For Shelly, it is a marriage problem. For someone else it is a problem with her "unenlightened" parents. For yet another it is a "chemical imbalance." For many it is a compulsion to ditch class or get "loaded," or to suddenly "blow off" an important exam. Maybe it is simply having "the blues" all the time. For marriage problems, depression, chemical abuse, fear of success, and family-of-origin problems there is, at least, a certain amount of collective wisdom about coping, changing, treating, managing. In my experience, the process of moving from the working class to the professional middle class is a highly personalized and tangled mess of psychological, sociological, and cultural confusion. As philosopher Ludwig Wittgenstein said, that which one has no language for is often not even perceived.

Geraldine Piorkowski made a rare attempt to describe the psychological barriers for the upwardly mobile student. She illustrates another aspect of the crossover experience and gives us a starting point for looking at cultural collision. She identifies as "survivor guilt" a phenomenon she observed in her work at a student-counseling center at Roosevelt University, in Chicago. "For low income, urban, first-generation college students, survivor guilt has emerged as a significant explanatory concept for academic difficulty." She goes on to say:

> One minority woman reported that her most stressful experience was being the only one in her south-side neighborhood going to college. Another student described her frustration in trying to persuade family members to take positive steps on their own behalf (e.g., to continue their education or get jobs) with no success. Other first generation college students who work at improving their English grammar find that their manner of speaking becomes the object of ridicule by family members who feel threatened by such differences from family norms. "So you think you're too good for us" is a taunt frequently directed at the family member who is trying to escape the family socio-economic level. Unless one is very comfortable with narcissistic strivings "to be special," survivor status tends to create conflict. Thus it is difficult for many of these students to pursue academic work, which represents an escape from the family level of functioning, without a great deal of internal struggle.[2]

Robert Lifton's work on survivors of natural and human disasters identifies the survivor's haunting and disabling dilemma: "Why did I live when they died?"[3] Piorkowski recast this dilemma for her troubled working class students: "Why did I succeed when they failed?" Piorkowski and her colleagues found the concept of survivor guilt to be a helpful explanation of why these students have difficulty with "higher attrition rates, lower GPA's, significant conflict with less affection toward parents, problems organizing time, lower self-esteem, and more psychosomatic problems than their [dorm-staying, middle class] peers." They also found that using (and explaining) the concept of survivor guilt in counseling sessions and in workshops helped those students and evoked testimony:

> Another student, a 26-year-old, married Black woman, heard about survivor guilt in a study skills workshop. She felt that the concept of survivor guilt was the most important thing she had learned in the workshop. . . . She said: "If you come from a family that didn't make it, you feel you shouldn't. My sister lost her job and I feel guilty—like why should I have a job. It's typical of my family—always somebody losing their job or something. We just don't have the same types of problems. When I'm around my family I feel I don't have any right to talk about anything positive. They don't have anything positive to say." The only member of her family attending college, she came in for help with chronic depression and marital problems.[4]

When I found Piorkowski's work, while writing a master's thesis on working class people and psychotherapy, I wept with sorrow and relief.

But the loss I felt was more complex than guilt. Eventually I combined her research with that of others and found my own conclusions: survivor guilt is one aspect in an array of psychological difficulties that working class students experience. Piorkowski's successful work in this area demonstrates her own thesis, and, in my view, it also illustrates the psychosocial results of a cultural chasm. For working class people who pursue middle class careers, part of the existential dilemma is that there is value in each culture, as well as drawbacks. For Shelly, who was previously happy with her husband and her working class life, there is a blazing new star on her horizon, a life of the mind. It complicates things because she wants both to keep her working class roots and to develop her intellectual abilities. She loves her husband, and she can barely stand the strain of not "doing it together." The ambivalence in her relationship is a mirror of her own gathering ambivalence, her own feeling of being "torn"—*torn not just between success and failure in college but between two different notions of what it means to succeed in life.*

I, and others, have tried to articulate what seem to be some of the valuable and central features of working class cultures and how these contrast with middle class culture. It is beyond the scope of this chapter to describe and support all of this, but here's my snapshot: working class people are raised with a more here-and-now sensibility, in activities and worldview; individuality (but not necessarily self) is downplayed in favor of a powerful sense of community and loyalty, and an internal sense of "belonging." Working class cultures also tend to be more embedded in ethnic (non-Anglo) traditions, and so are more diverse by nature. Conversely, middle class culture is more homogeneous (and Anglo) and tends to put a premium on individual accomplishments, on the achievement of planned (and publicly recognized) goals in general, and on earning self-definition by way of these achievements—what I called "becoming." These are fundamental differences in outlooks and approaches to life.[5]

I offer the following by way of example. In my counseling of mixed class couples, I see a lot of cultural clash. One working class woman, Carla, said to her middle class husband, Steve, "You're so cold to my family, they don't feel welcome." Steve replied, "Why do we have to spend so much time with them? We're grown-ups now!" In another session, Steve said, "Why are you spilling your guts to my boss's wife? I've got to project the right image here if I want to keep my job!" Carla retorted, "Well, why the hell do we have to go out with them anyway? On Saturday night! This is your idea of fun? Sipping white wine with your boss?" And round they went. Carla's life has taught her that social relationships are supposed to be supportive, not challenging. Keeping close family ties, in her culture, is not a sign of arrested development. She also has developed her social skills with the assumption that social relationships will be peer-based: it does not "feel right" to her, nor does she desire, to socialize across hierarchies, least of all work-based hierarchies. Working class women often talk with each other about intimate problems, even if they do not know each other well—this behavior *includes* the other person, makes her feel "like one of us." In the middle class, being polite and reserved is a way to show respect for others and one's self (on which there is a premium), and sharing confidences with someone you hardly know might be considered rude or at least déclassé. In turn, this emotional reserve often seems a coldness to working class people—a way of letting someone know you don't want them around or simply being rude. There are different meanings for the same behaviors.

Stephen Garger, in *This Fine Place So Far from Home*, a collection of essays by academics from the working class, describes how a colleague interrupted his presentation three times to argue against it in the same way:

> Where I came from, the immediate and practically the only response to a fellow ignoring or contradicting an explanation three times is to yell and go for the throat—literally and figuratively. Early in my college career silence was the only way to override that response, and this is exactly what happened. . . . All the verbal cues I was receiving indicated the questioner was insulting me and pushing for a fight. However, his physical demeanor most certainly contradicted that impression. The mixed message I was getting was further clouded by the fact that we were violating the unwritten [working class] rule that you don't fight with the people you hang with.[6]

After a friend of his explains that intellectual arguing is something of a recreational sport among academics, Garger muses, "John, the questioner, just may have been opening the door for fun. When I did not respond to the protocol, he tried again and again. Undoubtedly, *he* was receiving mixed messages, too." He concludes: *"It was as if we were engaged in different and separate rituals in which neither of us understood the rules the other was playing by"* (emphasis mine).[7]

As rules start to change for the crossover, family problems abound. Some parents push their children toward "good, clean jobs" as a way to show love and to make their own difficult work lives feel more meaningful. But their reward for this sacrifice is sometimes poignant. If their children succeed, more likely than not, they have adopted the culture, style, and *classism* of the professional/managerial class. Many parents shrink back in shame and confusion while the children they worked so hard to send to school become cultural strangers to them. They fear what is too often true; their children have become embarrassed by their "low class," "backward" family.[8]

Julie Charlip illustrates the painful class distinctions that start as soon as these children enter the halls of higher education:"I vividly remember visiting Bates College with my mother. It was winter, and it was cold in Maine. She wore her good wool coat, the one to which she had sewn a small pink collar, the one she had had all my life. The dean of students greeted us in his plush office and looked my mother up and down with a sniff of disdain. Clearly he thought we were so far beneath him that he didn't need to mask his scorn. I felt small and inadequate and terribly sorry for Mom. I was, as expected, rejected by Bates."[9]

Too often, these students escape the dissonance of clashing cultures and "survivor guilt," in school and later in their middle class careers, through the coping strategy of distancing themselves from their family. This is a tragedy not only for the parents; psychologically it tears the crossover up inside.

Other parents are frightened or insulted if their children get "too big for their britches." Perhaps this latter group—the people that Piorkowski identifies as sabotaging her students' success—creates the less tragic situation. At least these parents remain *engaged* with their children. The "ridicule" Piorkowski describes may be the family trying to bring this member back into the fold for the good of everyone involved. Working class people resist—*I resist*—seeing working class family life as merely something to "survive," or seeing working with one's hands as inherently inferior. It is middle class arrogance that takes the institutional injustices working class people face (less pay for new coats) and reduces their lives and culture to nothing *but* that.

"You'd think with all your education you could use an electric can opener!" my mother snapped at me, after I got my undergraduate degree. She seemed to resent me for going to college. Like Shelly, I was the first in a large and close extended family to go to college. My parents seemed genuinely disturbed when I first decided to go to college. "Why don't you do something useful and get a nice civil service job?" my father said with real concern. He thought I was throwing myself away. My mother, when I asked for a bit of financial help, asked me what the purpose of this "college deal" was. I said, "I don't know yet, I just want to learn." She was aghast: "We're not paying for anything if you are just going there to *learn*!" She said "learn" as if I had said I was going there to do heroin. Clearly (and culturally) my parents thought college was a waste of time and money. I think it is fair to say they were also afraid it would take me further away from them. It was out of their frame of reference and it conflicted with their values. And there I was, with all the enthusiasm of a religious convert, already "correcting" my mother's English at seventeen.

DOMINATION AND CULTURAL "CAPITAL"

My mother resisted my evangelical efforts to improve her perfectly good and colorful English. She was a fighter, and the struggle I'm describing is a matter not simply of *different* cultures but of one dominating the other. Is it any wonder that working class families do not easily surrender their children to the people who they know help make their own lives difficult? In the world of work the professional/managerial class is employed by the very wealthy to inflict appalling abuse and neglect on "lower class" workers. Working class people do not have equality of economic opportunity. This is, I think, the location at which survivor guilt, as Piorkowski describes it, is most accurate. Irvin Peckham, another contributor to *This Fine Place So Far from Home,* says this of his and his father's lives: "I have only to compare what it is like to spend one's day behind a counter with the boss more or less hanging over one to being an English professor. The comparison hurts my mind."[10]

This domination also happens, in more genteel settings, by way of what Bourdieu calls "cultural capital." Professional middle class social style, language, and knowledge constitute a kind of social currency. People who have learned these things can use it for entrance into, and access to some amount of power in, the academy (as in business and government). Cultural barriers may be as effective in shutting out working class people as are the (significant) economic ones, perhaps more so. I have said elsewhere that most working class people's native tongue is more metaphoric than literal, more personal and particular than abstract and universal. It is more implicit than explicit, more for members of a defined social group, also more pithy, colorful, and narrative.[11] It reflects cultural differences from the middle class. It is the opposite of how students are expected to write and speak to get good grades in school. This makes trying to "make it" in school considerably more difficult. Indeed, successful working class students are not necessarily "making it" in the sense that their parents, partners, and former peers understand that term. Cultural difference and prejudice against working class culture combine to frustrate the "upwardly" mobile student.

To succeed in higher education (and, often, in a middle class marriage) working class people must learn to adopt and represent middle class culture as their own. This culture does not grant dual citizenship. You must "leave behind" your "low class" ways, your "bad" English, your values of humility and inclusion (don't show off and be a "big shot," because it says you think you're better than others), and much more—not least the people you love! In early adulthood there are developmental tasks of differentiation at play that I suspect help fuel the leap the young crossover student is trying to make. But it is a cruel and unsuspected consequence to have that process set up a chasm that may never be bridged again. As Donna Burns Phillips, a long-time college teacher, said: "If finding a coherent identity is so difficult for me, one who has had an entire life as well as a career in which to reconcile the influences of hostile value systems, what must it be like for the students who come to our classrooms wholly unsuspecting, wholly unprepared for the changes we intend for them?"[12]

This suffering is invisible not only to others but, most poignantly, to those who bear it. "By Thanksgiving of my first year of college, I wanted to go home and stay there. What was I doing at this place for rich kids? What was I accomplishing? How was I helping my family? I was a mute, a heavy drinker, a class skipper," said Laurel Johnson Black.[13] A middle class counselor might see Black's situation in terms of success and failure, surviving or not surviving her own history. What the middle class perspective misses is the working class culture it can't see, as well as the contempt for that culture—based on razor-thin stereotypes that *are* "seen"—that this potential "survivor" experiences almost daily. Michael Schwalbe illustrates the dissonance of invisibility and classism.

> Once when I was talking to a professor in his office, another professor leaned in the doorway and said, "I just heard a new excuse for missing an exam. A student said he couldn't come in today because he had to move a trailer house." The professor to whom I was talking laughed and replied, "That's one I never heard before. I guess it tells you you're really at a blue-collar college." Part of me liked being privy to this exchange. I took it to mean I was being treated as an insider. But I also sympathized with the student. It made sense to me that you might have to miss an exam to move a trailer house. What was funny about that?[14]

As another contributor to the same collection puts it, "Being working class means never knowing with certainty why someone is laughing at you."[15]

As the consequences of choosing a professional path start to impinge on the student, confusion and ambivalence threaten not only her school success but the sense of self and identity she needs to feel anything like "whole."

DISSONANCE, DISTANCE, AND RESISTANCE

This subtle, slow, and unacknowledged process of crossing class-based cultures threatens "integration." Integration is the psychological process of layering new experiences on top of old ones to create an ongoing evolution of meaning—of one's personal story of life, of who I am and of what I might expect in the future. Take the basic cultural differences between the working and middle classes; stir in the unchallenged assumption, everywhere in the working class student's new culture, that it is far superior; fold in cherished national myths of equality and freedom for all people; and you have a recipe for personal *dis*-integration and profound "cognitive dissonance" (an acute mental and emotional confusion). "Nothing will ever be enough to stitch together the before and after of this life," despaired working class academic Renny Christopher as a graduate student.[16] For many working class students, this dissonance is so great, they are more likely to either *reject* the new culture (one reason for the high dropout rate among such students) or try to *eject* the former culture from their sense of self.

Throughout the literature of working class academics is the common thread of distancing oneself from family and former life, the most common means of resolving the dissonance of "the before and after of this life." For the ones who distance themselves there is loss, unstated and misunderstood. The problems I have described above appear to remain true for many of the people who have already crossed the class divide (especially if they still feel loyalty to their roots). Irvin Peckham, whose mind hurt when he compared his father's and his own work, says it plainly:

> A few of us manage to break with our origins, denying our "incorrectness" or the "incorrect" class into which we were born. I do not know how others manage the break but I erased my incorrectness by infrequently going home. In time, I more or less forgot who my parents and siblings were. Although I hesitate to admit it, I have to tell you that the only time my parents and I and my brother and my sister have all been together since I left home was for my parents' silver wedding anniversary. I suspect the next occasion will be a funeral. That's called erasure.[17]

Laurel Johnson Black, who "was a mute, a heavy drinker" in her first year in college, is now an academic who says, "When I speak to my siblings my world slips around until I am dizzy." Her essay in *This Fine Place so Far from Home* is called "Stupid Rich Bastards." She offers a palpable sense of the cognitive dissonance she feels: "Sometimes I sit in meetings and classrooms and wonder who else might like to cut the shit and say what they feel. I feel suspended, dangling. If I put my toe down at any point I might root there. I cannot move among the rich, the condescending, the ones who can turn me into an object of study with a glance or a word, cannot speak like them, live in a house like them, learn their ways without being disloyal to someone."[18]

Resistance is harder to track because it often manifests in *not* going to college, *not* writing papers, and so on. If working class culture is different from middle class culture, and if both have their strengths, then it is reasonable to *choose* to remain in the working class *despite* the severe economic and physical penalties imposed for doing so. I believe many people do just this. Unfortunately, most are punished with lower wages and less control. Others, like my big brother Eddie, manage to change not cultures, just work or income.

Eddie and I have both held professional jobs for most of our adult lives. But I went to college (and graduate school), and he was a mail carrier who gradually worked his way up to postmaster of several large post offices in Minneapolis. I became a left-wing type who did community organizing, and I now focus much of my counseling work on poor and working class kids and adults. I also developed a love of theater, Beethoven, and "fine dining." As a young adult, I became, ironically, both politically committed to working class people and increasingly ashamed to bring my new activist friends home to my "redneck" family. My brother became a right-wing type who nonetheless has worked hard to bring an "employee involvement" management style into the post offices he managed before his retirement. He still plays rockabilly guitar and sings karaoke, wears cowboy hats, and can't imagine paying as much money for an entire meal as I do for a tip (though he makes more money than I do). He never stopped enjoying the company of and connection with the many members of our extended family. Who is the more advantaged and who the disadvantaged one between us? If the answer is easy, it shouldn't be.

Perhaps my relatively cheery view on working class culture comes in part from the fact that I, like Garger, come from a relatively successful, "settled living," working class family and neighborhood. My father did skilled labor (meat cutting) in Minnesota. We had plenty of problems, as I have described elsewhere, mostly to do with the conditions of the work. But I grew up in the 1950s and 1960s, arguably the best time in American history for working class people. Jack Metzgar, who independently came up with ideas almost identical to mine about cultural differences, and who argues for the validity and equality of working class culture, is likewise from a family of skilled labor and even union activity.[19]

But these sentiments can be found among the very poor as well. Jay MacLeod, in his book *Ain't No Makin' It*, recounts his study of boys from a housing project in "a northeastern city." Many had parents who were chronically unemployed or who worked intermittently in so-called un-skilled labor that never brings in enough to pay all the bills. MacLeod studied two groups of teenage boys, the ones who pursued education as a "way out" and the ones who did not. Among the ones who neither attained nor desired academic success (the "hallway hangers"), there was a boy named Slick who was extraordinarily bright and sometimes thought of becoming a lawyer. He explained his existential choice:

Slick: What it is it's a brotherhood down here. We're all fucking brothers. There's a lot of backstabbing down here, down in the streets. But we're al-ways there for each other. No shit. There's not a guy in here who wouldn't put out for the rest of us. If he needs something and I got it, I'll give it to him. Period. That's the way it works. It's a brotherhood. We're not like them up there—the rich little boys from the suburbs or whatever. There's a line there. On this side of the line we don't fuck with each other; we're tight.

Frankie: We'd chump them off [rob] on the other side, though.

Slick: Fucking right. If he's got four hundred bucks in his pocket, there's more where that came from. Fuck him. But they also chump each other off; only they do it legally. How do you think they got rich—by fucking people over. We don't do that to each other. We're too fucking tight. We're a group. We don't think like them. We think for all of us.

Frankie: That's the fucking truth. If you don't have fucking buddies, where are you? You're fuckin' no one. Nuttin'.

Slick: *If I had the choice, and this isn't just me but probably everyone in here, if I had the choice between being a good person and makin' it, I'd be a good person. That's just the way I am. If I had my bar exam tomorrow and these guys needed me, I'd go with them. That's just the way it is down here.*

Shorty: Yeah, you wanna be here with your family, with your friends, they're good people. You're comfortable with them. You don't feel right with these other people. (Emphasis mine.)[20]

A "good person" in the professional middle class is too often a "brilliant" individual who achieves something mighty for "the good of [an ab-stracted] humanity"; that person often gets awards for his or her actions. A "good person" in the working class has time to hang out, wants to keep the circle of connection intact, and offers many small generosities to per-sonal and particular others. In a society in which virtually everything, and particularly education, is "classed," might not some decide to opt for a culture that emphasizes cooperation over competition? Might not some choose "hanging out" over pushing themselves to achieve? Might not some prefer Christmas cards that simply say "love, Aunt Mary" to Christmas letters that compile the year's achievements, evidence of one's worth (or brilliance, or ambition, or travel budget)? For me, this is not hard to imagine at all. Resisters to professional class culture may choose to live in their cooperative cultures, despite economic penalties. They choose to remain with the people and places that feel like home. But, in a society dominated by the very wealthy, and largely run by the professional middle class, the privileges and rewards of staying in the working class or moving into the middle class are far from equal.

CONCLUDING WITH CREATION

Somewhere at the center of all these arguments and abstractions sits Shelly, hiding and crying in a bathroom stall at a midwestern state university. It would be wrong-headed to try to tell her what her own decision and solutions might be. What we *can* do is clarify what those decision points are by seeing her dilemma more clearly. We can start by illuminating and validating both her past and her present. If she can see her and her husband's dilemma as a clash of cultures rather than a battle of good and bad, better and worse, normal and abnormal, she may even be able to avoid choosing decisively *between* the cultures. If she has someone to talk with about how she might reconcile them in her own life, she and her family might move forward in a way right for her and them.

Working class cultures have many humane, healthy, and life-giving qualities for which people from the middle class pine and search, at no small consequence to their bank accounts. Like most counseling psychologists, I have spent a part of my career helping both "failures" and "successes" from the professional middle class improve their mental health. We help them, often, to embrace a kind of humanity that values warmth over brilliance, "connectedness" over competition, and that helps them to find a self that exists in spite of personal achievements or failures. I do not intend to romanticize what can be, in many ways, a difficult working class life with limited options, but it is also easy for me to remember, and enjoy to this day, many positive aspects of working class life.

Donna Burns Phillips believes that "academics have to be just as clear and deliberate about the attitudes toward the students they teach as they are about the theories they teach."[21] In my view, it is exactly the job of college teachers, and other (perhaps unwitting) gatekeepers to the professional/managerial middle class, to help people remember, even see more clearly, where they came from and what value it has. Phillips suggests that "education sets up a dialogue between past, present and possible selves."[22] I want it to do just that for Shelly.

What college *should* give Shelly (and what it gives her middle class peers) is additions to herself, as Phillips points out—not subtractions from herself, or a "transformation." What she needs is an *integration* of new abilities and awarenesses, not a compartmentalized half-self plagued with doubt and addicted to success. This work is "creating" or "bridging," a third response to the clashing of cultures and the resulting confusion. If this is difficult, if it seems contradictory to people (like me) who long for a classless society, we still need to apply ourselves to the task.

We need to experiment and figure out how to help Shelly "stitch together the before and after" of her life. There is probably much she can teach us, if we listen. In this area, our role must be as much about facilitating as professing. Helping Shelly see and define *her* own cross-class experience is important. Shelly is not only seeing her husband with newly judgmental eyes, she is also distancing herself from her "old" self. Without a conscious appreciation of the complex journey she is making, without an appreciation for the working class woman she was and is, she could lose all of what was good about her working class life, as well as losing her husband and family. Shelley's success will be dubious, at best, if she must relinquish that much to achieve it.

NOTES

Introduction — Michael Zweig

1. The 2001 Bush tax cut provided the bottom 60 percent of the population, those with incomes less than $44,000 a year, an average $32.50 a year in tax relief (compared with $5,312 for those in the top 1 percent, with average annual incomes more than $1.1 million) (*New York Times*, February 25, 2002, A18). That was more than taken up in a single month just by the subway fare increase workers had to pay in New York City because government help was no longer available to support mass transit. Increases in health costs for Medicare and Medicaid patients, higher fees for government services, higher costs and reduced availability when government privatizes services—these and other consequences of the fiscal crisis make "tax relief" a burden for workers but a boon for capitalists.

2. Jeff Madrick, "Regardless of Progress of a Few, Many Nations Still Face Economic Despair," *New York Times*, August 7, 2003, C2.

3. United States Space Command, *Vision for 2020*, February 1997 (contains no pagination as downloaded from www.spacecom.mil/visbook.pdf).

4. For a detailed discussion of the class composition of the United States, on which these and the following findings are based, see Michael Zweig, *The Working Class Majority: America's Best Kept Secret* (Ithaca, NY: Cornell University Press, 2000), chap. 1.

5. Some middle class people are represented by unions, such as university professors in the American Federation of Teachers (AFT) and legal aid attorneys in the UAW. Most union members are in the working class.

6. Kate Bronfenbrenner, "The Effects of Plant Closing or Threat of Plant Closing on the Right of Workers to Organize" (Dallas, TX: North American Commission for Labor Cooperation, 1997).

7. Barry T. Hirsch, David A. Macpherson, and Wayne G. Vroman, "Estimates of Union Density by State," *Monthly Labor Review* 124, no. 7 (July 2001): 51–55 (accompanying data online at www.trinity.edu/bhirsch); and Edward N. Wolff, "Recent Trends in Wealth Ownership, from 1983 to 1998," in *Assets for the Poor: The Benefits of Spreading Asset Ownership*, ed. Thomas N. Shapiro and Edward N. Wolff (New York: Russell Sage Foundation, 2001), 34–73.

8. Lance Compa, *Unfair Advantage: Workers' Freedom of Association in the United States under International Human Rights Standards* (New York: Human Rights Watch, 2000); and Richard B. Freeman and Joel Rogers, *What Workers Want* (Ithaca, NY: ILR Press and Russell Sage Foundation, 1999).

9. Melvin Dubofsky, *We Shall Be All: A History of the Industrial Workers of the World* (Chicago: Quadrangle, 1969); Paul F. Taylor, *Bloody Harlan: The United Mine Workers of*

America in Harlan County, Kentucky, 1931–1941 (Lanham, MD: University Press of America, 1990); Janet Christine Irons, "Testing the New Deal: The General Strike of 1934 (PhD. diss., Duke University, 1988); Art Preis, *Labor's Giant Step: Twenty Years of the CIO* (New York: Pioneer, 1964); Joshua B. Freeman, *Working Class New York: Life and Labor Since World War II* (New York: New Press, 2000); Nelson Lichtenstein, "Taft-Hartley Symposium: The First Fifty Years: Taft-Hartley: A Slave-Labor Law?" *Catholic University Law Review* 47 (spring 1998): 763–89; Stephen Franklin, *Three Strikes: Labor's Heartland Losses and What They Mean for Working Americans* (New York: Guilford, 2001); JoAnn Wypijewski, "Audacity on Trial," *The Nation*, August 6, 2001; Jack Mulcahy, "Longshore Union Enforced 'No Work' Policy on the Docks—During Lockout," *Labor Notes*, no. 284 (November 2002); Steve Downs, "Transit Workers Prepare for Outlawed Strike," *Labor Notes*, no. 286 (January 2003); Christopher L. Tomlins, *The State and the Unions* (New York: Cambridge University Press, 1985); American Social History Project, *Who Built America? Working People and the Nation's Economy, Politics, Culture, and Society* (New York: Pantheon Books, 1990); and Robert V. Bruce, *1877: Year of Violence* (Indianapolis: Bobbs-Merrill, 1959).

10. David Brooks, "The Triumph of Hope over Self-Interest," *New York Times*, January 12, 2003, sec. 4, p. 15.

11. Calvin Coolidge, speech to Society of American Newspaper Editors, Washington, DC, January 17, 1925, Calvin Coolidge Papers, Library of Congress, Washington, DC.

12. Irving Bernstein, *The Turbulent Years: A History of the American Worker, 1933–1941* (Boston: Houghton Mifflin, 1971); Robert H. Bremner, "The New Deal and Social Welfare," in *Fifty Years Later: The New Deal Evaluated*, ed. Harvard Sitkoff (New York: McGraw-Hill, 1985), 69–92; Frances Fox Piven and Richard A. Cloward, *Poor People's Movements: Why They Succeed, How They Fail* (New York: Pantheon, 1977), chaps. 2 and 3.

13. On post–World War II labor history, see Stanley Aronowitz, *From the Ashes of the Old: American Labor and America's Future* (Boston: Houghton Mifflin, 1998); Mike Davis, *Prisoners of the American Dream: Politics and Economy in the History of the U.S. Working Class* (London: Verso, 1986); Michael Goldfield, *The Decline of Organized Labor in the United States* (Chicago: University of Chicago Press, 1987); and James Gross, *Broken Promise: The Subversion of U.S. Labor Relations Policy, 1947–1994* (Philadelphia: Temple University Press, 1995).

14. Cedric Belfrage, *The American Inquisition, 1945–1960* (New York: Bobbs-Merrill, 1973); Robert Justin Goldstein, *Political Repression in Modern America, 1870 to the Present* (Cambridge, MA: Schenkman, 1978); Ann Fagan Ginger and David Christiano, eds., *The Cold War against Labor: An Anthology* (Berkeley, CA: Meiklejohn Civil Liberties Institute, 1987); Ellen Schrecker, *Many Are the Crimes: McCarthyism in America* (Boston: Little, Brown, 1998).

15. Comments of George Strauss, founding member and past president of the IRRA, at the IRRA session "Is Class Relevant in Industrial Relations Studies?" Atlanta, January 2002.

16. Author's experience organizing the session.

17. See Zweig, *Working Class Majority*, chap. 3.

18. Steven Greenhouse, "DeLay Denies Role in Letter Riling Unions: Patriotism of Labor Called into Question," *New York Times*, February 8, 2003, A11.

19. Philip Dine, "Organized Labor Shows Increasing Distaste for War in Iraq: About 100 Union Locals Have Passed Resolutions Expressing Reservations," *St. Louis Post-Dispatch*, January 15, 2003, A1.

20. U.S. Labor Against the War, "Call to a National Labor Assembly for Peace," October 24–25, 2003, Chicago, posted on www.uslaboragainstwar.org.

21. Frank Bruni, "The 2000 Campaign: The Texas Governor; After Convention, Bush Chides Gore for Divisive Tone" *New York Times*, August 19, 2000, A1.

22. John Manley, "The Significance of Class in American History and Politics," in *New*

Perspectives on American Politics, ed. Lawrence C. Dodd and Calvin Jillson (Washington, DC: Congressional Quarterly Press, 1994).

23. Jeremy Brecher, *Strike!* rev. ed. (Cambridge, MA: South End, 1997); David Alan Corbin, *Life, Work, and Rebellion in the Coal Fields: The Southern West Virginia Miners, 1880–1922* (Urbana: University of Ilinois Press, 1981); J. Anthony Lukas, *Big Trouble: A Murder in a Small Western Town Sets Off a Struggle for the Soul of America* (New York: Simon and Schuster, 1997).

24. For a brief explanation, see Zweig, *Working Class Majority,* 103–7. For a full explanation, see Adam Smith, *An Inquiry into the Nature and Origins of the Wealth of Nations,* ed. Edwin Cannan (1776; repr., Chicago: University of Chicago Press, 1976); and Karl Marx, *Capital: A Critique of Political Economy,* vol. 1, *The Process of Capitalist Production* (1867; repr., New York: International, 1967), and vol. 3, *The Process of Capitalist Production as a Whole* (1894; repr., New York: International, 1967).

25. Karl Marx, "Letter to J. Wedemeyer," March 5, 1852, in *Selected Works,* by Karl Marx and Friedrich Engels (Moscow: Progress, 1969–1970), 2:410; and Karl Marx and Friedrich Engels, *The Communist Manifesto: A Modern Edition* (1848; repr., London: Verso, 1998).

Part I. The Mosaic of Class, Gender, and Race — Michael Zweig

1. See Michael Zweig, *The Working Class Majority: America's Best Kept Secret* (Ithaca, NY: Cornell University Press, 2000), 31–33.

2. U.S. Census Bureau, *Statistical Abstract of the United States: 2001,* 119th ed. (Washington, DC, 1999), table 682.

3. Theodore W. Allen, *The Invention of the White Race: The Origin of Racial Oppression in Anglo-America,* 2 vols. (New York: Verso, 1994 and 1997).

When Feminism Had Class — Dorothy Sue Cobble

1. Quotes from Dorothy Sue Cobble, *Dishing It Out: Waitresses and Their Unions in the Twentieth Century* (Urbana: University of Illinois Press, 1991), 12, 97–99, 128–30, 199–200; Edwin Lahey, "Myra, the Battling Belle of the Working-Man's Café Society," *Detroit Free Press,* July 24, 1966, 8–11; and Jean Maddern Pitrone, *Myra: The Life and Times of Myra Wolfgang, Trade Union Leader* (Wyandotte, MI: Calibre, 1980), 122–24. For more on Wolfgang, consult Dorothy Sue Cobble, *The Other Women's Movement,* 2–3, 31–33,180–81, 188–90, 201–2.

2. Leila Rupp and Verta Taylor use the term "doldrums" to describe the postwar decades. They focus on the National Woman's Party as the predominant carrier of feminism in those years. See *Survival in the Doldrums: The American Women's Rights Movement, 1945 to the 1960s* (New York: Oxford University Press, 1987).

3. For a fuller discussion of the gender biases of labor history, see Ava Baron, "Gender and Labor History: Learning from the Past, Looking to the Future," in *Work Engendered: Toward a New History of American Labor,* ed. Ava Baron (Ithaca, NY: Cornell University Press, 1991), 1–46.

4. For other scholarly work suggesting the need for new measures of "feminist consciousness," see, for example, Evelyn Nakano Glenn, "From Servitude to Service Work: Historical Continuities in the Racial Division of Paid Reproductive Labor," in *Unequal Sisters: A Multicultural Reader in U.S. Women's History,* 3rd ed., ed. Vicki L. Ruiz and Ellen Carol DuBois (New York: Routledge, 2000), 436–65; or Deborah King, "Multiple Jeopardy, Multiple Consciousness: The Context of a Black Feminist Ideology," *Signs* 14 (autumn 1988): 42–72. When I use the term "working class," I do not mean to suggest a rigid dichotomous class categorization of society. I am simply referring to that majority group in society whose members' income, whether from their own market work or that of family members, derives primarily from nonsupervisory wages or salary.

5. Cobble, *The Other Women's Movement,* 15–25.

6. "Women's Movement?" *Wall Street Journal*, January 22, 2002, A1.

7. For biographical sketches of these and other labor women reformers, consult Cobble, *The Other Women's Movement*, 25–49. Oral histories of Esther Peterson, Maida Springer-Kemp, Mary Callahan, and other trade union women of their generation can be found most readily in Brigid O'Farrell and Joyce Kornbluh, *Rocking the Boat: Union Women's Voices, 1915–1975* (New Brunswick, NJ: Rutgers University Press, 1996).

8. Quotes from Addie Wyatt, "'An Injury to One Is an Injury to All': Addie Wyatt Remembers the Packinghouse Workers Union," *Labor's Heritage* 12 (winter/spring 2003): 26–27; interview with Addie Wyatt by Rick Halpern and Roger Horowitz, January 30, 1986, United Packinghouse Workers of America Oral History Project, State Historical Society of Wisconsin, Madison, Wisconsin. See also Cobble, *The Other Women's Movement*, 32–33, 201–3.

9. Quotes from interview with Caroline Davis by Ruth Meyerowitz, July 23, 1976, "The Twentieth Century Trade Union Woman: Vehicle for Social Change," oral history project, Institute of Industrial Relations, University of Michigan, Ann Arbor; "Lady Labor Leader: To Keep Labor Peace and Prosperity in an Indiana Factory, the Boss of Local 764 Just Acts Like a Woman," *Life*, June 30, 1947, 83–85. See also Cobble, *The Other Women's Movement*, 37–42, 182.

10. I consider them "feminists" because they recognized that women suffer disadvantages due to their sex and because they sought to eliminate sex-based disadvantages. I call them "labor feminists" because they articulated a particular variant of feminism that put the needs of working class women at its core, and because they championed the labor movement as the principal vehicle through which the lives of the majority of women could be bettered.

11. Cobble, *The Other Women's Movement*, 34–36, 151–64, 181–82; and Esther Peterson with Winifred Conkling, *Restless: The Memoirs of Labor and Consumer Activist Esther Peterson* (Washington, DC: Caring, 1995).

12. The following discussion is based on Cobble, *The Other Women's Movement*, chaps. 2–6.

13. Quote from transcript, "Conference of Trade Union Women, April 1945," 103–6, box 898, file "WB Conf. 1945," Women's Bureau, U.S. Department of Labor, record group 86, National Archives and Record Center, Washington, DC.

14. Quote from Esther Peterson, "The Changing Position of Women in the Labor Force," in U.S. Department of Labor, *Labor Laws and Their Administration: Proceedings of the 41st Convention of the International Association of Governmental Labor Officials, Augusta, Georgia, August 24–28, 1958*, Bulletin 199 (Washington, DC: U.S. Government Printing Office, 1958), 22–23.

15. Nancy Fraser, "After the Family Wage: What Do Women Want in Social Welfare?" *Social Justice* 21 (spring 1994): 80–86.

16. For more on the debate over time, see Cobble, *The Other Women's Movement*, 139–44, 171–73, 186–90; and Dorothy Sue Cobble, "Halving the Double Day: The Labor Origins of Work-Family Reform," *New Labor Forum* 12 (fall 2003): 63–72.

17. For a fuller discussion of how labor is changing to meet the needs of women, see Dorothy Sue Cobble and Monica Bielski Michal, "'On the Edge of Equality'?: Working Women and the U.S. Labour Movement," in *Gender, Diversity, and Trade Unions: International Perspectives*, ed. Fiona Colgan and Sue Ledwith (London: Routledge, 2002), 232–56.

How Race Enters Class in the United States — Bill Fletcher Jr.

1. David Roediger, *The Wages of Whiteness: Race and the Making of the American Working Class* (London: Verso, 1991); W. E. B. DuBois, *Black Reconstruction in America, 1860–1880* (1934; repr., South Bend, IN: Notre Dame University Press, 2003); Theodore W. Allen, *The*

Invention of the White Race: The Origin of Racial Oppression in Anglo-America, 2 vols. (London: Verso, 1994 and 1997).

2. Lerone Bennett Jr., *The Shaping of Black America* (New York: Penguin, 1993).

3. J. Sakai, *Settlers: The Myth of the White Proletariat*, available from Crossroad Support Network, c/o Spear and Shield Publications, 5206 S. Harper, Chicago, IL 60615.

4. W. E. B. DuBois, *The Souls of Black Folk* (1905; repr., New York: Modern Library, 2003).

5. DuBois, *Black Reconstruction*.

The Tangled Knot of Race and Class in America — R. Jeffrey Lustig

1. Orlando Patterson, *The Ordeal of Integration* (New York: Basic Civitas, 1997), 24.

2. Seymour M. Lipset, *Political Man: The Social Bases of Politics* (Garden City, NJ: Doubleday, 1960), 230, 439.

3. See, for example, Stanley Aronowitz, "Does the United States Have a New Working Class?" in *The Revival of American Socialism*, ed. George Fischer (New York: Oxford University Press, 1971).

4. William Forbath's apt metaphor in "Caste, Class and Equal Citizenship," 98 *Michigan Law Review* 1 (October 1999): 3, 5.

5. Joel Olson, "DuBois and the Race Concept: Toward a Political Theory of Race" (paper presented at the Western Political Science Association annual meeting, Long Beach, CA, March 2002), 18; and "The DuBoisian Alternative to the Politics of Recognition" (paper presented at the American Political Science Association annual meeting, Washington, DC, September 2000), 20. Also Theodore Allen, *The Invention of the White Race: The Origin of Racial Oppression in Anglo-America*, 2 vols. (London: Verso, 1994 and 1997).

6. Asa Briggs and John Saville, *Essays in Labor History* (London: Macmillan, 1960); Raymond Williams, *Culture and Society* (New York: Columbia University Press, 1960), xv.

7. Karl Marx and Friedrich Engels, "The Communist Manifesto," in *The Marx-Engels Reader*, 2nd ed., ed. Robert Tucker (New York: W. W. Norton, 1978), 480, 485; Karl Marx, *The Eighteenth Brumaire of Louis Bonaparte* (New York: International Publishers, 1963), 124.

8. Marx and Engels, "Communist Manifesto," 476, 481–83.

9. Gunnar Myrdal, *An American Dilemma: The Negro Problem and Modern Democracy* (New York: Harper and Row, 1944), 11. On the view of racism as a passing epiphenomenon, see Michael Omi and Howard Winant, *Racial Formation in the United States: From the 1960s to the 1980s*, 2nd ed. (New York: Routledge and Kegan Paul, 1994), 9, 35.

10. Karl Marx and Friedrich Engels, "Contribution to the Critique of Hegel's *Philosophy of Right*," in *The Marx-Engels Reader*, 2nd ed., ed. Robert Tucker (New York: W. W. Norton, 1978), 64; and Marx and Engels, "Communist Manifesto," 482, 491.

11. Williams, *Culture and Society*, 325.

12. Ray Boshara, "Poverty Is More Than a Matter of Income," *New York Times*, September 29, 2002, section 4, p. 13. On wealth and income, see Michael C. Dawson, *Behind the Mule: Race and Class in African-American Politics* (Princeton: Princeton University Press, 1994), 7; and Lani Guinier and Gerald Torres, *The Miner's Canary: Enlisting Race, Resisting Power, Transforming Democracy* (Cambridge, MA: Harvard University Press, 2002), 44–49.

13. Donald R. Kinder and Lynn M. Sanders, *Divided By Color: Racial Politics and Democratic Ideals* (Chicago: University of Chicago Press, 1996), 90; Etienne Balibar, "Class Struggle to Classless Struggle?" in *Race, Nation, Class: Ambiguous Identities*, ed. Immanuel Wallerstein and Etienne Balibar (London: Verso, 1991), 156; David Brion Davis, *In the Image of God: Religion, Moral Values, and Our Heritage of Slavery* (New Haven: Yale University Press, 2002), 357.

14. Melvyn Dubofsky and Foster R. Dulles, *Labor in American History*, 6th ed. (Wheeling, IL: Harlan-Davidson, 1999), 73.

15. David R. Roediger, *The Wages of Whiteness: Race and the Making of the American Work-*

ing Class (New York: Verso, 1991), chaps. 3–4. See also Karen Orren, *Belated Feudalism: Labor, the Law, and Liberal Development in the United States* (New York: Cambridge University Press, 1991).

16. W. E. B. DuBois, *Black Reconstruction in America, 1860–1880* (New York: Atheneum, 1992), 700–701; Olson, "DuBoisian Alternative," 2; and Forbath, "Caste," 12.

17. Alexander Saxton, *The Indispensable Enemy: Labor and the Anti-Chinese Movement in California* (Berkeley: University of California Press, 1982), chap. 4. Tomas Almaguer, *Racial Faultlines* (Berkeley: University of California Press, 1994), 3, 154, 210.

18. Almaguer, *Racial Faultlines*, 3, 181, 205. "It is to the eternal shame of the American labor movement that . . . it always favored Euro-American racist solidarity over worker solidarity." Patterson, *Ordeal of Integration*, 7.

19. Olson, "DuBoisian Alternative," 15.

20. Cornel West, *Race Matters* (New York: Vintage, 1993), 156; Roediger, *Wages of Whiteness*, 95.

21. *Dred Scott vs. Sanford*, 19 How. 393; 15 L. Ed., 691 (1857).

22. Roediger, *Wages of Whiteness*, 57.

23. Guinier and Torres, *Miner's Canary*, 12, 294–98.

24. Olson, "DuBoisian Alternative," 20. In Forbath's words, black subordination bound "white Americans together as 'equals' across unacknowledged breaches of class" ("Caste," 3).

25. Roediger, *Wages of Whiteness*, 69. I discuss here only the dominant elements in organized labor. There were also serious attempts at cross-racial organizing during these years, both by southern unions and by the Knights of Labor. These were eventually defeated, however, and the emerging AFL took a decidedly racist tack.

26. Allen, *Invention*, 1:198. Guinier and Torres make the point in the present context: "The mechanisms that make it so hard for black people to accumulate assets in a way that changes their life chances are the same mechanisms that keep poor whites poor" (*Miner's Canary*, 49). Also see Roediger, *Wages of Whiteness*, 87, 178, 182.

27. Seymour Martin Lipset and Reinhard Bendix, *Social Mobility in Industrial Society* (Berkeley: University of California Press, 1959), 106.

28. Many unions discriminated against blacks and other minorities up through the 1970s, admitting them when ordered by the court, but often denying them voting or other membership rights, adequate grievance representation, and access to high-prestige jobs. Herbert Hill, *Black Labor and the American Legal System: Race, Work and the Law* (Madison: University of Wisconsin Press, 1996).

29. "The black man's career in any one subordinate subsector establishes preconditions for him to get inferior results from any other sector. . . . The racial functions of the different institutional sectors reinforce one another." Harold Baron, "The Web of Urban Racism," in *Institutional Racism in America*, ed. Louis L. Knowles and Kenneth Prewitt (Englewood Cliffs, NJ: Prentice-Hall, 1969), 160. A fuller model would take into consideration other institutions as well—welfare, the criminal justice system, the military, etc.

I focus on African Americans in this discussion because blacks are the paradigmatic racial formation in America. "Ethnic" groups, while also discriminated against, are regarded and treated differently, though there have also been attempts to racialize them historically. Blauner identifies one cause of the differences between race and ethnicity in the contrasting ways groups initially encountered American society—via violence and coercion (blacks and Indians) or voluntary choice (Europeans, Asians, and current Hispanic immigrants). Robert Blauner, *Racial Oppression in America* (New York: Harper and Row, 1972), 52.

30. David Wellman titles a chapter "Prejudiced People Are Not the Only Racists in America" in *Portraits of White Racism* (New York: Cambridge University Press, 1977). Also see Baron, "Web," 142.

31. George Lipsitz, *The Possessive Investment in Whiteness* (Philadelphia: Temple University Press, 1998), vii–viii and chap. 3 (on Proposition 187).

32. Forbath presents a fuller discussion of the concepts of social citizenship and material conditions of citizenship in "Caste, Class and Equal Citizenship."

33. DuBois, *Black Reconstruction*; and Eric Foner, *Reconstruction: America's Unfinished Revolution, 1863–1877* (New York: Harper and Row, 1988).

34. This interpretation follows Forbath's analysis. "Between the [New Deal's] constitutional mandate and its enactment fell the shadow of Jim Crow and the betrayal of Reconstruction." "Caste," 5, 26, 41–42. Michael Brown et al. extend this analysis into housing, urban renewal, labor, transportation, and agricultural policies. *Whitewashing Race: The Myth of a Color-Blind Society* (Berkeley: University of California Press, 2003), introduction.

35. Thus Almaguer writes that "race, rather than class, [has] served as the key organizing principle of hierarchical relations" but also adds that the capitalist context shaped this racializing process. Almaguer, *Racial Faultlines*, 3, 7, 170–72. Also see Omi and Winant, *Racial Formation*, 34, 66.

36. One-quarter of all immigration to the United States in the 1980s came to California, for a population increase reaching four hundred thousand a year, legal and illegal, late in that decade. Peter Schrag, *Paradise Lost* (Berkeley: University of California Press, 1998), 230. California's first constitution in 1849 was published bilingually, in English and Spanish.

37. Schrag, *Paradise Lost*, 239.

38. In 1991 the state spent $1.8 billion on undocumented residents, according to U.S. government reports, $1.3 billion of which went for schooling, their right under the Fourteenth Amendment (*Plyler vs. Doe*, 1982), not a social service per se. Taking into account the undocumented workers' federal income taxes, state taxes ($732 million in fiscal year 1992, in sales, property, and income taxes), their direct expenditures, and the spending generated by them, the Urban Institute calculated that they made a net *contribution* to the state of $12 billion annually. Jeff Lustig and Dick Walker, *No Way Out: Immigrants and the New California* (Berkeley, CA: Campus Coalition for Human Rights, 1995); "The Immigration Blame Game," *Los Angeles Times* editorial, November 11, 1992; Jeffrey Passel, Rebecca Clark, and Manuel Garcia y Griego, "How Much Do Immigrants Really Cost?" (Riverside, CA: Tomas Rivera Center and the Urban Institute, 1994); and Jeffrey Passel et al., "Fiscal Impacts of Undocumented Aliens: Selected Estimates for Seven States" (Washington, DC: Urban Institute, 1994). Also see Lipsitz, *Possessive Investment*, chap. 3.

39. Wells Fargo Bank economists reported a "hemorrhage" of a half million jobs from the state in 1991–1992, totaling almost 5 percent of the workforce by 1994. "Special Report: Defense Cuts and the California Economy," *Wells Fargo Monitor*, April 30, 1992; "The California Economy: A Mid-Year Review," *Wells Fargo Monitor*, June 30, 1992; "One Step Forward, Two Steps Back," *Wells Fargo Monitor*, July 31, 1992. By February 1994, California's unemployment rate was two points above the national rate (8.7 compared to 6.4 percent). Sam Stanton, "Hard Times Driving Governors' Race," *Sacramento Bee*, February 27, 1994. During the 1980s the gap between rich and poor widened and the poverty rate nearly doubled. The income of the wealthiest fifth increased 15 percent, that of the middle-income group gained 3 percent, and that of the bottom fifth plummeted by 8 percent. Center for Budget and Policy Priorities findings, reported by R. G. McLeod, "Income Inequality Worsening," *San Francisco Chronicle*, August 28, 1992, A9. The gap between rich and poor in California widened primarily because of a "precipitous drop" in male earnings (20 percent in 1994 dollars, from 1967 to 1994). Between 1969 and 1989, California moved from the twenty-first to the sixth most income-polarized state. Deborah Reed, M. G. Haber, and Laura Mamesh, *The Distribution of Income in California* (San Francisco: Public Policy Institute of California, 1996), vi, viii.

40. Howard Gardner, "Paroxysms of Choice," *New York Review of Books*, October 19, 2000, 49; Frank Webb, "Zip Codes Shouldn't Determine Our Students' Future," *CTA California Educator*, May 2001, 6–8. "The pertinent debate concerning black hiring is never 'merit vs. race' but whether hiring decisions will be based on merit influenced by race-bias against blacks, or on merit influenced by race-bias but with special consideration for minorities and women." West, *Race Matters*, 78.

41. Derrick Bell, "Racial Realism," in *Critical Race Theory: The Key Writings That Formed the Movement*, ed. Kimberle Crenshaw et al. (New York: New Press, 1995), 306. The important measure, again, is wealth. While middle class African Americans made up 9.2 percent of the nation in 1995, they held only 2.9 percent of its wealth, including a mere 1.3 percent of its financial assets. Melvin Oliver and Thomas Shapiro, *Black Wealth, White Wealth: A New Perspective on Racial Inequality* (New York: Routledge, 1997), 103. Also see Spencer Rich, "Whites Ten Times Wealthier Than Blacks, Hispanics," *The Washington Post*, January 11, 1991; Guinier and Torres, *Miner's Canary*, 44–47; and Brown et al., *Whitewashing Race*.

42. Kinder and Sanders, *Divided By Color*, 32.

43. Davis, *In the Image*, 357; also see Blauner, *Racial Oppression*, 28–29.

44. Balibar, "Class Struggle," 161–62, 178.

45. This was the central thesis of E. P. Thompson's magisterial *Making of the English Working Class* (New York: Vintage, 1963): "The making of the working class is a fact of political and cultural, as much as of economic history" (194). Aronowitz similarly emphasizes "the primacy of social time over social space: spatial arrangements are sedimented outcomes of struggles over class formation and, since social time is not reversible, are marked by contingency." *How Class Works* (New Haven: Yale University Press, 2003), 56.

46. Aronowitz, *The Politics of Identity* (New York: Routledge, 1992), 72. David Halle describes the multiple identities of his fellow workers in *America's Working Man* (Chicago: University of Chicago Press, 1984). See also Gary Gerstle, *Working Class Americanism: The Politics of Labor in a Textile City, 1914–1960* (New York: Cambridge University Press, 1989).

47. *Regents of the University of California vs. Bakke*, 438 U.S. 265 (1978), dissenting opinion.

48. "The 'politics of identity' . . . fail[s] to recognize that interests and identities are constructed upon a terrain of inegalitarian distribution of social and economic power." Joseph Schwartz, "Reconstructing the Left in an Age of Globalization and Social Differentiation" (paper presented at the American Political Science Association annual meeting, Washington, DC, September 2000), 3.

Neoliberalism and Anticorporate Globalization as Class Struggle — William K. Tabb

1. On keywords see Raymond Williams, *Keywords: A Vocabulary of Culture and Society* (London: Oxford University Press, 1983). For such usage as applied to globalization and a discussion of definitions of globalization see William K. Tabb, *Unequal Partners: A Primer on Globalization* (New York: New Press, 2002), chap. 1.

2. William K. Tabb, *Economic Governance in the Age of Globalization* (New York: Columbia University Press, 2004).

3. Naomi Klein, "Revolt of the Wronged: Argentina Was a Model Student. And It's Still Suffering as a Result," *Guardian* (London), March 28, 2002, Internet edition.

4. See Joseph E. Stiglitz, *Globalization and Its Discontents* (New York: W. W. Norton, 2002), in which the former chief economist at the World Bank, Nobel Prize winner in economics, and chair of President Clinton's Council of Economic Advisers offers a not dissimilar evaluation.

5. John Williamson, "What Washington Means by Policy Reform," in *Latin American Adjustment: How Much Has Happened?* ed. John Williamson (Washington, DC: Institute for International Economics, 1990).

6. The phrase is from Charles Gore, "The Rise and Fall of the Washington Consensus as a Paradigm for Developing Countries," *World Development*, fall 2002, 791.

7. William K. Tabb, "After Neoliberalism?" *Monthly Review*, June 2003.

8. John Williamson, "The Political Economy of Policy Reform," in *The Political Economy of Policy Reform*, ed. John Williamson (Washington, DC: International Institute of Economics, 1994).

9. Three accessible evaluations are found in William Finnegan, "The Economics of Empire: Notes on the Washington Consensus," *Harper's*, May 2003; Dani Rodrik, "Trading in Illusions," *Foreign Policy*, March–April 2001; and William Easterly, *The Elusive Quest for Growth* (Cambridge: MIT Press, 2001).

10. John Williamson, "What Should the World Bank Think about the Washington Consensus?" *The World Bank Research Observer*, August 2000, 255.

11. David Rock "Racking Argentina," *New Left Review*, September–October 2002.

12. See the important essay by World Bank economist Branko Milanovic, "The Two Faces of Globalization: Against Globalization as We Know It," www.networkideas.org/themes/inequality/aug2002/ie21_Globalisation.htm.

13. E. P. Thompson, *The Making of the English Working Class* (New York: Random House, 1985).

September 11 and Its Aftermath—Leo Panitch

1. Editors' preface, *Working Classes/Global Realities: The Socialist Register 2001*, ed. Leo Panitch and Colin Leys with Greg Albo and David Coates (London: Merlin; New York: Monthly Review Press, 2000), viii–ix.

2. Edward Wyatt, "At Ground Zero, A New Divide, Some of 9/11's Neediest Get the Least Government Aid," *New York Times*, June 5, 2002, B1.

3. See, for instance, Robert Reich, "Take a Guess: Who's Going to Pay for the Terror Economy?" *Los Angeles Times*, October 23, 2001, B13.

4. Branko Milanovic, "True World Income Distribution, 1988 and 1993: First Calculation Based on Household Surveys Alone," *Economic Journal* 112, no. 475 (2002): 51–92.

5. See John Pilger, "The Real Story behind America's War," *New Statesman*, December 17, 2001, 14–15.

6. Maxwell Geismar, ed., *Mark Twain and the Three R's: Race, Religion, Revolution—and Related Matters* (New York: Bobbs-Merrill, 1973), 178–79.

7. "G-7 Countries Find Their Public Supportive of U.S. Military Action in Afghanistan But Serious Opposition Appears in Other Countries," Ipsos-Reid Media Center, December 21, 2001.

8. Robert Cooper, "The New Empire," *Prospect*, October 2001, 22–26.

9. Harold Innis, *Essays in Canadian Economic History* (Toronto: University of Toronto Press, 1956), 407.

10. "Address on Foreign Economic Policy, Delivered at Baylor University," March 6, 1947, *Public Papers of the Presidents*, www.trumanlibrary.org/trumanpapers/pppus/1947/52.htm. On the preparations for this crucial speech see Gregory A. Fossendal, *Our Finest Hour: Will Clayton, the Marshall Plan, and the Triumph of Democracy* (Stanford: Hoover, 1993), 213–15.

11. Quoted in William Appleman Williams, *Empire As a Way of Life* (New York: Oxford University Press, 1980), 189; and see Gabriel Kolko, *Century of War* (New York: New Press, 1994), 397.

12. See Robin Blackburn, "Terror and Empire," www.counterpunch.org/robin1.html.

13. Ellen Meiksins Wood, "Contradictions: Only in Capitalism," in *A World of Contradictions: The Socialist Register 2002*, ed. Leo Panitch and Colin Leys (London: Merlin; New York: Monthly Review Press, 2001), 291.

14. See my essays "Rethinking the Role of the State" in *Globalization: Critical Reflections,*

ed. James Mittelman (Boulder, CO: Rienner, 1996); "The State in a Changing World: Social-Democratizing Global Capitalism?" *Monthly Review* 50, no. 5 (October 1998): 11–23; and "The New Imperial State," *New Left Review* 2 (March/April 2000): 1–15.

15. Stephen Lewis, interview by Jim Wurst, "The United Nations after the Gulf War: A Promise Betrayed," *World Policy Journal*, summer 1991, 539–49.

16. See Samir Amin, "The Political Economy of the Twentieth Century," *Monthly Review* 52, no. 2 (June 2000): 9.

17. Naomi Klein, "Farewell to 'The End of History': Organization and Vision in Anti-Corporate Movements," in Panitch and Leys, *World of Contradictions*, 9.

18. See my *Renewing Socialism: Democracy, Strategy and Imagination* (Boulder, CO: Westview, 2001).

Global Strategies for Workers — Katie Quan

1. U.S. Department of Labor, *The Apparel Industry and Codes of Conduct: A Solution to the International Child Labor Problem?* (Washington, DC: U.S. Department of Labor, Bureau of International Affairs, 1996).

2. Penchan Charoensutthipan, "Factory's Sister Firms Collapse: Textile Plants Lay Off 1,231 Workers," *Bangkok Post*, September 10, 2000.

3. Katie Quan, "Legislating Sweatshop Accountability," April 20, 2001, www.nelp .org/docUploads/quan.pdf.

4. Norris Willatt, *Multi-National Unions* (London: Financial Times, 1974).

5. "Banana Union Feminism: Women's Networks, International Solidarity, and the Transformation of the Banana Labor Movement in Honduras and Central America" (paper presented at Institute of Labor and Employment conference, University of California, Los Angeles, May 20, 2003).

6. Jon Erik Dolvik, *An Emerging Island? ETUC, Social Dialogue and the Europeanisation of the Trade Unions in the 1990s* (Brussels: European Trade Union Institute, 1999).

7. Edna Bonacich and Richard P. Appelbaum, *Behind the Label: Inequality in the Los Angeles Apparel Industry* (Berkeley: University of California Press, 2000).

8. Jason Judd (AFL-CIO Solidarity Center), personal communication with the author, May 2003.

9. Human Rights Watch, "Trading Away Rights: The Unfulfilled Promise of NAFTA's Labor Side Agreement," April 2001, www.hrw.org/reports/2001/nafta.

10. See for example Diao Xinshen and Agapi Somwaru, "Impact of the MFA Phase-Out on the World Economy: An Intertemporal Global General Equilibrium Analysis," October 2001, www.ifpri.org/divs/tmd/dp/tmdp79.htm.

11. Tamara Kay, "Raising Wages Globally" (paper presented at Sweatshop Watch conference on Living Wages in the Global Economy, University of California, Berkeley, July 1998).

12. Frank Borgers, "Global Unionism—Beyond the Rhetoric: The CWA North Atlantic Alliance," *Labor Studies Journal* 24, no. 1 (spring 1999): 107–22.

13. John Russo and Andy Banks, "How the Teamsters Took the UPS Strike Overseas," *Working USA* 2, no.5 (January/February 1999): 75–87.

14. Stanley Gacek, untitled presentation (University of California, Berkeley, Center for Labor Research and Education conference on Labor in the Americas, 1997).

15. Katie Quan, "A Global Labour Contract: The Case of the Collective Agreement between the Association of Flight Attendants (AFL-CIO) and United Airlines," *Transfer* (Brussels), spring 2000.

16. Kitty G. Dickerson, *Textiles and Apparel in the Global Economy* (Englewood Cliffs, NJ: Prentice-Hall,1995).

17. Jared Bernstein et al., "Pulling Apart: A State-by-State Analysis of Income Trends,"

Center on Budget and Policy Priorities, and Economic Policy Institute, Washington, DC, April 2002, www.epinet.org/studies/Pulling_Apart_2002.pdf.

18. Dana Frank, *Buy American: The Untold Story of Economic Nationalism* (Boston: Beacon, 2000).

19. Ibid.

20. Ibid.

21. Alethea Yip, "Remembering Vincent Chin," *Asian Week*, June 5–13, 1997.

22. Tamara Kay, "Global Governance and Transnational Labor Cooperation in North America" (paper presented at the American Sociological Association annual conference, Atlanta, August 2003).

23. May Chen, interview with author, 2001.

24. Robert E. Scott, "Phony Accounting and U.S. Trade Policy: Is Bush Using Enron-like Tactics to Sell Trade Deals to the Public?" October 23, 2002, www.epinet.org/content .cfm/Issuebriefs_ib184.

25. Katie Quan, "NAFTA Realities and FTAA Dangers," *On the Move* (University of California, Berkeley, Center for Labor Research and Education Newsletter), spring 2003, 6–7.

Part III. Class and Working People — Michael Zweig

1. See Michael Zweig, *The Working Class Majority: America's Best Kept Secret* (Ithaca, NY: Cornell University Press, 2000), chap. 4.

2. Edmund L. Andrews, "Economic Inequality Grew in the 90's Boom, Fed Reports," *New York Times*, January 23, 2003, C1.

Neoliberal Social Policy and Labor Market Discipline — Frances Fox Piven

1. For a review, see Robert L. Borosage, "Class Warfare, Bush Style," *The American Prospect*, March 2003, 25–26.

2. See Stefanie Chambers, "Urban Education Reform and Minority Political Empowerment," *Political Science Quarterly* 17, no. 4 (winter 2002–2003): 643–65.

3. Jonathan Kozol, *Savage Inequalities: Children in America's Schools* (New York: Crown, 1991). The Education Trust recently published "The Funding Gap Report," showing that the poorest 25 percent of school districts in each state average $966 less in state and local funds per pupil than the richest 25 percent. The Education Trust, www.edtrust.org.

4. U.S. Census Bureau, *Statistical Abstract of the United States: 2001*, 119th ed. (Washington, DC, 1999), table 537.

5. David Stockman, *The Triumph of Politics: Why the Reagan Revolution Failed* (New York: HarperCollins, 1984).

6. Mickey Kaus, "The Work Ethic State," *The New Republic*, July 7, 1986, 22–23.

Economic Crisis, the Working Class, and Organized Labor — Michael D. Yates

1. Real wage data can be found in Lawrence Mishel, Jared Bernstein, and Heather Boushey, *The State of Working America 2002/2003* (Ithaca, NY: Cornell University Press, 2003). Economists at the Economic Policy Institute (www.epinet.org) provided me with the most recent data, showing a continuation of real wage gains through 2001, although there are signs of slower wage growth since September 11. Unemployment rates can be found at the Bureau of Labor Statistics Web site, www.bls.gov. The rates for May 2003 are also from this source. Poverty rates are shown at the U.S. Census Bureau's Web site, www.census.gov. Some evidence of a slowdown in the growth of income inequality in the latter part of the boom can be found in Mishel, Bernstein, and Boushey, *State of Working America*.

2. See Michael Yates, *Why Unions Matter* (New York: Monthly Review Press, 1998).

3. See Mishel, Bernstein, and Boushey, *State of Working America*, 189–95.

4. Data on union density can be found in a convenient table at www.lraonline.org/tables/states_density.php. See also Stephen Lerner, "Three Steps to Reorganizing and Rebuilding the Labor Movement," *Labor Notes*, no. 285 (December 2002), available at www.labornotes.org/archives/2002/12/e.html.

5. See Michael Yates, *Longer Hours, Fewer Jobs* (New York: Monthly Review Press, 1994), and Kim Moody, *An Injury to All* (London and New York: Verso, 1988) for details.

6. Data on wage gains in the first year of collective bargaining agreements were kindly provided to me by BNA PLUS, the research division of the Bureau of National Affairs in Washington, DC.

7. U.S. Census Bureau, *Statistical Abstract of the United States: 2001*, 119th ed. (Washington, DC, 1999), table 537.

8. For information on employment, unemployment, and poverty, see the sources cited in endnote 1 above.

9. See Evelyn Iritani, " A Giant Awakens," *Los Angeles Times*, October 20–22, 2002, A1.

10. See Bruce Feldacker, *Labor Guide to Labor Law*, 4th ed. (Upper Saddle River, NJ: Prentice Hall, 2000); and Michael D. Yates, *Power on the Job: The Legal Rights of Working People* (Boston: South End, 1994).

11. On state fiscal crises, see Max B. Sawicky, "Altered States: How the Federal Government Can Ease the States' Fiscal Crisis," Economic Policy Institute issue brief 187, February 26, 2003, www.epinet.org/content.cfm/Issuebriefs_ib187.

12. For a good discussion of the war in Iraq and the U.S. economy, see the speech by Economic Policy Institute president Lawrence Mishel, titled "The Economy, the War, and Choosing Our Future" (keynote address to Society of American Business Editors and Writers, April 17, 2003, Cambridge, MA), www.epinet.org/webfeatures/viewpoints/mishel_war-economy-future.pdf.

13. See Mark Landler, "West Europe Is Hard Hit by Strikes over Pensions," *New York Times*, June 4, 2003, A9.

14. Michael Yates, "A Note from the Associate Editor," *Monthly Review*, January 2002, www.monthlyreview.org/nftae01.htm.

15. More than one hundred examples are described at www.aflcio.org/issuespolitics/bushwatch/.

16. David Bacon and Freda Coodin, "Bush Threatens West Coast Dockers' Right to Strike," *Labor Notes*, no. 282 (September 2002), available at www.labornotes.org/archives/2002/09/b.htm. On the union involved, the International Longshore Workers Union, see Steve Rosswurm, ed., *The CIO's Left-Led Unions* (New Brunswick, NJ: Rutgers University Press, 1992).

17. See Lee Sustar, "AFL-CIO Criticizes War," *Socialist Worker Online* 443, March 7, 2003, www.socialistworker.org/2003-1/443/443_11_LaborAndWar.shtml.

18. Hal Leyshon, "AFL-CIO Stays the Course," *Labor Notes*, no. 274 (January 2002): 1, 12–14; JoAnn Wypijewski, "Labor in Las Vegas," *CounterPunch* 8 (December 1–15, 2001), 1.

19. For an excellent summary of the problems facing organized labor, especially with respect to the issues of imperialism and race, see Bill Fletcher, "Can U.S. Workers Embrace Anti-Imperialism? Trade Unionism and Anti-Imperialism in the Current Situation," *Monthly Review* 54 (July/August, 2003): 93–108.

20. JoAnn Wypijewski, "What Workers Talk About When They Talk About War," *CounterPunch* 8 (November 1–15, 2001): 1.

21. See Tom Robbins, "Waiting for Labor to Rise," *Village Voice*, December 26, 2001–January 1, 2002, www.villagevoice.com/issues/0152/robbins.php.

22. Lee Sustar, "Labor's Challenge in the Recession," *International Socialist Review*, January–February 2002, 57–63.

23. Chris Kutalik and William Johnson, "Within Unions, Anti-War Forces Mobilize

Opposition," *Labor Notes*, no. 289 (April 2003), available at www.labornotes.org/archives/2003/04/a.html.

24. See David Bacon, "Global Labour Rejects an Iraq War," *Spectrezine*, www.spectrezine.org/war/Bacon.htm.

25. See Fletcher, "Can U.S. Workers."

26. See James Petras, "The Unemployed Workers' Movement in Argentina," *Monthly Review* 53 (January 2002), 32–45.

Part IV. Class and Young Adults — Michael Zweig

1. Daniel P. McMurrer, Mark Condon, and Isabel V. Sawhill, "Intergenerational Mobility in the United States" (1997 unpublished paper available from the Urban Institute), 8. For a broader discussion of class mobility in the United States, see Michael Zweig, *The Working Class Majority: America's Best Kept Secret* (Ithaca, NY: Cornell University Press, 2000), 39–46.

2. U.S. Census Bureau, *Statistical Abstract of the United States: 2001*, 119th ed. (Washington, DC, 1999), table 217.

3. Greg Winter, "College Loans Rise, Swamping Graduates' Dreams," *New York Times*, January 28, 2003, A1.

4. C. L. Barney Dews and Carolyn Leste Law, eds., *This Fine Place So Far from Home: Voices of Academics from the Working Class* (Philadelphia: Temple University Press, 1995); Sherry Linkon, *Teaching Working Class* (Amherst: University of Massachusetts Press, 1999); Ira Shor, *When Students Have Power: Negotiating Authority in a Critical Pedagogy* (Chicago: University of Chicago Press, 1996); Janet Zandy, *What We Hold in Common* (St. Paul, MN: Consortium, 2001).

Young Workers, Economic Inequality, and Collective Action — Gregory DeFreitas and Niev Duffy

1. Howard Fullerton Jr. and Mitra Toosi, "Labor Force Projections to 2010: Steady Growth and Changing Composition," *Monthly Labor Review* 124, no. 11 (2001): 21–38.

2. The authors are grateful for the skillful research assistance of Daniel Golebiewski.

3. Public Agenda, *Kids These Days: What Americans Really Think about the Next Generation* (New York: Public Agenda, 1997).

4. David S. Johnson and Mark Lino, "Teenagers: Employment and Contributions to Family Spending," *Monthly Labor Review* 123, no. 9 (2000): 15–25.

5. David G. Blanchflower and Richard B. Freeman, "The Declining Economic Status of Young Workers in OECD Countries," in *Youth Employment and Joblessness in Advanced Countries*, ed. Blanchflower and Freeman (Chicago: University of Chicago Press, 2000), 19–56. See also Paul Ryan, "The School-to-Work Transition: A Cross-National Perspective," *Journal of Economic Literature* 39 (2001): 34–92.

6. Lawrence Mishel, Jared Bernstein, and John Schmitt, *The State of Working America 2000/2001* (Ithaca, NY: Cornell University Press, 2001), table 2.22.

7. Jared Bernstein and Jeff Chapman, *Time to Repair the Wage Floor* (Washington, DC: Economic Policy Institute, 2002). Workers aged 19 and younger can legally be paid a "sub-minimum wage" of just $4.25 per hour during their first ninety days with each employer, under the 1996 federal minimum wage law.

8. By 1997, the inequality of the wage structure and the shrinking share of full-time jobs had become major issues for the union. UPS Teamsters' locals spent the spring and early summer of 1997 educating their members and the public about the unfair pay policies of UPS, the $65 billion giant of the delivery industry. On August 4, 185,000 Teamsters launched a nationwide strike against UPS that crippled the company's operations but still won majority approval in public opinion polls. After a fifteen-day walkout, the workers won their key demands in a landmark five-year contract. It included: (1) hourly wage increases of $4.10 for part-timers and of $3.10 for full-timers; (2) conversion of 10,000 part-

time jobs to full-time; and (3) a company pledge that at least five out of six of the new full-time positions would be filled by people already working part-time for UPS. Louis Uchitelle, "Strike Points to Inequality in 2-Tier Job Market," *New York Times*, August 8, 1997.

9. Gregory DeFreitas, "Recession and Rebuilding in the New York Economy," *Regional Labor Review* 4 (2002): 3–18.

10. See the detailed estimates in Niev Duffy, "The Coming Health Care Crisis for New York Parents," *Regional Labor Review* 4 (2002): 29–33; and Niev Duffy, "A Crisis in Coverage: Falling Adolescent Health Insurance: Its Impact on Youth and Their Health Care Providers," *Mount Sinai Adolescent Health Center Policy Report* (New York: Mount Sinai Adolescent Health Center, 2002).

11. Michael S. McPherson and Morton O. Shapiro, *The Student Aid Game: Meeting Need and Rewarding Talent in American Higher Education* (Princeton: Princeton University Press, 1998). See also National Center for Public Policy and Higher Education (NCPPHE), *Losing Ground: A National Status Report on the Affordability of American Higher Education* (San Jose, CA: NCPPHE, 2002).

12. Michael Zweig, *The Working Class Majority: America's Best Kept Secret* (Ithaca, NY: Cornell University Press, 2000), 45.

13. Advisory Committee on Student Financial Assistance, U.S. Department of Education. *Empty Promises: The Myth of College Access in America* (Washington, DC: U.S. Department of Education, 2002), 31.

14. National Center for Education Statistics, *The Condition of Education, 2002* (Washington, DC: U.S. Department of Education, 2002), 174.

15. For more on analysis of "solidaristic sentiments" as an indicator of class consciousness, see the major recent study of American class relations by Erik Olin Wright, *Class Counts* (New York: Cambridge University Press, 1997).

16. See the analysis of the 1977 Quality of Employment Survey findings in Richard B. Freeman and James Medoff, *What Do Unions Do?* (New York: Basic Books, 1984).

17. Katia Hetter, "Organized State of Mind: Poll Shows Enduring Support for Unions," *Newsday*, September 3, 2001.

18. Henry Farber and Daniel Saks, "Why Workers Want Unions: The Role of Relative Wages and Job Characteristics," *Journal of Political Economy* 88 (1980): 349–69.

19. Freeman and Medoff, *What Do Unions Do?*

20. Bob Ortega, *In Sam We Trust: The Untold Story of Sam Walton and How Wal-Mart Is Devouring America* (New York: Times Books, 1998); Wendy Zellner, "How Wal-Mart Keeps Unions at Bay," *Business Week*, October 28, 2002.

21. Steven Greenhouse, "Activism Surges at Campuses Nationwide, and Labor Is at Issue," *New York Times*, March 29, 1999.

22. Rochelle Sharp, "What Exactly Is a Living Wage?" *Business Week*, May 28, 2001.

23. Union Summer figures from AFL-CIO Web site: www.aflcio.org (July 2002).

24. Quoted in Greenhouse, "Activism Surges."

25. See, for example, Vernon M. Briggs Jr., *Immigration and American Unionism* (Ithaca, NY: Cornell University Press, 2001). However, other historical research has amply documented the lengthy record of union involvement by immigrants. See James D. Cockcroft, *Outlaws in the Promised Land: Mexican Immigrant Workers and America's Future* (New York: Grove, 1986); Hector Delgado, *New Immigrants, Old Unions: Organizing Undocumented Workers in Los Angeles* (Philadelphia: Temple University Press, 1993); and Robert Asher and Charles Stephenson, eds. *Labor Divided: Race and Ethnicity in U.S. Labor Struggles, 1835–1960* (Albany: State University of New York Press, 1991).

In empirical research on a large longitudinal data set of young workers, DeFreitas found that, when migration status and other factors are controlled, there are no significant differences in demand for unionization among Asians, whites, and Hispanic immigrants. He concluded that young immigrants have had significantly less opportunity to translate their union preferences into actually acquiring union jobs. This may reflect in part their limited access to the highly unionized public sector and stronger management resistance to organizing efforts in the small firms where the foreign-born are more concentrated. But it also no doubt reflects continued union neglect of and occasional criticism of immigrant labor. Like black and female workers before them, immigrants have often been victims of discriminatory stereotypes that have cast doubt on whether they are even organizable. There has also long been apprehension that they are too easily manipulated by employers and thus weaken worker solidarity, depress wage levels, and displace incumbent workers. While there are certainly historical precedents for this view, it is also the case that most recent economic research has shown that immigration's benefits tend to outweigh its costs, resulting in no net wage or employment impacts on native workers. See Gregory DeFreitas, "Unionization among Racial and Ethnic Minorities," *Industrial and Labor Relations Review* 46 (1993): 284–301; and *Inequality At Work: Hispanics in the U.S. Labor Force* (New York: Oxford University Press, 1991).

26. See Gregory DeFreitas, "Can Unions Win at Region-wide Low-wage Organizing? An Interview with Hector Figueroa," *Regional Labor Review* 4 (2001): 12–24.

Promises to Keep—Michelle M. Tokarczyk

1. John Alberti, "Returning to Class: Creating Opportunities for Multicultural Reform at Majority Second-Tier Schools," *College English* 63, no. 5 (May 2001): 565.

2. I am not suggesting that the appalling status of many service jobs is inevitable. Such jobs should be unionized, pay living wages, and offer benefits. Hopefully, one day they will. But given the current nature of these jobs, it is logical that many poor and working class students look to a college education to better their lives.

3. See Jane Gross's series of articles in the *New York Times*: "Different Lives, One Goal: Finding the Key to College," May 5, 2002; "Preparing Applications, Fine Tuning Applicants," May 6, 2002; "At Last, Colleges Answer, and New Questions," May 7, 2002.

4. Alberti, "Returning to Class," 563.

5. Stephen Garger, "Bronx Syndrome," in *This Fine Place So Far from Home: Voices of Academics from the Working Class*, ed. C. L. Barney Dews and Carolyn Leste Law (Philadelphia: Temple University Press, 1995), 46.

6. Richard A. Greenwald and Elizabeth A. Grant, "Border Crossings: Working-Class Encounters in Higher Education," in *Teaching Working Class*, ed. Sherry Lee Linkon (Amherst: University of Massachusetts Press, 1999), 35.

7. For analyses of working class students' education in elementary and middle schools, see Jonathan Kozol, *Savage Inequalities: Children in America's Schools* (New York: Crown, 1991); and Lisa D. Delpit, *Other People's Children: Cultural Conflict in the Classroom* (New York: New Press, 1996).

8. Alberti, "Returning to Class," 573.

9. Mike Rose, *Lives on the Boundary: A Moving Account of the Struggles and Achievements of America's Educational Underclass* (New York: Penguin, 1990).

10. Caroline Pari, "Just American: Reversing Ethnic and Class Assimilation in the Academy," in Linkon, ed., *Teaching Working Class*, 123–41.

11. This attitude toward class among African Americans has been examined in bell hooks's *Where We Stand: Class Matters* (New York: Routledge, 2000).

12. Mary Prieto-Bayard, "First Generation Student Success Program" (paper presented at the National Conference on Race and Ethnicity in Higher Education, Santa Fe, NM, May 2000).

13. Gloria Morrow, "African-American First-Generation Students" (paper presented at the National Conference on Race and Ethnicity in Higher Education, Santa Fe, NM, May 2000).

14. Ann Wichman, "The Ecology of First-Generation Students and Their Families" (paper presented at the National Conference on Race and Ethnicity in Higher Education, Santa Fe, NM, May 2000).

15. Prieto-Bayard, "First Generation."

16. While the findings about mentoring preferences among different racial and ethnic groups at the University of La Verne are provocative, more research would have to be done before we can generalize from them.

Across the Great Divide — Barbara Jensen

1. Basil Bernstein, *The Structuring of Pedagogic Discourse* (London: Routledge, 1990).

2. Geraldine K. Piorkowski, "Survivor Guilt in the University Setting," *Personnel and Guidance Journal* 61(1983): 620.

3. See, for example, Robert J. Lifton and Eric Olson, *Living and Dying* (New York: Praeger, 1974).

4. Piorkowski, "Survivor Guilt," 620–21.

5. Bernstein, *Structuring;* and Basil Bernstein, *Class, Codes, and Control,* vol. 1: *Theoretical Studies towards a Sociology of Language* (London: Routledge, 1971); Pierre Bourdieu, "Cultural Reproduction and Social Reproduction," in *Power and Ideology in Education,* ed. J. Karabel and A. H. Halsey (New York: Oxford University Press, 1977); Barbara Jensen, "The Silent Psychology," *Women's Studies Quarterly* 26, nos. 1 and 2 (1998): 202–15; and "Becoming versus Belonging" (unpublished, 1997); Jack Metzgar, *Striking Steel* (Philadelphia: Temple University Press, 2000); Irvin Peckham, "Complicity in Class Codes: The Exclusionary Function of Education," in *This Fine Place So Far from Home: Voices of Academics from the Working Class,* ed. C. L. Barney Dews and Carolyn Leste Law (Philadelphia: Temple University Press, 1995), 263–76.

6. Stephen Garger, "Bronx Syndrome," in Dews and Law, eds., *This Fine Place,* 40–50.

7. Ibid.

8. Richard Sennett and Jonathan Cobb, *The Hidden Injuries of Class* (New York: Random House, 1973).

9. Julie Charlip, "A Real Class Act: Searching for Identity in a 'Classless' Society," in Dews and Law, eds., *This Fine Place,* 34.

10. Peckham, "Complicity," 265.

11. Bernstein, *Class, Codes and Control,* vol. 1; Bourdieu, "Cultural Reproduction"; Jensen, "Silent Psychology" and "Becoming versus Belonging."

12. Donna Burns Phillips, "Past Voices, Present Speakers," in Dews and Law, eds., *This Fine Place,* 230.

13. Laurel Johnson Black, "Stupid Rich Bastards," in Dews and Law, ed., *This Fine Place,* 21.

14. Michael Schwalbe, "The Work of Professing: A Letter to Home," in Dews and Law, eds., *This Fine Place,* 309–31.

15. Rosa Maria Pequeros, "*Todos Vuelven:* From Potrero Hill to UCLA," in Dews and Law, eds., *This Fine Place,* 96.

16. Renny Christopher, "A Carpenter's Daughter," in Dews and Law, eds., *This Fine Place,* 137–50.

17. Peckham, "Complicity," 274.

18. Black, "Stupid Rich Bastards," 24–25.

19. Metzgar, *Striking Steel.*

20. Jay MacLeod, *Ain't No Makin' It: Aspiration and Attainment in a Low-Income Neighborhood* (Boulder, CO: Westview, 1995), 34–35.

21. Phillips, "Past Voices," 230.

22. Ibid.

CONTRIBUTORS

DOROTHY SUE COBBLE is Professor of Labor Studies and Employment Relations at Rutgers University.

GREGORY DEFREITAS is Professor of Economics and Director of the Center for Labor and Democracy at Hofstra University.

NIEV DUFFY is Research Director at the John F. Kennedy Jr. Institute for Worker Education at the City University of New York.

BILL FLETCHER JR. is President of TransAfrica Forum.

BARBARA JENSEN teaches at Metropolitan State University in Minneapolis.

R. JEFFREY LUSTIG is Professor of Political Science at California State University, Sacramento.

LEO PANITCH is Distinguished Research Professor of Political Science at York University.

FRANCES FOX PIVEN is Distinguished Professor of Political Science at the Graduate Center of the City University of New York.

KATIE QUAN is Chair of the Center for Labor Research and Education in the Institute of Industrial Relations, University of California, Berkeley.

WILLIAM K. TABB is Professor of Economics at Queens College, City University of New York, and on the political science faculty at the CUNY Graduate Center.

MICHELLE M. TOKARCZYK is Professor of English at Goucher College.

MICHAEL D. YATES is the Associate Editor of the *Monthly Review* and Professor Emeritus of Economics at the University of Pittsburgh, Johnstown.

MICHAEL ZWEIG is Professor of Economics and Director of the Center for Study of Working Class Life at the State University of New York, Stony Brook.

INDEX